REMEMBERING
JEWISH
AMSTERDAM

REMEMBERING JEWISH AMSTERDAM

Philo Bregstein
&
Salvador Bloemgarten

Dutch textual composition
by Johanna Katharina Barends

Translated from the Dutch
by Wanda Boeke

Holmes & Meier
New York/London

Published in the United States of America 2004
by Holmes & Meier Publishers, Inc.
160 Broadway • New York, NY 10038
www.holmesandmeier.com

Copyright © 2004

This book has been printed on acid-free paper.

Designed by Brigid McCarthy
Typesetting by JoAnne Todtfeld

Library of Congress Cataloging-in-Publication Data

Herinnering aan Joods Amsterdam. English.
  Remembering Jewish Amsterdam / compiled by Philo Bregstein and Salvador
  Bloemgarten; Dutch textual composition by Johanna Katherina Barends;
  translated from the Dutch by Wanda J. Boeke.
    p. cm.
  ISBN 0-8419-1425-7 (cloth)
    1. Jews—Netherlands—Amsterdam—Social life and customs—20th century.
2. Jews—Netherlands—Amsterdam—Social conditions—20th century. 3.
Amsterdam (Netherlands)—Social life and customs—20th century.
4. Amsterdam (Netherlands)—Social conditions—20th century. 5. Jews—
Netherlands—Amsterdam—Interviews. I. Bregstein, Philo, 1932- II.
Bloemgarten, Salvador, 1924- III. Barends, Johanna Katherina. IV. Title.

DS135.N5A53713 2004
949.2'352004924—dc22

                                                          2004054222

Manufactured in the United States of America

Narrators

Emmanuel Aalsvel
Maurits Allegro
Jeanette Alvarez Vega-Keizer
Lodewijk Asscher
Bertha Barnstein-Koster
Wilhelmina Beatrix Biet-Meijer
Barend Bril
Gerrit Brugmans
Werner Cahn
Rosa Cohen-De Bruijn
Joël Cosman
Barend De Hond
Abraham De Leeuw
Mozes De Leeuw
Aron De Paauw
Jan De Ronde
Salomon Diamant
Barend Drukarch
Carel Josef Edersheim
Joop Emmerik
Max Emmerik
Simon Emmering
Suze Frank
Arthur Frankfurther
Mozes Heiman Gans
Mirjam Gerzon-De Leeuw
Simon Gosselaar
Hartog Goubitz
Alexandre Joseph Goudsmit
Joannes Juda Groen
Ruben Groen
Hubertus Petrus Hauser
Julia Heertjes-Van Saxen
Hermine Heijermans
Abel Jacob Herzberg
Salko Hertzberger
Henri Isidore Isaac
Jo Juda
Eduard Charles Keizer

Isaac Kisch
Barend Kroonenberg
Toos La Grouw-Gosselaar
Loe Lap
Marius Gustaaf Levenbach
Isaac Lipschits
Johanna Louman-Groen
Barend Luza
David Mindlin
Meijer Mossel
Aron Peereboom
Ben Polak
Karel Polak
Sylvain Albert Poons
Carel Reijnders
Max Reisel
David Ricardo
Abraham Salomon Rijxman
Leen Rimini
Ben Sajet
Dick Schallies
Hijman (Bob) Scholte
Ben Sijes
Jacob Soetendorp
Nathan Stodel
Max Louis Terveen
Eduard Van Amerongen
Elizabeth Van De Kar-Stodel
Rosine Van Praag
Abraham Van Santen
Max Van Saxen
Bernard Van Tijn
Alexander Van Weezel
Liesbeth Van Weezel
Aaron Vaz Dias
Joop Voet
Ali Voorzanger-Suurhoff
Sal Waas

Contents

Preface   ix
Introductory Remarks   x
Translator's Introduction   xi
A Historical Perspective   xiii

I   OCCUPATIONS
          Street Vending   2
          Retail and Wholesale   9
          Trades   17
          Professions   26

II   RELIGION
          Practice   32
          Music   47
          Synagogues and Rabbis   52
          Education   59
          Philanthropy   65

III   THE OLD JEWISH QUARTER
          Living and Housing Conditions   73

IV   EMANCIPATION
          Politics and the Labor Movement   85
          Culture and Upbringing   92
          Socialism and Religion   104
          Liberals and Liberal Democrats   111
          New Neighborhoods   115

V   JEWS AND CHRISTIANS
          Anti-Semitism   124
          Integration and Assimilation   136

VI   ENTERTAINMENT AND RECREATION
            Theater and Music   148
            The Lighter Muse   157
            Sports   164

VII   IMMIGRATION
            Jewish Immigrants from Eastern Europe   168
            German Jews after 1933   174

VIII   ZIONISM
            In General   186
            Socialist Zionism   193

IX   WAR
            The Years Prior to 1940   200
            1940–1945   208
            After 1945   220

       Illustrations   229
       Place Names   231
       Organizations and Publications   235
       Glossary   239
       Biographical Notes on Interviewees   243

Preface

In preparing the film *In Search of Jewish Amsterdam,* which I made in 1975 on the occasion of the seven-hundredth anniversary of the city of Amsterdam, I recorded a large number of interviews in consultation with my close friend, historian Salvador Bloemgarten.

When the film became shorter and simpler than originally intended due to time and financial constraints, I decided to make a very personal selection. Only a small portion of the interview material could have been used for the film in any event.

After reviewing the interviews, Salvador and I were convinced that these first-hand accounts of a continually shrinking group of "survivors" had to be made accessible to the reading public. As a source of historical knowledge, they provide important additional information to existing publications and throw light on many unknown aspects of prewar Jewish Amsterdam.

Actual memory has the advantage of being a living contact with the past. Of course, memory sometimes incorporates factual errors as actual fact. Salvador has attempted to correct as many factual errors in the text as possible. This book does not pretend to be historically exhaustive, in spite of the fact that Salvador and I undertook several additional interviews. I posed questions based on my own personal interest and usually got to hear only what I inquired about. The responsibility for the text as we assembled it lies completely with Salvador and myself. Johanna Katharina Barends, who helped us prepare the text, attempted to retain the oral flavor of the original recordings as much as possible. Lively story-telling seemed to us more important than stylistic integrity.

We composed the book as an act of collectively bearing witness. It struck me again how little it is generally known today what Amsterdam meant to Jews and what Jews meant to Amsterdam. Unfortunately, the unpleasant conclusion is that despite this integration of Jewish and non-Jewish Amsterdammers, the Nazi persecutors were able to do their job so efficiently after 1940. Since 1978, a new generation of Dutch historians has conducted much research on this painful question. However, until today they have not been able to provide a satisfactory answer.

My deep gratitude goes to those who have entrusted me with their memories.

—PHILO BREGSTEIN

Introductory Remarks

In this book of interviews that Philo Bregstein and I put together, we attempt to present an image of what Amsterdam and the Jews meant to each other during the period after 1900. For clarity's sake, we divided the material into a number of sections in which particular subjects are discussed in some detail. Fragments that to our feeling were most typical and informative were extracted from the various interviews and placed in different chapters.

In choosing the fragments, our point of departure was the actual experience of the interviewees. Nevertheless, in several instances we utilized the knowledge that an interviewee had gained from books and study.

We do not have any illusion of presenting a complete picture of the position of Jews in prewar Amsterdam, nor is it our intention to do so. For instance, the list of Jewish occupations in the section that deals with this subject, is not only not exhaustive, but moreover it makes no mention of the fact that prior to 1940, Jews increasingly found work in occupations that had previously been performed mainly by non-Jews.

We imagine that sections of the book can be read separately, although the book can certainly be read from cover to cover. For those who know little if anything about prewar Amsterdam, we are furnishing a few reading aids. These are my historical introduction, brief introductions to each section, biographical notes on the interviewees, and a glossary.

—SALVADOR BLOEMGARTEN

Translator's Note

Translating the exceptional interviews you are about to read was challenging on many levels. The hurdles would have been harder to overcome and much of the detail would have been lost to readers of the English edition without the tireless guidance of Salvador Bloemgarten, whose input is present on every page, literally or figuratively.

To aid the reader, I have supplied additional footnotes and I have also compiled lists of place names, organizations and publications.

I appreciate the gracious assistance of Solon Beinfeld, translator of *Girl with Two Landscapes: The Wartime Diary of Lena Jedwab, 1941–1945*, who helped me to establish consistency in spelling Hebrew and Yiddish terminology. In this respect, Ashkenazic spelling has been used to reflect the culture in Amsterdam.

My thanks also go to editor Maggie Kennedy, whose close reading revealed inadvertent ambiguities.

—WANDA J. BOEKE

A Historical Perspective

When the Germans overpowered the Netherlands in 1940, there were about 140,000 people living in the country who were considered to be Jews according to National Socialist standards—which meant that they had at least three Jewish grandparents who were members of a Jewish congregation. More than half, a total of 80,000, were located in Amsterdam. The percentage of Jewish inhabitants (ten percent) was higher in Amsterdam than in any other city in Western Europe.

The social makeup of the Jewish sector of Amsterdam also differed from that of other Western European urban centers. For a long time, Amsterdam was the only city in Western Europe where the majority of Jews consisted of a proletariat of laborers and street vendors. After 1880, when a large wave of poor Jews fled from czarist Russia to the West (North and South America, but primarily to the United States), London also acquired a large Jewish working class.

As early as the middle of the seventeenth century, there were a considerable number of Jews living in Amsterdam who were barely, if at all, in a position to support themselves. The city, which during this century built up a trading empire of imposing magnitude, was at the time run by a certain number of patrician merchant families, or regents, who were proponents of free trade and freedom of religion and thought. Those who could not bear it elsewhere for one reason or another could set up shop in Amsterdam, as long as they did not come to the city's administrators begging for financial support. Also, a restrictive ruling applied to Jews whereby they could not become members of an existing trade or professional guild.

Thus, during the seventeenth and eighteenth centuries, the economic base for most Jews who settled in Amsterdam was extremely narrow. As a rule, Jews were allowed to engage in only those occupations that had not been organized into guilds. Jewish craftsmen who produced mainly for the Jewish market, such as printers of texts in Hebrew, Portuguese, Spanish, and Yiddish, were permitted to do so. For the rest, Jews had recourse primarily to commerce and certain kinds of business connected with industries that either did not previously exist in Amsterdam, or that barely did.

The Jews who came from Spain and Portugal around 1600 to settle in the Netherlands included quite a few rich merchants who, thanks to their contacts in Mediterranean countries and in the New World, made decisive contributions to the flourishing of the Dutch Republic and Amsterdam in particular. The Portuguese, as they were called, laid the foundation for the diamond and tobacco trades and associated industries in Amsterdam. During the seventeenth century, the Portuguese also turned Amsterdam into a famous center for Hebraic typography. During the eighteenth century, it was once again the Portuguese who brought about the development of the then new method of securities trading. This small elite of wealthy Portuguese, some of whom belonged to the nobility, attempted to keep their Spanish and Portuguese cultural traditions alive in Amsterdam. They steeped themselves passionately, for the most part, in Jewish religious culture, but at the same time remained open to new trends in the thought and culture of Western Europe. Consequently, these Portuguese were able to associate freely with foremost Dutch scholars and artists while still retaining their own identity.

The glory of the Portuguese, to which the stunning and monumental synagogue on Jonas Daniël Meijerplein (Jonas Daniël Meijer Square) bears witness, might erroneously create the impression that all the members of the so-called Portuguese Jewish Nation were wealthy. Not only was there poverty among the Portuguese to start with, but the backsliding of Amsterdam's position in international trade later, during the second half of the eighteenth century, was especially disastrous for many Portuguese. Accordingly it has been revealed that in 1799, at least fifty-four percent of the Sephardic Jews lived on charity.

Sephardic Jews cleared the way in Amsterdam for the Ashkenazic or High-German Jews who came primarily from Germany and Poland. The latter first settled in Amsterdam in 1620, almost a quarter of a century after the arrival of the first Sephardim. When the High-German Jewish Nation's Great Synagogue on today's Jonas Daniël Meijerplein first opened in 1671, the congregation in Amsterdam already included 7,500 members and was thereby about three times larger than that of the Portuguese. After 1730, the largest immigration of poverty-stricken Jews from Eastern Europe took place, and the census of 1797 showed that there were over 20,000 High-German Jews and 2,800 Portuguese Jews living in Amsterdam. In other words, there were over seven times as many Ashkenazim in Amsterdam as there were Sephardim. At the time, the total population of Amsterdam was about 200,000.

Ashkenazic Jewish families that became wealthy and gained social prestige during the seventeenth and eighteenth centuries had, as a rule, worked themselves up from nothing. They had far fewer economic opportunities than the Sephardic Jews, and often had to resort to dealing in second-hand goods, street vending in the form of peddling and selling at the marketplaces. At the end of the eighteenth century, two out of three Ashkenazic Jews lived partly on charity, meaning charity from their congregation. Among Christians in Amsterdam, it was "only" thirty percent. Among the richer Ashkenazim in eighteenth-century Amsterdam, one encountered primarily dealers in precious metals and brokers in colonial products.[1] The only truly major entrepreneur among them at the end of the eighteenth century was the tobacco merchant and planter, later banker, Benjamin Cohen, grandfather of the lawyer Jonas Daniël Meijer for whom the square in Amsterdam was named.

Before the so-called Batavian Republic was established in 1795 with the help of the revolutionary French army, destitute Jews had recourse only to the boards of trustees of their respective congregations for assistance. The communities of both the Portuguese Jewish Nation and the High-German Jewish Nation had been self-governing during the old Republic of the Seven Provinces (1576–1795). The laws and ordinances of both Jewish nations had simultaneously applied as city ordinances, which meant that the congregation trustees, or *parnassim*, could summon violators of Jewish law before the Amsterdam court. Thanks to the backing of the Amsterdam magistrates, the parnassim had been able to act as absolute rulers within their communities. Of course they had to if something like aid to the needy was to function to any reasonable extent.

The supervision by the parnassim of both Jewish nations was undoubtedly facilitated by the fact that practically all Amsterdam Jews lived in a single neighborhood, with today's Waterlooplein (Waterloo Square) lying at its center. At the end of the eighteenth century, the area of this so-called Old Jewish Quarter was significantly smaller than at the beginning of the twentieth century. Sint Antoniesbreestraat was still predominantly Christian then, and only the section of Weesperstraat directly bordering on Jonas Daniël Meijerplein (then the Deventer Lumber Market) was predominantly Jewish. The Old Jewish Quarter was not a real ghetto and was never populated exclusively by Jews. Jews chose to settle there because of the synagogues and also to be among their own. Only 200 Jews, according to the census of 1797, lived outside the so-called ghetto.

The Batavian Republic came into being in 1795 under the auspices of the French military occupiers, or, as the bulk of the population thought of them, liberators from the aristocratic regime of stadtholder William V, Prince of Orange (who, fled to England upon the arrival of the French troops). The Batavian Republic wrought an important change in the political position of Dutch Jews, including those in Amsterdam. On September 2, 1796, the National Assembly, a Dutch parliament elected according to universal male suffrage, recognized the Jews settled in the country as Dutch citizens with the same civil and political rights as all other Dutch citizens.

---

[1]The colonial products Amsterdam Jews traded in came from the East and West Indies, particularly tobacco, sugar, coffee, and cocoa. Also, red coral was traded on a large scale by way of Livorno, Italy, where there was a large Jewish community.

The large majority of Amsterdam Jews was not very happy with this change and hardly aware of what it meant for them. Most of them saw the new rulers, the revolutionary Patriots, mainly as opponents of the stadtholders—members of the House of Orange in the service of the former Republic of the Seven Provinces—who had always protected them. It was precisely because the adversaries of the last stadtholder, Prince William V, were promoting Dutch citizenship for the fiercely pro-Orange Jews that the latter were largely *against* the equal rights of citizens. Also, the parnassim and the rabbis were afraid of losing power within the Jewish community and that the Jews of the Netherlands would gradually lose interest in religious matters as a result of the new system of government. Promoting citizenship for Dutch Jews was, however, a logical consequence of the separation of church and state, which had taken place shortly before. Jews could now be considered simply as members of private church congregations because of this separation, and the Jewish nations lost their reason for being separate political entities. In the new system, the government recognized only individual citizens having equal rights and did not recognize separate political entities, such as the Jewish nations, that obeyed their own laws.

Starting in February 1795, a small group of enlightened Jews organized the Patriot group *Felix Libertate* and committed themselves to zealously lobbying for the civil equality of Jews. They expected that with civil rights, the poor and, in their eyes, uneducated Jewish workers and small business operators would develop themselves socially, economically, and culturally to become the equals of their fellow Christian citizens. Moreover, with the disbanding of the trade and professional guilds in 1798, the last of the legal obstacles to raising the social and economic standards of the impoverished Jewish population of Amsterdam appeared to have been cleared away. Mozes Asser, chairman of *Felix Libertate*, summed up the situation in which Jews had found themselves during the time of the Republic of the Seven Provinces with the words, "We were granted the right to sing psalms in public and to starve to death." In the new state, organized according to the principles of the French Revolution, it therefore seemed that Jews no longer had to starve to death. The fact that they were no longer allowed to "sing psalms in public," that is, allowed to practice religion in public places, was something the men of *Felix Libertate* gladly put up with.

Soon the Jewish Patriots' high hopes were dashed. For about a century, the necessary economic conditions to successfully combat poverty among working-class Jews would remain absent. Amsterdam's economic backsliding through the end of the French Napoleonic era (1813) made the circumstances of the Jews of this city, forced to be so strongly dependent on trade, even more dire. Even after the Napoleonic Wars were over in 1815, however, when Amsterdam was able to recuperate its trading relationships with colonies and overseas regions, the economy of the city continued to languish. As long as Amsterdam was not embraced by modern industrial capitalism, Amsterdam's poor, both Jews and Christians, had little or no opportunity to improve their economic position. And even though a Jew was now allowed to register as a carpenter or a smith, for instance, he couldn't go very far with his new right if he couldn't attract any clients.

Obviously there was some improvement in the socioeconomic position of Amsterdam Jews. Even before 1870, more and more Jews started successful professional careers by becoming physicians, lawyers, and journalists. The first Jews joined the faculties of Dutch universities during this period. Jews succeeded in gaining social prestige as merchants, contractors, and bankers more so than during the eighteenth century. Some, like the physician Samuel Sarphati, developed initiatives that provided a strong stimulus for Amsterdam's business world as well as for the welfare of the common people. Nevertheless, the overwhelming majority of Amsterdam Jews continued to live in dreadful poverty. This caused not only the immigration of penniless Jews from other countries to come to a halt during the nineteenth century, but also quite a number of poor Amsterdam Jews left to try their luck outside the Netherlands. Thus, an enclave of poor Amsterdam Jews arose in London's East End as early as the 1860s, even prior to the arrival there of Eastern European Jews.

Although not much changed in the socioeconomic position of most Amsterdam Jews during the rule of King William I (1815–1840) or that of his son King William II (1840–1848), there was some change on a cultural level. With the unqualified approval of the religious leaders of the Jewish congregation, Dutch replaced Yiddish as the language of instruction in Jewish religious schools. Moreover, many Jews also started attending the city's schools for the poor, where primary school education was, of course, conducted in the Dutch language. The initiative for this came from the government, which hoped that Jews would start assimilating. Increasingly, even notable Jews started to regard Yiddish as a primitive dialect, even if, from a religious perspective, they were orthodox. So, it was not surprising that they gladly worked together with the government in its attempts to assimilate Jews by means of language. Yiddish soon disappeared entirely as a written language. After 1850, Dutch became the official spoken language of Amsterdam Jews, albeit that this Dutch was still so riddled with Yiddish that a non-Jew or an assimilated Jew would find it hard to understand. One consequence was, however, that during the nineteenth century, Amsterdam Jews became alienated from the large communities of Jews in Eastern Europe with whom they could no longer communicate in Yiddish.

Assimilation through language did not particularly aim to alienate Jews from their religion. Until 1861, the government subsidized Jewish religious schools, so that a reasonable knowledge of Jewish religious culture could be retained, even among the poor. Prior to the end of the nineteenth century, assimilation was understood to mean formal adaptation to Dutch ways rather than actual abandonment

REMEMBERING JEWISH AMSTERDAM

of identity. As long as poor Amsterdam Jews had recourse to congregation charity, continued to practice for the most part specifically Jewish occupations, and
continued to live in a single neighborhood as adherents to one religion, they con-
stituted a closed community with its own clearly recognizable character.

For now, doubting the existence of God was still a luxury that only the rich in
Amsterdam could afford. But even non-believers of note remained loyal members
of the congregation, often becoming its leaders. The congregation, under the religious and political leadership of Orthodox rabbis and Liberal Jews, continued to
be the natural center of Jewish life in Amsterdam until the final decades of the
nineteenth century.

Between 1870 and 1914, Amsterdam was roused from its stupor by the developments in modern capitalism. The sleeping beauty on the Amstel and IJ, with its
sharp but unquestioned contrasts between rich and poor, was swept along in the
wake of other Western European peoples by the power and force of capital. The
new activity in trade and industry led to a fundamental change in the pattern of
life for everyone in Amsterdam, especially for Jews. Through the modernization
of the business world and the expansion of possibilities for commerce, larger
amounts of cash were freed up for individuals to buy consumer goods, which in
turn stimulated production and sales.

Many Jews, who worked their way up during this period, advanced in their
own occupations, as it were. A cigar maker who made cigars at home with a few
assistants could work himself up to become the head of a cigar factory where the
cigars were produced largely by machine. Some diamond cutters became jewelers who rented diamond-grinding mills and had others work the rough diamonds
into beautifully faceted stones. The ultimate level was that of jeweler-baron, like
Abraham Asscher, for instance, who had his own factory built, one with ultra-
modern machines and room for hundreds and hundreds of diamond workers. A
small textile shop like Bijenkorf on Nieuwendijk was able to expand into an
impressive chain of department stores during this period. Former Jewish ragmen
or dealers in second-hand goods became antiquarians or antique dealers. By
means of these occupations, some ended up in the art trade. Of course, such a
climb up the social ladder was possible only for a small minority.

After 1870, it was particularly the diamond trade that gave poor Jews the
opportunity to work themselves up to being skilled industrial workers who were
well paid at times, although poorly paid at other times.[2] The impressive growth
of Amsterdam's diamond trade after 1870 resulted from the discovery in South

---

[2] Diamond workers were initially well paid due to the rapid expansion of the diamond
industry. Competition then drove wages down. After 1894 the ANDB helped improve the
workers' lot for ten years until fluctuations in the diamond markets caused cyclical unemployment.

Africa of large quantities of high-quality rough diamonds and a growing demand for superior cut diamonds (especially brilliants) in the United States after the Civil War. Amsterdam's diamond workers were the most skilled in the world and they worked for relatively low wages. The diamond trade thus became "The Trade" in Amsterdam, and it is a reasonable assumption that by 1914, roughly half of the Jewish population depended on it.

The new economic structure introduced significant changes in social, political, and cultural relations. Social welfare slowly left the realm of congregational and private charity, which had been so well developed among Jews. The Jewish workers' society Handwerkers Vriendenkring (HWV), founded in 1869, was the first society of Jewish workers that tried to raise the social and educational standards of workers in practical ways—doing so completely outside religion. At the turn of the century, the modest social work of a small society like Handwerkers Vriendenkring was increasingly taken over and encouraged by the trade union movement, progressive political parties, and the government.

During the 1880s, Jewish workers continued to remain deaf to the revolutionary call of Ferdinand Domela Nieuwenhuis and his Social Democratic Union (SDB). Then, between 1892 and 1894, the tide turned. Three young Jewish diamond workers, Henri Polak, Adolf De Levita, and Jos Loopuit, succeeded in transforming their fellow diamond workers into an important factor in the labor movement. First, they breathed new life into the moribund socialist Dutch Diamond Workers Society, then they implored the Jewish diamond workers not to regard their Christian colleagues as intruders in the trade, but rather as comrades with whom they had to join forces in the struggle against their employers. The socialism propounded by this threesome was not the same as that of the revolutionary Domela Nieuwenhuis, but was instead inspired by the ideas of their slightly older friend Frank Van der Goes. Followers of Van der Goes first attempted to win the Social Democratic Union over to the so-called parliamentarian viewpoint. They hoped to get social legislation going by means of a strong social-democratic party with representation in parliament, even though they did not discount the notion of revolution. In practice, but not in theory, they became—with the exception of Van der Goes himself—reformers who wanted their capitalist society to evolve into a socialist one gradually, without revolutionary violence. Polak, De Levita, and Loopuit made an important contribution in Amsterdam to the establishment of the Social Democratic Labor Party (SDAP), a new labor party with a parliamentary orientation, which got a modest start to its political activities on August 26, 1894, under the leadership of attorney Pieter Jelles Troelstra.

Later that year, the publicity campaign run by the small Dutch Diamond Workers Society bore fruit. The diamond workers, whose wages had fallen far below a living wage due to increasingly sharp competition among hundreds of small-time jewelers, all went on strike in November; first the Christians and then the Jews. That very month, strike leaders founded a new union, the Dutch Diamond Workers Union (ANDB). The ANDB soon organized the overwhelming majority of diamond workers, at that time still a unique phenomenon for the Netherlands, and Henri Polak immediately became chairman, remaining its leader until May 1940. It was particularly by means of the ANDB'S *Het Weekblad*, a newspaper that was edited by Polak from 1895 to 1940, that the diamond workers received an education in the ideology of the modern union movement and parliamentarian socialism. In the first ten years of its existence, during which time it continually struggled with predominantly Jewish employers, the ANDB grew to become the most important and most effective union in the Netherlands and consequently a model for other Dutch unions. In 1905, thanks mainly to the efforts of the ANDB and its chairman, Henri Polak, the first modern federation of its kind, the Dutch Federation of Unions (NVV), was founded.

To what extent union and political activities were interrelated is revealed by the fact that until 1900, the overwhelming majority of SDAP members consisted of Jewish diamond workers.

The influence that the SDAP and the ANDB had on the Jewish proletariat in Amsterdam and Jewish diamond workers in particular is hard to overestimate. In fact, socialist leaders took over the educational work from religious leaders. A new secular culture that was not based on Jewish tradition or religion—one that may have meant cultural impoverishment as well as enrichment at the same time—was imparted to workers. The ANDB, and particularly Henri Polak, successfully provided workers with not only greater material well-being and improved working conditions, but also brought workers closer to science, art, and nature. Secular artists and scientists, such as the writers Multatuli, Emile Zola, and Herman Heijermans, along with architect Hendrik P. Berlage, and biologist Jacob P. Thijsse, became the new idols of Amsterdam's newly conscious Jewish proletariat, now more than ever alienated from its old religious culture.

This alienation was in no small measure due to the fact that around 1900 most of the rabbis had little concern for the social circumstances of the Jewish working class. Moreover, they were often the all too willing lackeys of Jewish and non-Jewish authorities. The blatant propaganda of Jewish congregation leaders and the Jewish press promoting the conservative Liberal Union also contributed to this alienation. The VDB (Liberal Democratic League), a party operating between the conservative Liberal Union and the progressive SDAP socialists, found a following primarily among Jewish intellectuals and the educated middle class.

However, even though the ties of Jewish workers (as well as much of the Jewish middle class and intellectuals) to religion and congregation loosened after 1894, this certainly does not mean that these ties were completely severed. In fact, many socialist leaders officially remained congregation members. Despite the fact that they operated largely outside the framework of Judaism, they did not necessarily want to undertake a direct attack on religion and the synagogue. One would be hard put to find a single anti-religious statement made by Henri Polak. Those people who, like Abraham Reens, believed that when Jews converted to socialism they stopped being Jews, continued to make up a very small minority.

Socialism undoubtedly lifted numerous social and religious barriers separating Jews and non-Jews in Amsterdam between 1894 and 1940. The SDAP, the ANDB, and, after World War I, the Workers Youth Federation (AJC) not only brought Jews and non-Jews together ideologically, but also encouraged mixed marriage. The secularization of culture in general during the twentieth century tended to promote mixed marriage. The less educated category of Jewish skilled workers, however, usually remained more strongly tied to Jewish tradition and consequently remained more isolated from the non-Jewish environment than their more educated fellows. This applied even more to the Jewish lumpenproletariat, which still continued to make up an important percentage of the Jewish population in Amsterdam until 1940.

It is certainly true that before 1940, the centrifugal forces pressuring Amsterdam Jews to assimilate were becoming stronger. Only rarely, however, did this lead to total assimilation with the non-Jewish environment and the complete loss of Jewish identity. In fact, there is evidence of mutual influence. Quite a few Christians who lived and worked among Jews were influenced by them. The Christian secretary of the ANDB, Jan van Zutphen, for instance, liked to pepper his letters to fellow directors with Yiddish expressions, while the epistles of the Jewish president of the union, Henri Polak, were textbook examples of pure and proper Dutch.

Between 1870 and 1940, Amsterdam Jews were fully integrated into Dutch society while maintaining their Jewish identity. During this period, the majority moved to newly built neighborhoods in Amsterdam East and South that were relatively close to the Old Jewish Quarter. Few Jewish families decided to settle in the western and northern extensions of the city because they were further away from the so-called ghetto. Most Jews preferred to live near the Old Jewish Quarter in order to keep in touch with friends and family still living there.

Prior to 1940, most Jews in Amsterdam felt they were Amsterdammers, Jews, and Dutch—in that order—regardless of political opinions or ideologies. Along with most non-Jews, they were very shortsighted regarding developments in other countries. The Jews deemed themselves safe and secure in the complacent isolation of the Netherlands, which had not been involved in any wars for over a century. It was primarily Zionists and left-wing socialists who became truly alarmed at the outbursts of anti-Semitism, occurring initially in czarist Russia and, after 1918, in the Polish republic.

Refugees from Eastern Europe and, after 1933, from Germany and Austria did not find a particularly warm welcome among their Jewish brothers and sisters in Amsterdam. Help was offered, of course, but only a few really listened to what these immigrants had to say. Very few Jews in Amsterdam considered the establishment of the National Socialist regime in Germany and the rise of National Socialism (the NSB party) in the Netherlands to be a real danger. In 1940, the Jews along with the rest of the Dutch were ill prepared for the German occupation and were therefore perhaps more vulnerable than they might have been. It is striking that the Jews who participated in the Dutch resistance during the World War II (quite a number), were as a rule either Zionist or left-wing socialists.

Three-quarters of the Jews in the Netherlands did not survive the war. Those who did attempted with admirable courage to give meaning to their lives again after the war. The contributions of Dutch Jews to postwar Dutch society have been remarkably valuable. Notwithstanding that fact, those who survived the war in hiding or in concentration camps, as well as the generation of Jews born after the war—along with children from mixed marriages—have continued to wrestle with this wartime past.

—SALVADOR BLOEMGARTEN

I

OCCUPATIONS

Jewish occupations in the true sense are of course only occupations that are directly tied to religion, such as being a rabbi or a cantor. In this chapter, however, the focus is on occupations that were practiced by many Jews and opted for on the basis of a situation that grew historically. It is impossible to draw a clear distinction between Jewish and non-Jewish occupations. Many Jews were employed in public education in prewar Amsterdam. This was a new development, however, which proves that due to their emancipation, many Jews began to prefer the profane climate of public education to the traditionally religious climate. Contrary to popular belief, Jewish bankers were not numerous in prewar Amsterdam. They were practically unheard of at the large banks. Jewish bankers ran primarily small family banks. These often had their origins in branches of business and trade in which Jews had specialized, sometimes as early as the eighteenth century. For these reasons, we can talk about such a thing as a Jewish occupation.

In this chapter, obviously only those occupations that were practiced by Amsterdam Jews are mentioned. However, some occupations typical for specifically Amsterdam Jews, for instance those of antique dealer, antiquarian book dealer, or jeweler, hardly ever come up.

Between 1900 and 1940, moreover, the percentage of Jews employed in occupations that were not specifically Jewish quickly increased. It was especially in the administrative occupations, both within the private sector as well as within the burgeoning public sector, that more and more Jewish employees were to be found. Between 1920 and 1940, the number of diamond workers, both Jewish and non-Jewish, decreased drastically due to the precipitous decline of the diamond industry in Amsterdam.

For some reason, Jews were practically wholly absent from a number of occupational groups until 1940. Thus, in heavy industry, construction, the dockyards, as well as the police force and the military profession, Jews were definitely the exception.

Street Vending

◆ BAREND BRIL

My mother was left with six small children. So, Mother had to go out on the street with a cart full of fruit. Apples, plums, oranges, whatever there was. At four o'clock in the morning, Mother had to take her really run-down old push-cart to the produce market—it was still on Marnixstraat then—to do her buying. And she wouldn't get back until practically nine o'clock. So, if there wasn't any money then, well, we wouldn't get any breakfast; we'd be out of luck.

That street vending went on from four in the morning till sometimes twelve at night, her going around with one of those vending carts selling fruit. Just to get rid of it, that was the trouble. And to top it off, it was forbidden to stop anywhere with your vending cart. In those days there were police everywhere. Well, she knew every last one of them, but if she didn't pay off one of those officers, she'd automatically get fined. To pay that fine right then and there, the bedding—we had nothing else—had to be brought down to the pawnshop so my mother wouldn't have to go to jail. We had to go through that time and again, of course.

◆ LEEN RIMINI

They went around peddling and they were able to purchase their produce "to suit." They didn't have the money to pay the supplier for a whole crate of fruit—you know, those big crates with 240 apples in them—so they'd "call out" their orders. "To suit" means that you can get, say, fifty apples. They would go get their produce from one of those wholesalers. Well, when they'd sold that, they'd have earned peanuts, as you can imagine, because an apple only cost a penny or two. They'd have tough luck if there were bruised ones in there; they'd have to sell those for a song if they could manage. You'd get two for a penny or some-thing. But that's how those people lived.

As far as peddling goes, with one of those carts, it wasn't allowed, see. If they stood in one spot and a police officer came by, they'd get fined. Now, if they'd gotten, say, ten fines, they'd let those ten fines add up since they didn't have the money to pay. They'd do time for a day instead and be rid of the penalty.

A police detective from Jonas Daniël Meijerplein would walk down

Jodenbreestraat to get the money from those people. A fine was fifty cents, and they'd let it add up so that when it happened to snow, say, they'd do their time.

◆ EMMANUEL AALSVEL

Mose's brother-in-law was a ragman and Mose was a diamond worker. That ragman earned a good living, but Mose was unemployed because it was bad times for the diamond workers and a ragman is a ragman. So, Mose's brother-in-law said, "Mose, come on out with the rag cart. You'll earn good bread tomorrow." So, his brother-in-law walks along with that rag cart and he calls out, "Rags, rags." And Mose, the diamond worker, he walks behind and says, "Me too, me too."

Now, that was typically an Amsterdam thing, that "me too, me too," because he was ashamed to say, "Rags."

◆ JOOP EMMERIK

Lots of Jewish people went around with rag carts and they'd call out, "Who's got rags? Rags, bones, metals!" I started out by selling out of my home. Those rags were first sorted into woolen, worsted, or flannel, then sold like that to Italy, to Prato. There were great big factories there and they carefully sorted it all by color and put it in compartments. The stuff would be ground up and then respun and rewoven, and this is how they turned it into new bolts of cloth.

Then you've got another kind of rag, which is white cotton. Paper is made from this. And from really cheap kinds of rags, they make balata—a kind of linoleum. And they also turned them into that kind of asbestos board they used to use for the backs of radio sets.

◆ BAREND DE HOND

I was friends with Hartog Mof. He was a rag dealer, and every Sunday morning we'd go to the Jewish Quarter. As early as five AM, there would already be strawberries, cherries and pears and apples out there at Waterlooplein (Waterloo Square). Those people, they'd go out with a cart on Sundays and sell that stuff. And then you'd get to the Tip Top movie theater. That's where the market began. There you had Tijpie selling eggs. "Four for a dime," she'd call out. Hard- and soft-boiled eggs, four for a dime. You'd hear those hawkers already right where the market began. And then you had Cross-eyed Ko. He was a man who sold watches and all that nonsense, except it was all cheap imitation, let me put it that way. But he did earn his living.

Then there was Hollander. He worked the stand next door. Toothache pads he sold. He also had his stand at Amstelveld, but on Sundays he was at the Jewish Quarter. He'd have pieces of leek he'd chopped up really fine and put in tissue paper. He'd get right up on his stand and make his pitch, "If there's a tough guy out there with a toothache, he should come on over here, up on top of the stand."

Well, there was always somebody with a toothache, and then he'd say, "So, you take this, what I've got here in this paper. You take that. And then you rinse and spit it out here in this bowl." So then, the farmer fellow would spit it out, and Hollander would say, "See those little white things? Those are the worms, and they just came right out of your tooth." And he'd sell this stuff for a quarter, like that, in little packets. There was nothing but little pieces of leek in them.

Back in those days, I had a stand at the market myself. I'd buy old inner tube rejects at Vateman's on Camperstraat, old brand-name tires, like Dunlop, Hevea, Engelbrecht. I'd fix these up at home by sticking patches on them, and I'd sell them for two or three quarters apiece. Sunday mornings, in a stand that was maybe twenty-two square feet, I'd demonstrate them, and if a tire happened to be bad and pop, I'd say, "Now, that's what they look like on the inside." You had to do something. Visitors came from all over. They called it the Jewish Quarter, but the visitors were Christian folk. Of course there were Jewish people who came by for the company, but most of the people by far were Christian and generally came from the Zaan. I knew one who came from Zaandam, who'd say, "If I don't take a look around that market, my whole Sunday'll be ruined." But then, you couldn't pass a stand where there wasn't some kind of entertainment. There was a little fellow there, also happened to be named De Hond, and you could go see how he rolled cigars. He had one of those long wooden boxes, and that's what he rolled those cigars in. Then he let them dry. He sold three or four for a quarter. They were real working man's cigars, but they were still made of real tobacco.

◆ LOE LAP
The market ran all the way down to right by Foeliestraat and over the Oude Schans, like that, around the whole district—it was all one big market.

There were people there selling bicycles—loads and loads of new bicycles— and rags; it's incredible what all was there. It was the biggest market in the country. But you couldn't walk there, you shuffled. You did that automatically, because it was packed with people. You could just about lift your feet and let the crowd carry you.

On Jodenbreestraat and Sint Antoniesbreestraat, all the shops were open on Sunday mornings, which meant you could buy food. The butcher shop, the poultry shop, the bread bakery, the candy shop, everything was open. Snattager's pastry shop and the fabric stores on Sint Antoniesbreestraat were open. And right up along there lay the market. On Vissteeg, people had fruit and fish stands. I'd say there were at least thirty or forty hawkers at that market selling all kinds of things, from playing cards to penny whistles.

If you entered the Jewish Quarter by way of Uilenburgerstraat, that's where it started; over the bridge to Uilenburgerstraat. And then, right on that bridge, there were two Jewish people, a man and a woman. They sold all kinds of chocolate, although their specialty was nougat bricks. Those two people did nothing all morning but sing out, "Nougat here, two cents a brick!" That's what she would sing out, and then he'd start in with, "Nougat here, two cents a brick!" and then she'd start in again with, "Nougat here, two cents a brick!"

A market vendor would tout his wares with, say, "Buy here!" or "It's cheapest over here!" There were people who did that in a singsong chant, "Max, he got the finest fabrics!" and "Max's fabrics, seventeen cents a yard!" But they weren't hawkers. They were what we called "steady vendors." They generally had an assorted stall with all kinds of things on the table—there'd be somebody with different kinds of tools, or somebody with different kinds of fabric.

A hawker always had just one particular article he bet on. It might be a box of cigars, it might be a knickknack, or something like pocketknives, pliers, or gauges. Or he would focus on a joke article, like the mysterious "miracle radio stylus." I remember that somebody who drank from a glass this pen-like thing had been put in would get little "shocks." But it was all one big con—they'd demonstrate with a couple of friends who would act like they'd gotten shocks.

Hawkers sold fabric, too, once in a while; English fabric, "made in England." They'd wear British sailor's jackets, sailor suits, or fishermen's sweaters and black coats. That really took the cake. So then they'd start talking "English." They'd know all of ten or twelve words of English. The story goes that a class of schoolchildren passed by one time with their teacher, who said, "Kids, listen a minute! Those are Englishmen. You might learn something from them!" But those "English" words—it was all Yiddish. This teacher went over to them. "Are you English?" he asked in English, and they said, "Yes!" So then the teacher said to the children, "They're speaking some kind of dialect. They must come from a very strange part of England!"

A steady vendor had a big stall, and that cost a bundle. A hawker hardly needed a penny. He could travel with a small sack or a little case. He was much more mobile. He could come and go as he pleased. A steady vendor was usually tied down with a cart, a pedal cart or barrow-bike or something like that. Hawkers were probably vendors who were poorer to start with.

A lot of the time wholesalers gave you credit. That's how most of the hawkers did it, but they still got by on that.

Their acts were all different. One would sing out in a comical way, another in a serious way, depending on what they were selling. And in those days they used "shills," and they'd be the first to buy. Then other people would automatically come over. The shills were "accomplices," "flunkies." There were hawkers who made the job as cut-and-dried as possible, which meant they only cared about the money. But you also had these really funny hawkers. They got a kick out of goofing around, and the crowd would laugh. Of course it's not absolutely true, but usually it's easier to sell something to people who are laughing than to people who are in a lousy mood. Some of those hawkers got such a kick out of it, they'd just keep on goofing around, at which point it turned into a game.

You had "cranes." That's what Meijer Linnewiel, alias Kokadorus, did. He had a small stand, a board and a couple of sawhorses, and he'd get up on it and tell his stories. Meijer Linnewiel, alias Professor Kokadorus, worked like that at the market sometime around 1908, 1910. I think he got the idea of hawking from his family in England where he'd seen them do that. He'd been schooled in England, too. Over here he was one of the first, a pioneer.

He'd tell the craziest stories and say all kinds of funny things. For instance, he'd sell watches that weren't exactly classy, so he'd say they were "genuine gold-brick." They weren't gold at all, you see! And he said things like, "I dropped by the palace to visit the Queen, and I was received and ate a delicious steak there." Stories like that he'd tell.

Then there was the "swimmer." He was a hawker who'd toss his wares in the middle of a little tarp and walk around it in a big circle. And then you had your "normal" hawkers. They were the guys who told stories behind their little stands. The cigar sellers did that, although they preferred to sit on chairs if possible because that made more of an impression—cigars were a serious item. Then there was the young guy with the knickknacks, pocketknives, razor blades, or pieces of shaving soap. He'd "swim" halfway through—make a big circle. And if a fellow was offering something really classy, he'd stand up on something—if he had to sell a pen or a special watch or maybe a cough syrup for some company. The quacks all stood up on something when they worked.

They'd all get as far away as possible from one another so they wouldn't bother each other. Hawkers are loud! They chided each other a lot, "Hey! Now is that any way to work? You're squeezing me out. I can't earn a thing thanks to you because your people are blocking my stall!" Spots were also worked in "combinations." Two or three guys worked with partners and all three teams would draw straws for one spot. That way they always had one! A lot of these guys went to the market without bringing anything to sell. They had no money. So, they'd get chummy with a vendor at his stand and say, "You want to work together?" A guy like that would have a little case with him, but there'd be nothing in it. Pretty sad, really.

Just about the whole hawker elite would be at that famous Sunday morning market in the Jewish Quarter. You could go from one stand to the next in stitches. They really lived it up there. The crowd went for it because it was a piece of entertainment that couldn't be had anywhere else in the world. So, they'd give one person a quarter and buy from somebody else for a dime. These guys were all semi-performers. The crowd would have a couple of guilders apiece on them, which they'd spend on a Sunday morning. I know from my father-in-law that every Sunday morning he'd buy a packet of razor blades for a guilder—he had razor blades coming out of his ears! But then, of course, they also had entire cabinets filled with knife-sharpeners. All kinds of crazy tie racks they had, at least five or six! These were all hawkers' articles. People would buy these things just because they were at this market.

◆ DICK SCHALLIES

At Waterlooplein there were generally only a few hawkers. The hawkers' markets in the country were mostly annual fairs and weekly markets, like Amstelveld in Amsterdam, for example. *After* the war[1], Waterlooplein became a bit more of a hawkers' market. It used to be "the little fruit square," which is all gone now. That's where the subway tunnels run. But after the war, some ten or twelve hawkers regularly showed up there.

Before the war, Waterlooplein was a real flea market. Everything that was bought up from private homes, say when spring-cleaning was done, went to Waterlooplein. Whatever the well-to-do had no space for anymore was sold at Waterlooplein to people who could still make good use of it at least. It's still done some now. These days people even go there to look for antiques!

At Amstelveld there were, for example, people selling ice cream. Montezinos and some other guy. They would compete with each other with that ice cream. But when it was over, they would shake hands, and I believe they even split their profits, too. They put on a play together, as it were.

"I'll add a scoop for five cents!"

"You'll get a heap on top from me!"

And then that mound of ice cream would get bigger and bigger the longer this went on, and finally they would go and sell it for five cents.

Once you had everything set up, there had to be somebody in the crowd who "played patsy." That's why they had the "shills" around. They were just "patsies." Later on, the real patsies came all by themselves, and *they* came for free so you could keep your money in your pocket. But the "shills" would come by with their things to settle up afterwards, and they'd get a couple of guilders for their efforts because they really did have to work and spend their time on it.

◆ DAVID MINDLIN

On Sunday mornings, there was a market in the Jewish Quarter, and it drew people from all over the country. On Mondays, there was a market out at

---

[1]World War II

Amstelveld, and the place would be terribly busy. Zuurbier had a stand there. He attracted the most people.

Zuurbier was an anarchist, but always smartly dressed with a handsome black hat on. And he'd say, "So you see, ladies and gentlemen, thousands of soldiers headed to the front. Luckily I couldn't read or write, so I got to stay and just sit on my duff in Amsterdam. The rest were killed in action, but I'm still here to tell you what the future will bring!"

Retail and Wholesale

◆ SIMON EMMERING

My father was a diamond polisher. There was a strike, and of course Father went on strike as well—he was so Red. And that strike went on and on, and of course there weren't any strike funds or anything.

Still, bread had to be put on the table. So, what did my father do? He rented a little stall at Nieuwmarkt and offered his own books for sale there.

And don't forget, a Jewish boy who's living in an even slightly orthodox family is raised on books. Jews have to read an awful lot, you know, if they want to practice their faith. Even Jewish laymen read a lot more than faithful Christians do. Jews have always had a bond with the book as such. On top of this, of course, the book trade was always unrestricted. At one time there was a guild for booksellers, but they weren't second-hand booksellers. Old books, used books, second-hand books, as well as the fruit and the fish business were free trades of old. But my father's interest was books.

As soon as things were going pretty well, he started buying books, too—with the firm intention of selling them. A couple of years later, he rented a stall, or "booth," as it was called, in the Oudemanshuispoort arcade. He stayed there until 1904, and then he opened his first shop on Langebrugsteeg.

He had a good story he'd tell about a small bookseller who also had a stand there, a Jewish bookseller, and this man could barely read or write. One day a little old lady came over to him with a Bible and asked, "Salesman, do you want to buy this Bible from me?"

And the man looked at the little Bible in his hand, smelled it, and said, "I'm not going to buy it, it's Lutheran, nobody's going to buy that."

After a while she asked, "How do you know it's Lutheran?"

"Oh, I can smell it." And he was right, too!

◆ MAURITS ALLEGRO

Pickling was mostly in the hands of Jews—that whole profession. In Amsterdam in those days, there wasn't a single non-Jewish pickling business. Later on one came in. And, believe it or not, the guy running the business had actually been a National Socialist during the war. But after the war, those pickling businesses were all gone, so other ones automatically came along.

9

Pickled foods were eaten a lot on Friday evenings. It would typically be pieces of pickled gherkin or something, or yellow dill pickles. Dill pickles practically aren't made here anymore.

◆ JOOP EMMERIK

Every Sunday evening a pickleman came to Kerkstraat. Heimie was his name as I recall. And he always called out, *"Karrotje in waje waaj, karrotje!"* That just means red cabbage pickled in vinegar.

◆ EMMANUEL AALSVEL

My father started out as a diamond worker in Belgium. After the Great War, he went to Amsterdam, but there were no jobs in the diamond trade. So, he started up a pickling business through one of my mother's brothers who had already worked in the trade. Gradually our business became very popular in Amsterdam. It was on Tugelaweg. We worked there with my father.

When I was in middle school and high school, there were barrow-boys who went around with our pushcarts. One of them would go to South Amsterdam, another to East Amsterdam, and one went to the Watergraafsmeer district, next to the Jewish Transvaal district. "H. Aalsvel, Transvaal Pickling, Tugelaweg" was written on those carts. I would find clients for my father at lunchtime when I was twelve. And then this teacher at school would ask me, "So, did business go well today?" And I'd say, "Yes!"

Actually the tastiest pickle you used to eat in Amsterdam—and it's not made at all anymore—is a brine pickle. That's a brine-pickled gherkin, and it was made in wine vats. We would buy empty wine vats that couldn't be used for wine anymore at a wine shop in Limburg or Groningen and had our own cooper repair them, and that's what those gherkins would be pickled in. Because the flavor of the wine went in along with the water and the salt—they had to ferment for six weeks—it was delicious, that wine taste in those gherkins.

◆ AARON VAZ DIAS

Practically all of my mother's family was in the cattle business. Every school vacation, I went to the cattle markets with my grandfather. That was always a blast for me. They were always cracking jokes I didn't always get, but I was always up for them.

Most cattle dealers were Jews and because of this, the bidding was always done using Jewish terms—the non-Jewish dealers and farmers did that too. I've been told that it's still done that way nowadays. If somebody bid too low, they would say, "What, you want to have it for *kuf-nun?*"

It's a well-known fact that the Jews were not allowed to practice a profession or skilled trade at one time, so that's why they were forced to go into business.

◆ Max Louis Terveen

The name Terveen was not Terveen in 1652, but just like all the other names at that time. You'd have a first name, and your father's first name would be your last name. For instance, Mordechai Ben Mordechai, is Max Maxson.

At a certain point, a license was issued to sell binding and ribbon in the neighboring village of Amstelveen. That's why the man was said to be "vending *ter* or 'in' Veen." And so the name Terveen came about. In Napoleonic times, Jews, in particular, were forced to take on a last name since they often didn't have one. This gave rise to strange names, like Gherkinsman.

The Terveens always had large businesses. They bought chintz—that's a kind of shiny printed cotton—in England. They also bought a machine there to fill blankets with cotton batting. They would parcel out those blankets to piece workers in Amsterdam's Jordaan neighborhood to be quilted. They sold those blankets all over the country. So, that's how they became blanket manufacturers. Consequently they were importers of packaged cloth, and little by little they also started selling that cloth by the yard.

The fabric world was made up of people who were not organized into a trade union. They were competitors and very well traveled. Once a month, my grandfather took a train from Weesperpoort Station to Germany and from there to Silesia, now Poland, where there was a huge textile industry. It ran up to Lodz, a stretch of over one hundred and twenty miles. He would come home a week later, after doing his buying there.

My grandfather completed his studies at the *Hvis met de Zeven Hoofden,* a trade school. That's where he took his final exams. He spoke fluent French, German, and English. He would also spend a week in Lancashire and Yorkshire and stay in Manchester or Bradford, where he had friends and acquaintances. In Leeds, there was a large Jewish community he did business with. In Bradford, some of the businessmen were Jewish, some weren't.

He would also spend a week in France and go to Amiens and Mulhouse. These were textile centers where he visited some fifty mills. That was a wholesaler's job. My father did the same thing. He bought nothing but fabric—there was no ready-made clothes industry in those days. A shopkeeper would receive an order and take in five thousand yards of fabric to fill it. Now, those shopkeepers buy fifty yards of fabric. At that time, though, they sold everything by the yard—every suit and every dress was made at home.

The fabric business was huge! Here at Nieuwmarkt, for instance, there was a stand run by Stoppelman's aunt and father, the Stoppelman who now has four stores. But there used to be at least two hundred fabric stands on the square. They sold wool tweed, for instance, for making suits. They would sell a good ten rolls of that in a single morning. People from out of town came to buy at Nieuwmarkt, too. At that time, Sint Antoniesbreestraat was a street lined with shops that had private apartments above them—a very respectable street, where coaches neatly pulled up right in front of the door and where you could say the "better" class lived. Then those storekeepers started wholesaling, and the apartments above them were vacated and replaced by offices. Those wholesalers would sell fabric for fifty suits at a time to a single client—more and more of that went on—and the apartments were turned into stockrooms to store the fabrics.

On the other side of Sint Antoniesbreestraat, there was a market that attracted thousands of visitors. It was in the Jewish Quarter. On Sundays, people from out of town came to see it. It was one of the sights. The shopkeepers on Sint Antoniesbreestraat would be open then, because there were a lot of market vendors who worked Monday through Saturday and who could do their buying only on Sundays.

Store personnel was mostly Jewish. Around 1912, they began to "peddle" Jewish orphans. People from the Jewish orphanage would come by to ask if you'd hire one of those boys. You couldn't say no to that.

So, around 1929, there were a lot of Jewish vendors in Amsterdam who had no capital, which is precisely what's most important for a vendor. Now if one of them heard that there was some store stock for sale somewhere (a shop that had gone bankrupt, so its inventory could be sold on the market), he would go in search of "partners," who all had to pay in five guilders. Then the ten of them would buy that stock for fifty guilders. But if those ten didn't have five guilders, and that was usually the case, they would each have to find another ten partners who had fifty cents.

After the money was collected, the first fellow would go for that inventory, although nobody was supposed to know anything about it. The shop would be emptied and everything inside loaded onto pedal carts. Then they still had to find people to sell the goods. This resulted in tremendous fights, because when the "take" (the money they got) was counted, it first had to be divided into ten and then into ten again.

There would be arguments, like the one where a man said to one of these vendors, "You have to give me a share, too, because I always go in on it. Except you didn't ask me this time. If you *had* asked me, I'd have gone in on it too!"

◆ Mozes De Leeuw

In their line of work, Jewish textile wholesalers dealt more with non-Jews than many people in other more or less typically Jewish professions.

Wholesalers began to have more textile products ready-made. They would buy twenty or thirty thousand yards of muslin, for example, and have that worked up because at a certain point there was a greater need for sheets than for yardage.

They had that done by contract seamsters, smaller business people, in the city at first and later out of town as well. The farther away you went, the less Jews entered into it.

In the textile world here, relationships before the war were much more personal than they are nowadays. As a merchant, you might have such a good relationship with a client that you supplied the person for years. That particular merchant and that particular client did nothing without consulting each other. My father had clients like that too. That doesn't happen anymore now. My father had a client who was in The Hague, and when that man came to the city on Sundays—*the* big day in the textile world—they would both bring their wives, who were specially dressed for the occasion, and the women would go to the Schiller Cafe while the men went off to do business on Jodenbreestraat or somewhere. Most textile businesses were closed on Saturdays because there wasn't any point in opening up.

They all had clients they swore by. If my father wanted somebody to have a "lot," he would call him up and say, "I'm saving it just for you," and he would, too. These clients didn't necessarily have to be Jewish, although they usually were. They were often Jews from Rotterdam or Brabant or Limburg. During and after the war, of course, it all changed—got wiped out in one fell swoop. There's nothing left of it.

Reiss's was one of the oldest firms on Breestraat. It still exists. The Reisses were wholesalers, pretty important wool wholesalers. Mrs. Reiss was already a very dignified lady at that time, and she ran stands at two markets: at Nieuwmarkt and in Utrecht. She did that for a very long time. They were an extremely prominent family and had a house of their own built on Sint Antoniesbreestraat. When I was a boy, everybody looked up to them.

It was a very normal thing that she had a stand at the market. Other wholesalers' wives had stands too. I don't know if they needed to do that to earn money, but it was just something they felt they had to do. That's also probably how they started. Those people were a big name at the market. There were a good three hundred stands there, but somebody would come from Wormerveer or Haarlem just to buy at Mrs. Reiss's.

◆ ELIZABETH VAN DE KAR-STODEL

I went to the vocational school for saleswomen, which, I believe, is now called the Retail Business School. I was there for three years. Then I started working at De Vries Van Buuren, in the office, because it was 1927 and already at that time it was hard for an Orthodox girl or boy to get a job where you were off on the Sabbath. De Vries Van Buuren was a very big business, a textile wholesaler that used to be on Jodenbreestraat, next to the Rembrandt House. If you got a job there, you were off on the Sabbath and for *yontif*.

I got to know my husband there, too. It was a very Jewish business and a kind of marriage market for girls at the same time, because the majority of the girls who worked there got married to boys from De Vries Van Buuren. I went to Nieuwmarkt to see my father, who had a stall there, and when I said that the company had taken me on, everybody came over to congratulate me. My father and my mother were terribly happy—because if "heaven forbid" I shouldn't get married, I would still be out of the woods for life because the company had a pension fund.

The company's personnel was primarily Jewish, from the upper to the lower echelons—except for shipping. That department also worked on Saturdays, because the cloth had to go out, so the personnel at that department was Christian.

◆ KAREL POLAK

I wanted to be a window dresser, because I was very adept at drawing and painting and writing. Well, that didn't work out, because if you want to be a window dresser, you really have to work for a company where window displays are being done all day long, say at De Bijenkorf, Gerzon's, Vroom and Dreesman's, or Hema. But these are businesses that are open on the Sabbath, and a Jewish boy from an orphanage can't go and work on the Sabbath; he just can't. So, in the meantime, you just have to find a company where you can learn a trade. I started working on Jodenbreestraat and learned the fabric trade. From there, I moved on to Hirsch's on Leidseplein as a salesclerk in their fabric department. The management was Jewish and actually had an exceptionally Jewish social orientation. Mrs. Kahn—she was the wife of Mr. Kahn, the president—was a trustee of the Dutch Israelite Orphanage for Boys. That's how I ended up at Hirsch's, as a matter of fact. It was all patronage and protection in those days because it was so hard to get a job.

The most important thing to me, though, was to be off on the Sabbath and for *yontif*. Obviously that was very important, because where else could you go? Hirsch's was open until one o'clock on Saturdays, and that was impossible for me. So, they hired me with the promise that I would have Saturdays off. Unfortunately they kept their promise to me for only three months, since the other employees were jealous that I had more days off than they did.

◆ MIRJAM GERZON-DE LEEUW

The father of the Gerzon brothers was originally a sales representative who sold paper—wallpaper and such—in the province of Groningen and he died young. The oldest brother was my father, Joseph Gerzon, and he was more or less responsible for the whole family, together with his brother Maurits, the next one down. One day he said, "Boys, you younger ones are going to have to learn a trade abroad and perhaps one day you'll come back with the knowledge you picked up there."

So, the Gerzon brothers Eduard and Leon ended up in Cologne. Right away they got jobs at a very good company where they were able to learn a lot—tricot and hosiery and such. They were there for a time, married the owner's two daughters, and came back to Amsterdam with these two women.

Eduard Gerzon was a striking figure. He always reminded me of the Calvinist Abraham Kuyper, leader of the Antirevolutionary Party—his face looked a little like that. Eduard was without a doubt the more intelligent of the two. The other brother, Leon, was the handier one and the salesman. The combination was excellent. Eduard was a very well-read man. He co-founded the Institute for Efficiency.

Fabric purchasing, fashion, and styles were what Leon did. For instance, he would go sit out on a Parisian boulevard for half a day with his daughter Emmie. At some point, he'd say, "Look, here comes one—that woman who's walking over there. She's wearing something new. *That* I have to have!" And he'd go straight to the city of Lyon, buy the fabrics, and make sure that the styles he had seen in Paris also came to Amsterdam. He was extraordinary in the fabric department, and he also had a very good rapport with the personnel. If one of the girls was planning to get married, he'd know about it and make sure that there was something special for her.

Leon was very attuned to the mentality of Dutch buyers; starting with his first day on Nieuwendijk when he tossed every possible kind of stocking into the display window, saying, "Now people here in Holland are going to say, 'They're crazy. There's nothing but stockings in there!' Well, that's exactly what I need. They have to see that we have all kinds of stockings." Eduard, on the other hand, he was the administrator, the financier.

There was a time that businesses closed for Yom Kippur. I see this as a sign that they wanted to testify outwardly to being Jewish. They also took on a lot of Jewish personnel. This was sometimes held against them, Leon told me once. "But," he says, "I can't do anything about that. The Jewish staff often has a better feeling for the business than the non-Jewish staff." And it just so happened to be true, too—they were excellent saleswomen.

◆ HENRI ISIDORE ISAAC

The founder of the department store De Bijenkorf was my grandfather, S. P. Goudsmit. He wasn't from Amsterdam, but from one of the islands of South Holland. His father was a goldsmith down there. His name was Goudsmit (Goldsmith), but he also happened to *be* a goldsmith.

The Bijenkorf was originally a kind of dry goods business: fabrics, haberdashery, and fashion. That's really what it started with and then it gradually expanded.

De Bijenkorf was on Nieuwendijk, but over the course of years they were constantly buying other buildings on the street because the space kept getting too small. When they decided to construct a new building on Nieuwendijk, they temporarily housed on Damrak. Once they were there, though, the growth of the business was so significantly much better than on Nieuwendijk that they decided not to go back. So, the permanent Bijenkorf building was constructed on the site of the temporary building, and it opened in August 1914, just when the First World War started.

In the very beginning, the business closed Friday afternoon, opened again Saturday evening, and was open on Sunday. So, it was a very typical Jewish business, hiring mostly Jewish employees. They must already have stopped doing that before 1909, before the move.

It is definitely not true that De Bijenkorf took on exclusively Jewish personnel, although by coincidence the majority was. Or maybe not by coincidence; I don't know. Still, there was a certain affinity—on the part of the applicants, too. They really preferred to work for a Jewish company.

That went on for a very long time, but obviously not after World War II—we lost a lot of people during the war. The company's entire management changed too, although I stayed on until 1969 as a member of the board of directors.

Trades

◆ Ben Sijes

My father was a cigar maker, and he earned something like nine or ten guilders a week, maybe, which meant more income was needed. That extra money came from two sources: the first being that my mother sewed buttonholes in military coats—this was done at home—and the second, that my father made cigars, also at home.

Before making cigars, you had to make what they called "bunches," and you did this on a metal plate. Then those bunches—the first rough form of the cigar without a cap—have to dry. After that, a leaf wrapper is put around each one, and then various other processes follow.

In the evenings after dinner, the tablecloth was taken off the table, and the stemmed tobacco would be laid out on a big piece of paper. So, I learned how to make those so-called bunches. The stemmed tobacco was mixed with a tiny bit of tobacco from Brazil. Then a first binder was wrapped around those bunches—a leaf from Delhi if I remember right—but then, of course, that was my father's job.

◆ Hartog Goubitz

Diamond workers were the most well-off as a group. Diamonds are a luxury item after all. Those workers went through times of great unemployment, but when the economic climate was favorable and there was a lot of demand for diamonds, their wages were incredibly high compared to wages earned in other businesses. It wasn't rare in those days—if there was no unemployment—for a diamond worker to earn forty guilders a week.

In our neighborhood, most of the people supported themselves by peddling and vending, and it was a big step up if you could get into "the trade" (meaning diamond cutting). And if that didn't work out, let's say because your eyesight was bad, you became a cigar maker, because that was work you could do at home, too. Tobacco was really cheap. If you could make cigars and there was work, you could work at a factory, although it was also possible to make cigars at home. You only had to buy a little tobacco, and then you could sell the cigars or trade them at the butcher's for some meat, say, or at the grocer's.

Cigar making was an occupation that didn't count as a trade, as opposed to, say, being a metalworker or furniture maker. Sure, you needed training to be a cigar maker, but it was easier to get into the profession. You could get work as a

17

"stem boy," for instance, and then you were already earning one to two and a half guilders a week. Making cigars at a factory, you had ten-, eleven-hour work-days. You might just manage to earn twelve, thirteen guilders if you were a good craftsman, but that was a high wage at the time, really. So, if you had a large family, you just had to get by on that.

◆ LIESBETH VAN WEEZEL

My father originally cut brilliants. He worked at home at first—those are my ear-liest memories—in a room. I think I was two or three, and he would sit in front of a "balloon," a globe of water that sat on a square, wooden stand. There was an alcohol flame, too. He'd stick his cement sticks in there, and soon the glass-powder cement would start to melt. My father would cool the cement by blow-ing on it, and then the sound of the sticks grinding on each other would start.

◆ JOOP VOET

My father went straight into diamond work. He was an intelligent kid, but at twelve, when he'd finished grade school, that was it. There were two options at that point: either you went on with your studies, becoming a doctor or a lawyer—but there wasn't any money for that—or you learned a trade, and for Jews this was likely to be the diamond trade.

For my mother, it was exactly the same thing. When she finished grade school, she was sent to the factory to learn "cutting." Apparently there wasn't enough money to feed all the children. Once you properly graduated from grade school, you had to start earning money. My mother didn't want to, so she kicked up a fuss—although it didn't do any good. There was no other way.

◆ MAX EMMERIK

It was an incredible honor to become a diamond worker. Diamond workers, I might add, the older ones at least, all have that feeling. It was instilled in them at their mother's breast. It was passed from generation to generation. Those people, each and every one, including the big employers, started that way, as apprentice diamond workers.

If you had any money at all, you were supposed to pay to learn the trade. I was dirt poor and during *yontif* I had to go to my master, Leman Mulder, on Prinsengracht, to bring him a three- or three-and-a-half-guilder chicken. He was later on the board of Helpt Elkander.[2]

You couldn't get into the trade if your father wasn't in it. This meant you couldn't become a diamond polisher if your father wasn't "in diamonds."

---

[2]Help One Another (Helpt Elkander) was an early private insurance company that geared itself toward covering the health care costs of workers. It was founded in 1903 and its membership consisted primarily of Jewish diamond workers.

◆ KAREL POLAK

In those days, you couldn't get into the diamond trade unless your father and your mother were diamond workers. It was a kind of caste, a closed shop. What did exist was the AJV, the General Jewelers Union. Members were assigned two protégés per year to learn the trade from a master jeweler. So, I went to the Diamond Exchange, to Mr. Van Amerongen, who was a trustee of the orphanage at the time and always called me Kareltje (Charlie), and he said he would try to get me into the diamond trade.

I became a brilliant polisher with Asscher, his brother-in-law. All the others had to apprentice for three years, I believe it was, but if you were a protégé, you were allowed to apprentice for two. The others would get a guilder pocket money, but I got two and a half because I was a protégé. It meant you finished apprenticing faster and got your certificate sooner.

Not every jeweler was assigned two protégés. They drew lots. If a jeweler won two new diamond workers, he was allowed to choose: polisher, cleaver, cutter, or sawyer—these were all separate specialties. Nobody can do everything all at the same time in the diamond trade.

◆ RUBEN GROEN

The majority of diamond workers were Jewish. I really enjoyed working there. My apprenticeship lasted three years, and then you had to take your exam. So, I did that at Asscher's and passed. I worked there for about a week on two small lots of stones, and crafted them all. After that, Asscher's manager gave me a little certificate so I could go to the Union to get my registration booklet. That was tremendous, because when you picked up your registration booklet, you were a professional, you could start working, and in those days you'd make about twenty to twenty-three guilders a week. That was a decent income for a skilled worker in those days. I finished my apprenticeship when I was about seventeen or eighteen. That was a wage that the ordinary working man would have trouble earning.

It's the kind of work where you produce something you can see, the way furniture makers at one time made beautiful pieces and looked at them with pleasure. That's how it is in the diamond trade, too. You take a raw product and turn it into something truly beautiful. And, of course, the larger the stone, the greater the satisfaction you get from it.

◆ MOZES DE LEEUW

The diamond polishing factories were simply awful places. Behind here, in that old Boas factory on Valkenburgerstraat, people sat in long halls, all of them at a wide leather belt, in this incredible racket. Then whenever the sun came out, the factory was absolutely stifling—and that was the most modern factory around when I was a boy. Asscher and his new factory came after that.

Still, if you were a diamond polisher, you were somebody. The conditions were bad, but didn't seem out of the ordinary because it was tough for everybody—for lots of people in any case.

◆ ARON DE PAAUW

My father was a diamond polisher, too, same as I was. He was actually a "rose polisher." Dutch rose cuts were very thin diamond chips on which people made twenty-four facets. These were called "roses." That's a very rare cut nowadays.

Every year they decided how many apprentices would be allowed to go into the diamond trade. You had to be fourteen. I was almost fourteen, and I was taken on in 1917. It was customary for the apprentice to pay the master something for this, but at Asscher's, management paid the master. Abraham Asscher would ask, "Who can this boy apprentice with and which personnel team should he go to?" and then he would pay the master.

At Asscher's, there were three kinds of "personnel." You had personnel who made exclusively "small" stones. They were Christian. Then there was personnel who made exclusively intermediate sizes or "melees." And then there was "big personnel." They worked large stones. I joined them and was very happy with this, because they were the best.

Small diamonds were produced "for a rate," piecework pay, and if you were pretty quick you could earn a very decent salary doing this. It wasn't any less than if you worked "big," because "big" was based on steady hourly pay. And if you got steady pay, you regularly had to ask for a raise from your boss, and that wasn't about to happen very quickly.

We lived in a patriarchal society, and good craftsmen often just didn't get the chance to work on bigger stones. Asscher's big personnel were really a privileged caste.

From 1921 through 1929, there were some three hundred polishers and about one hundred cutters and sawyers at Asscher's alone. There were good craftsmen among them since you couldn't give "big" to just anybody. Still, some of them knew so little about the work, that Abraham Asscher let them polish only a portion, a little bit of the "tables" of the diamonds so they could stay on with him. They may not have gotten a high wage, but they still earned well enough. The assistant manager's brother worked there like that, as what was called a "bit polisher" in polishers' terminology. Then the good ones did all the final work.

Before 1940, life at the factory hall was very different than it was after the war was over. They used to sing together. They horsed around together. After '45, the radio made its entrance and as a result conversation stopped and personal communication along with it. It was my experience before 1940 that after months of unemployment, people would be at work again, and the hall would resound with songs. People were happy again. . . . There were patriarchal situations at Asscher's, but Asscher himself got along with people very well, and people were definitely not afraid of him. The older ones addressed him as Bram.

I remember once when it was snowing, Asscher stepped out of the factory to get into his car. There was an apprentice out in front, throwing snowballs. One snowball went off-course and hit Asscher's hat, which fell off.

So, Abraham Asscher drew himself up squarely in front of his door with his hands in his vest pockets and said to that boy, "You, come over here for a second!" The boy goes over to him, shaking in his shoes. Then Asscher takes a guilder out of his vest pocket and says, "Here's a guilder for you because you're such a good shot; but if you do that again, I'll throw you out on your ear." That's what things were like!

◆ SUZE FRANK

I was a diamond cutter for forty-one years, a brilliant cutter and a rose cutter. A "rose" was waste that could still be worked. My master was very good. He never cut small diamonds. Even if they're not any bigger than pinheads, though, they still have to be worked in the same way the large stones do.

In three years, I had learned the trade. After that, you earned half-wages for six months to start. I always had work, and I had different bosses at the same time. That was lovely! On Sunday afternoons, the diamond exchange would close, and the bosses would have done some trading. They'd come by with a few stones and ask me, "Suze, would you start on these tomorrow?" That's how come I pretty much always had work.

Polishing went like this: there were fifty-eight facets on one of those stones, but if one of those facets was "blemished," it was ruined, so the cutter would have to fix the facet. Well, this happened a lot, but the boss wasn't supposed to know, because a blemished diamond "lost"—they were always weighed. This meant a splinter had chipped off, so I'd have to repair it very inconspicuously.

We also had "runners." They were people who were maybe too old to practice a trade. So, we'd tell them, "Could you go get a half a challa and two ounces of cheese?" And then somebody else would say, "They must be meshugge over at the baker's, cutting up two challas!" So, one of those runners would go off with a very long list for itsy-bitsy pieces of meat: two ounces of sausage. All of us wanted just two ounces, see, although there were also times I ordered nothing on my bread.

My younger sister and I sat beside each other for twenty-six years. She was a very "fine" worker. She was much more precise than I was. The boss would sometimes say, "Suze, do you mind if Anita does this?"

You'd get one of those rough stones. It looks like a piece of rock candy at that point. And we would have to find a way to get as much of a large surface out of it as possible.

We had an enormous respect for our craft. When my father was still alive, all evening it would be, "What kind of work do you have? Do you have 'pure' work or is it a little 'impure'?" Whenever you ground an "impure" diamond with another diamond, what we called the "salt," which means the "impurity," would drop off.

One carat equals one hundred points, and the boss might say, for example, "It's nice, choice work." That meant that it was "pure," a valuable diamond that was allowed to lose a couple of points at most in working it. Some people got very valuable work, blue-white diamonds, and others got slightly impure work that had a tiny fracture or a speck in it. Then you had to manage to work it in such a way that things like this ended up on the side of the stone.

Not everybody had good tools. When you went to work for a boss, you got a few tools that you had to hand in when you left. But I had my own tools, the finest, a whole table full of them. Nobody had anything like that! On occasion they'd sometimes borrow a dop from me, a holder. I could fix a dop again myself. I'd set it on the machine—I had a file to go with it—and I'd scrape over it so that a new hole appeared in the dop. The diamond and your glass-powder cement had to go into that little hole.

The bosses did rush you occasionally and paid poorly then, but I always had luck with my bosses. If you get to work for a boss for twenty-five or forty guilders a week, that boss wants you to produce a lot. "Could you still just do this?" and that would be at ten to six, and at that time we worked from eight to six. So then I'd think, "I don't believe that lot's at all as nice as he says it is!" But there were also bosses who were very difficult, and if you didn't do what they asked, you'd simply be fired. Then you'd have to wait a week for your money from *that* boss, or you'd have to be fully unemployed for two days to get money sooner.

The quicker you were, the more you delivered, of course. I was quick and I was good, but not always both quick *and* good; that's impossible. My younger sister was a lot "finer" than I was, but also a lot slower and more timid, too. Not me! When I got a stone in my hands, I'd occasionally break off a piece and think, "Well, I won't have to cut *that* off anymore!"—because it takes a long time to do that.

Occasionally we had very poor diamonds, too. They just had to be patched together somehow. That would be for really small-time bosses, schlemiels who wanted to earn their own bread. That was great; I'll take those little jobs any day, they're more fun—the kind of boss who employed two or three people. I didn't feel at home with big bosses.

Cutters set the diamonds themselves. You had to do a good job. The glass-powder cement wasn't supposed to come up over the edge of the dop too far, and you had to make sure that the diamond stuck out well above the cement so you could really work on it. It couldn't be sitting crooked, either. You had to see to it that the diamond was level because you had to lay a little girdle around it, and the girdle wasn't supposed to be cut too wide or else the diamond would lose too much weight.

The worst was really the hours spent looking for stones the size of a pinpoint. You'd get a certain number of little stones in a little "diamond paper" and naturally you had to give all of them back—after they'd been faceted, of course. But how many times didn't one get away? You'd think it was lying right in front of you, but it would be over in the corner. You'd have to look for *hours* among the machines with a little brush; that was torture, but I had an incredible knack for it. I'd say, "Oh, Suze will come help out for a minute. How did it fall?" Sometimes I'd retrieve one from a man's tie. Sometimes it would be under somebody's shoe. There was this one guy who didn't want to take off his shoes. So we said, "Show us your filthy, black feet!" We got him down on the floor, pulled off his shoes, and peeled off his socks.

It happened to me once that a large stone got away, and it fell into a hole along a pipe and down into the hall on the floor below, and I kept on looking even *after* six. When I got home, my mother was leaning out the window. Everybody in my whole building felt bad for me.

Oftentimes when a lot of diamonds was finished, people wouldn't have another boss right away, and that cost them money, because a diamond worker was entitled to benefits only after a week of unemployment. Lots of times, a boss would buy just a small lot of "big," and there wouldn't be work for everybody. The question then was: who was going to be the schlemiel who got fired? So then that person would quickly have to go look for another boss. You also had to be as honest as gold, because if stones kept being lost, a boss might think, "I wonder, are they really being honest over there?" And if you were fired for that— rightfully or not—nobody had any use for you.

You also had stones that were called "whole." They were like shiny beads, and you'd have to cut them in the most advantageous way. You had to let the impurity drop off to get the beauty out of it. That was the craft: to be able to look *through* them!

Back then we didn't have money to buy clothes. Everything was mended by the mothers or the wives. There were little patches on everything. One time, I was once again looking for one of those little stones another polisher had lost. I felt all his "patches," which ones had come loose and which ones were stitched up, because a little stone like that could get lodged anywhere. And where had that little stone gotten to? His fly! That evening the entire factory knew: "Suze pulled a stone out of Arie Hartog's fly!" Boy, did we have a good laugh about that!

◆ HIJMAN (BOB) SCHOLTE

Of course, there were also times of terrible unemployment. On top of this, my father had a little accident at work. While he was polishing, he got something in his eye, and he went completely blind in that eye. He couldn't work anymore as a diamond polisher like that, so he began working at the factories as a "commissionair," as they say in Belgium, running errands on commission for people. A diamond polisher might say, "Scholte, go get a cheese roll for me." Then, when the week was over, he'd get some money from all those people he'd done errands for, and that's what his income amounted to. It wasn't much, of course. We had no money to spare for fun or trifles.

◆ ALEXANDER VAN WEEZEL

Beggar Gans was an extraordinarily dignified figure, striding across Dam Square in a threadbare coat, like a prophet, with a long staff in his hand. He made his living by passing through all the diamond factories, and everybody would give him some of their wages. One time a man put a nickel out for him, and Gans said, "Sir, it costs a dime."

◆ RUBEN GROEN

If you were a diamond worker, you really needed another job on the side, something to fall back on in case there was a slump. That's when they'd fire people. Back then it could happen overnight. The boss might well come up to you on a Friday afternoon and say, "You don't need to come back Sunday." And that was the end of that. You could go to the union (the Dutch Diamond Workers Union, or ANDB), and if you got official unemployment compensation from them, you got eighteen guilders a week at most. The union dues, on the other hand, were very high back then. If you earned twenty-five to thirty guilders, you paid three guilders in dues.

A second job was supposed to make up the shortfall. That was the case with me, too. I always sensed ahead of time when things would be coming to an end, and then, as a musician, I'd look for bookings. I worked my way through practically the whole chain of Heck cafe-restaurants.

◆ CAREL REIJNDERS

When I was little, a diamond polisher by the name of Delmonte lived above us. The entire time I lived there, and that was something like twelve years, I never saw that man work a single day. He was permanently unemployed. Just his wife, who polished roses, had work now and then. But that man had an unshakable optimism. He always whistled up the stairs and joked about the newspapers we read. Every day, you see, a Catholic paper and *Het Volk,* which was socialist, and a Protestant paper landed at the bottom of the stairs to the three apartments. He thought that was a really funny, and he'd say, "They never bite each other!"

I often played with the neighbor kids Dikkie, Rietje, and Jopie. Those names actually already showed that they weren't orthodox Jews. The wife who was terribly poor with the husband who was always unemployed told my mother once, "If God is good to you, you better live it up!"

Professions

◆ BERNARD VAN TIJN

Medicine is, of course, a very old tradition. When Jews weren't able to do anything else in the various countries of Europe but a little trading or whatever, that's when, aside from studying the Torah and the Talmud, medicine was *the* field they could go into. You saw plenty of Jewish doctors during the eighteenth century; in the Netherlands, too, and not just in Amsterdam but also elsewhere.

The study of law is, of course, somewhat in keeping with the way the Torah and the Talmud were studied. These texts contain little theology, although they cover a lot of customs and legal rules. The true function of a rabbi is administering justice, which means resolving disputes, disputes that often have a theological aspect but are still mundane matters. So, making the transition to studying law is obviously easier than making the transition to other studies. It's a kind of preliminary exercise: the father's a Talmudist and his son's a lawyer, isn't that how it goes?

And then, medicine is *the* academic profession into which Jews were first accepted and one in which they worked on an academic level, while for the most part other practitioners were still engaged in quackery. During the Middle Ages, there was a time when, besides Jews and Arabs, none of the doctors had an academic background.

◆ LOE LAP

One of the most appealing professions that Jewish parents thought was the be–all and end–all for their son was being a lawyer. "My son has to be a lawyer!" Or a doctor.

Although there were a good number of Jewish doctors, relatively speaking, there were especially lots of Jewish lawyers. Those were the professions in which you knew your rights, and knowing that made you feel confident. A Master of Laws; they used to look up to that in those days! Now, we laugh at it.

◆ MARIUS GUSTAAF LEVENBACH

The law school and the medical school always included a Jewish professor, as far as I know. I'm referring to the time when there was a university. My grandfather, who received his doctorate in 1848, studied at the same time as a young man named Stokvis, also a Jewish student. He became a professor in internal medicine.

As far as lawyers were concerned, T. M. C. Asser,[3] as a professor at Amsterdam's Atheneum Illustre, stayed on when it became the University of Amsterdam in 1877. I don't know whether he'd already been baptized by then or not, but in any case he was a Jew. Then, during the nineteenth century, came Den Hartog, Max Conrad, and J. A. Josephus Jitta. When I was going to the university, I had Hijmans for Roman law and Van Embden for economics.

In Leiden, Groningen, and Utrecht, this happened a lot less, but that was also due to the fact that many more Jews were involved in the academic milieu here at the University of Amsterdam. Amsterdam as a university always had a much larger number of Jewish professors in proportion to the number of Jews in the population.

You know the story, don't you, about how the Dutch Constitution of 1815 came into being? Just as many Protestants as Catholics were supposed to be on the Constitutional Committee , so they had an equal number of each. Then there had to be a secretary. Well, was that supposed to be a Catholic or a Protestant? And the story goes that the sovereign ruler, William I, himself said, "But we've got that eminent lawyer Jonas Daniël Meijer, don't we? He's an Israelite. Let's make him secretary!"

◆ ABRAHAM SALOMON RIJXMAN

Dr. Samuel Sarphati and Alexander C. Wertheim were two Jewish Dutchmen who totally committed themselves to their homeland. They were both in prominent social positions through which they succeeded in giving Amsterdam the impetus that would, after 1870, ultimately lead to a flourishing era that equaled seventeenth-century Holland's Golden Age. They were regarded as pioneers in the Netherlands, as far as the emancipation of the Jews was concerned.

The course of their lives made it clear to Amsterdam Jews how far Jews could go in the Netherlands without anti-Semitic opposition, as it existed in Germany, for instance. They were also able to achieve this because they fully committed their talents.

I believe both men were deeply sympathetic to the fate of their poorer fellow citizens, even though neither of them came to the point of social criticism. They were really very charitably oriented. This is evident, for instance, in the fact that Wertheim left a rather small inheritance, something on the order of a half a million. That isn't so much for the powerfully rich man that Wertheim made himself out to be! When I told this to old Mr. Christiaan Van Eeghen, the attorney, he couldn't believe his ears! The inheritance was small because Wertheim had given away practically all of his income to charity and social work.

---

[3]Tobias Michael Carel Asser received the Nobel Peace Prize in 1911.

Sarphati had done that to a lesser degree thirty years earlier, but Wertheim continued and expanded on Sarphati's work. The most important thing was that they established the Crédit Mobilier, a bank that was to provide industry with funds after the example of the Pereira brothers who were doing that in France, supported by Napoleon III. In those days, the banks sometimes did offer *crédit immobilier,* meaning credit for land and fixed property, but they considered extending credit for industrial activities to be too dangerous.

The Pereira brothers showed that *crédit mobilier* was just the thing to give the country an enormous boost. Sarphati established a bank like that back then in the Netherlands and Wertheim followed in his footsteps. Emerging Dutch industry was also given a strong impetus because of this.

Regarding their being Jewish, Sarphati was a very conservative Jew who still lived completely according to the religious codex. Wertheim, however, was extremely freethinking in the area of religion, which nevertheless did not prevent him from accepting the chairmanship of the Dutch Israelite Congregation.

Sarphati was a driven person who couldn't tolerate the impoverishment he saw around him in Amsterdam. The remarkable thing is that wherever people said, "That's impossible!" he persisted anyway. Evidently he was such a convincing character that he almost always managed to win people over for his plans. From the establishment of the first business school to the Rubbish Removal Service of Amsterdam, everything he set up operated extremely well. While a good number of nineteenth-century institutions disappeared in twentieth-century Amsterdam, most of Sarphati's creations are still going strong!

The Amstel Hotel, for instance. At the time, it was considered madness to build a hotel so far out of town when there were so many good lodgings to be found in town. It's still in operation. Rubbish incineration and the slaughterhouse have been taken over by the city, but Sarphati laid the foundations. Simply the fact that he saw that there had to be separate higher education for the benefit of the citizenry—the business school and later the public high school, for youngsters who didn't want to go to the university but who needed more advanced schooling—testifies to his visionary insight.

In the meantime, this Jewish doctor had also done important work in the area of socioeconomics. In 1865, the excise tax on milling was abolished, so people no longer had to pay tax on grain. This motivated Sarphati, struck by the physical and moral destitution of workers at the time, to establish a bread factory. It was the first bread factory in the Netherlands. Although he shortened workers' hours, he still managed, due to his flair and dynamism, to step up production to ninety thousand loaves a week, which was an enormous amount in those days. Also, the price of the factory bread was so low that private bakeries were forced to adjust their prices.

Sarphati made plans for the Paleis voor Volksvlijt (Cultural Palace for Industrial Workers) after visiting the 1851 industrial fair in London. Evidently the time was right for this, because the square in Amsterdam that is now Frederiksplein was immediately made available by the city, on the condition that there were sufficient funds for construction. Three hundred thousand guilders were needed, a tremendous amount of money in those days. King William III as well as his uncle Prince Frederik signed on for large sums, however.

Wertheim, on the other hand, was an Amsterdammer at the heart of Amsterdam's commercial life and was at the same time a man with an exceptionally developed artistic sensibility. When he was a boy, he contributed a lot to language arts at the distinguished writers' guilds, to which he had access due to his ancestry and birth. As an adult, he built this up into a love of art in general, theater, music, and literature. Those in Amsterdam who needed funding for art, first went to Wertheim. Amsterdam bankers generally had no eye for art in those days, so that Amsterdam was destitute in that respect, even though there were already plenty of theaters, orchestras, and museums in Paris and London. However, if there was a group of people in Amsterdam that wanted to get something like that started here in the capital city as well, they would say, "Go and talk to Wertheim! He's bound to be for it!" Which usually was the case, too.

For instance, theater in Amsterdam was very bad. Whatever was offered to the upper middle class by way of plays was presented in French. The well-to-do did not go to "common" plays. It went without saying that an actor was someone of the very lowest kind, and likewise, actresses were prostitutes. Then, too, vulgar Amsterdam Dutch was spoken, and the upper middle class didn't want to listen to *that*. Then poet and playwright Hendrik Jan Schimmel founded the Dutch Theater Alliance. Wertheim helped him in setting up the Theater School.

When the Amsterdam Municipal Theater burned down in 1890, Wertheim commissioned architects Springer and Van Gendt to build a new theater, the one that now stands on Leidseplein.

Since there had to be a decent museum for our greatest art treasures, he, along with poet and novelist Josephus Albertus Alberdingk Thijm and others, took care that the Rijksmuseum came into being. When people in the Netherlands spoke disparagingly about the fact that nothing was happening in the area of music, he helped found the Concertgebouw. He also had a hand in attracting the first Concertgebouw orchestra members.

How well-known he was in the Netherlands is revealed among other things by the fact that it was possible for the most beautiful art objects in the National Museum of Antiquity in Leiden to be acquired only with his support—because he had the right connections in Paris.

What made all this possible? First of all, Wertheim was a man of exceptionally pleasant character; secondly, as a banker, he knew how to tackle this kind of thing. Consequently he was extremely well suited to act as a mediator, particularly in the world of art and culture, which he had such an eye for.

The actress Betsie Van Gelder-Holtrop (1867–1962) told me that during the big fire at the Municipal Theater in 1890, the actors' and actresses' entire wardrobes were lost. In those days, this had to come out of their pay. Those people were at their wit's end, in tears, not only because they now had no income, but also because they had lost all their costumes.

So, Wertheim went to them and told them, "I'll make sure that your pay is continued and that you get new costumes." Of course, that came as a godsend at a time when there were no social services, and so it wasn't surprising that Wertheim was worshipped by those people.

◆ ARTHUR FRANKFURTHER

My family on my mother's side was intimately acquainted with the Wertheim family going back a couple of generations. One member of this family was a well-known notary. The most well-known Wertheim was Alexander, after whom the Wertheim Public Gardens were named. This banker, Alexander Wertheim, a member of the Wertheim and Gomperts firm, was a great art lover, was interested in theater, and he also subsidized acting companies at the Municipal Theater out of his own pocket.

As a banker, you joined underwriting syndicates, and you had a large number of clients' assets to manage, as the Lissa and Kann Bank in The Hague did at the time. Alexander Wertheim's interest in art was passed on to his offspring Job Wertheim, the sculptor. He sculpted his niece Mathilde Visser, one of the daughters of the attorney Lodewijk Visser, president of the Supreme Court. Her mother was also a Wertheim.

The Wertheims were very philanthropically oriented. They had a lot to do with the Bisschofsheim Foundation and the Rothschilds in Paris, and together they were in all the major European foundations that benefited the general public—orphanages and the like. The late Hendrik Wertheim, a notary and a good friend of mine, went to one of those meetings at the Rothschilds' in Paris just last year.

Philanthropic work outside Jewish circles was important, particularly for the Wertheim line, which had such a great interest in theater. The Wertheim family was again related to the Hijmans family from Arnhem. So, whenever somebody showed up named "Hijmans Van Anrooy" or "Heijmans Van Wadenoijen," then notary Wertheim would say, "That's my goy family!" because these people were in "mixed" marriages and had taken their wife's name as well.

The founder of the Amsterdam Bank was F. S. Van Nierop. He came from a family of cattle dealers from Nieuwdorp that had made a lot of money. The bank was founded in 1870, I think. This man had studied law. He was Frederik Salomon Van Nierop, attorney, and member of the Dutch Senate. He lived at 1 Sarphatistraat, later the location of the student club. That was his family home.

II

RELIGION

This chapter presents primarily the memories of Jews who were involved with religion in some way. It shows that within the two official congregations, the Dutch Israelite Congregation and the Portuguese Israelite Congregation, there was a wide array to be found, from orthodox to extremely "flexible" Jews who called themselves liberal. These so-called liberal Jews should not be confused with the members of the current Liberal Jewish Congregation. While the prewar liberal Jews were really only liberal because they no longer strictly adhered to the traditional rules, the proponents of Liberal Judaism in the Netherlands nowadays essentially regard orthodoxy as outdated. Their ideas spring from the nineteenth-century Reform, which was very popular in Germany and England. It was therefore also primarily German Jews who established the Liberal Congregations in Amsterdam and The Hague a few years before the war.

The fact that the Reform did not find firm footing in the Netherlands is in itself a curious phenomenon. It is also curious that until the end of the nineteenth century, the leaders of the Jewish congregations did not oppose religiously neutral public school education, unlike the leaders of the Protestant and Catholic congregations who demanded equal subsidy for parochial schools. In 1898, Chief Rabbi Dünner first launched an initiative in favor of subsidizing schools providing religious education to Jewish children, which was therefore a campaign against public schools being the only schools to receive public funds. Angry Social Democratic voices claimed that Dünner had waited to do this until after the chairman of the Dutch Israelite Congregation, the liberal banker A. C. Wertheim, had passed away.

Practice

◆ ABEL JACOB HERZBERG
A good number of Amsterdam Jews were employed in the diamond trade. The only diamond exchange in the world that was closed on the Sabbath was the exchange in Amsterdam. That was unique.

I still clearly recall from my childhood that at a certain point there was a proposal to open the exchange on Saturday and close it on Sunday, which unleashed a storm of indignant protest. It was also rejected by an overwhelming majority.

Most if not all the Jewish diamond workers adhered to the SDAP (Social Democratic Labor Party) and were at the factory on Sundays. My father had a number of rented diamond "mills," as these old steam-driven grinding machines were called,[1] here on Zwanenburgerstraat. On Sundays, the workers went to the polishing factory, on the Sabbath they sat around drinking coffee and talking at cafes on Rembrandtplein like The Crown or Mille Colonnes, and on Friday evenings they ate chicken soup.

Friday evening is the evening that precedes the Sabbath, during which there must be absolute peace and quiet. Very religious Jews pretty much feel Friday evening to be the moment when the universe comes to them, when they become part of the whole. The white tablecloth and the chicken soup are, of course, no more than established traditions, or something like symbols. It's really mostly about the atmosphere, though. On the Sabbath, a Jew has a *neshamah yeterah,* a special soul. He becomes a different person. He is free and at peace. He is filled with joy. He becomes part of the cosmic whole.

There is also a mystical element in this. So, if he sings of welcoming the angels from on high who are coming to greet him and who come in, well, the spirit has stepped into his apartment.

The day preceding the evening of the Seder during the celebration of Pesach or Passover, the lady of the house, I believe, places little pieces of bread all over the house, after which the man of the house collects that "soured" bread with his children. I did that with my father, too, with a candle and a goose feather.[2] The

---

[1] These milling machines, cumbersome by today's standards, were units that had a table with a grinding disk, a large belt driven by a motor, and the motor itself.

[2] On the evening before Passover, the family gathers with a candle to light the way, a feather for brushing up the leavened bread (the *chametz*), and a small bag into which all the crumbs are swept by the head of the household. The following morning, the crumbs are burned together with the bag and the feather.

next day, on the morning before Seder evening, the bread is burned. Here in Amsterdam, you used to be able to see outdoor fires here and there near the synagogues in the Jewish Quarter, and the flames got pretty high, too.

A distinction is made between unsanctified time, which is now coming to an end with the leavened bread, and the holiday that begins tomorrow, with the unsoured or unleavened bread. This commemorates the flight from Egypt. It is said that they had no time to "leaven" the bread, to let it rise, so they ate it while it was still unleavened.

◆ ROSA COHEN-DE BRUIJN

I can recall how, on Friday afternoon, everything was prepared for the Sabbath, and in the winter, the room would already be dark. My mother was a rose cutter, and she would be finishing up her lots, as they were called, and counting them. She would have a big glass globe and that was the only light source. When I came home and saw that, I knew: it was Friday, it was the Sabbath. That really appealed to me, seeing my mother working that way and seeing the maid busy with the last preparations, setting the table and all that. Still, we weren't really orthodox. At home, we were what people here now call "white-tablecloth Jews." I have the nicest memories of Fridays, though, coming home from school, then going to do some needlework, and then lying down in front of the fireplace. My father would come home from work, my brother and my sister would come home from school, and then the special plates would be put on the table. To think I used to complain that we had to eat so much on Friday evenings. I thought that was awful: a couple of kinds of this, double vegetables. . . . I didn't understand why. We were never told. It was Friday evening, so that's the way things were done.

The shop was closed on the Sabbath, my father didn't work, and we would always go for a proper, traditional walk, even though we were liberal, not orthodox at all.

My mother upheld them unconsciously, I think, all the Jewish customs. Milk and meat were never eaten together, for instance. That wasn't done. There was an established fish evening. And, of course, on Thursday evenings you ate dairy foods, to the absolute disgust of my sister and myself. We thought that was atrocious, made big productions over it. But in the end, we had no choice.

◆ WILHELMINA BIET-MEIJER

My father came from a very orthodox family. He was the only one of the nine children who still upheld Jewish traditions at home in some way. At first, my parents kept a kosher home, but they slowly let that go more and more as things improved for my father financially, as he entered other social environments and traveled more with us as a family.

After a while, we were no longer eating kosher at home, although we still didn't eat pork, and we didn't eat butter together with meat. From an orthodox stand-point, of course, that's utter nonsense because we weren't keeping kosher any-more anyway. But then, that's what we later called "God on a rubber band," where God moved up, along with the circumstances. You did X, you didn't do Y. All of us did say our prayers at night and in the morning. I didn't go to school on *Shabbes* or on the Jewish holidays until I was a sophomore at the girls' high school. It turned out that I was missing certain classes and that I would never be able to pass to the next grade that way. So then I was allowed to go to school on *Shabbes,* but I wasn't allowed to go by bike and I wasn't allowed to write. And, well, after a while it was obvious that that wasn't going to work, so I finally started writing, and at that point I didn't understand why I shouldn't be allowed to ride my bike as well.

At my parents' house, Jewish holidays were celebrated to the extent that we always had Seder. Then the whole family would come over to our house, thirty people or something: uncles, aunts, cousins. That was a lot of fun. Even as kids we were allowed to drink four glasses of wine along with everybody else. The older members of the family would sit at the head of the table, and we would sit at the other end. We'd be laughing and having a great time. Those were really big family celebrations.

I went to shul on the first day of the Jewish New Year at least, not on the sec-ond, and I wouldn't stay very long. That was the shul on Jacob Obrechtstraat. Usually I thought it was boring, because I couldn't understand what was going on and the Dutch translation was so old-fashioned. On the other hand, I really thought it was nice when I saw that my father was allowed to perform certain activities at shul.

When the Jacob Obrecht Shul was set up, silver plating was put on the black ebony doors that kept the Scrolls safely out of sight. There were two large knobs on that silver plating and my father had the names of his parents engraved on them. To me this was a little something that was also part of me. When my grand-father was still alive, my father would go to the Great Shul on Jonas Daniël Meijerplein, and then we would always spend the evening at my grandfather's. I remember one time my mother and I were waiting for my father in front of the synagogue on Yom Kippur, the Day of Atonement. It was very crowded. Then, the doors opened, and I remember that the cantor and the rabbi were wearing long white robes and had beautiful tall white hats on, and I said—and this was a big hit in our Jewish family—"Oh, Momma, look! There's a chef in the shul!"

◆ MARIUS GUSTAAF LEVENBACH

My parents had consciously assimilated. Occasionally a Jewish expression was used, but we didn't observe Jewish customs at all anymore, except for three things: *bris* (from *Brith Milah*) which is the circumcision of boys, then *chasseneh,* marriage, and *levaya,* the Jewish funeral. They weren't devout, but they didn't want to shut themselves off from the community either. One of my parents' rules went without saying: that I would have to be circumcised. Imagine, I might want to marry a Jewish girl later on, and what if I weren't circumcised?! The girl's parents might say, "No, we won't allow it, he isn't a real Jew because he's not circumcised."

My grandfather had one other custom. He would have his children and their husbands and wives over on Friday evening and they would have dinner with him. The grandchildren didn't go. So, he would have his little evening, and then they'd play whist. People didn't go out much, and there was no movie theater, so you visited one another, and Friday evenings would be spent at my grandfather's on Muiderstraat. On Sundays, all his children would bring the grandchildren to visit him. We always got a "chasséetje," a little *chausson* or turnover, from that Jewish bakery on Jodenbreestraat. They would take a head count. There were thirteen grandchildren, so there would be a little cake or a *chasséetje* for each of the grandchildren, and in the back room we would get a fruit drink. We weren't allowed to make too much noise, what with all the uncles and aunts there. My grandfather had been a doctor for the poor. He was a liberal Jew. He believed in nothing. He was a man of the nineteenth-century Enlightenment: Molenschot and Natural Science. He was a prestigious person. He was still a member of the congregation, though, or chairman of the congregation's board of trustees or something, because he was a man of note.

◆ RUBEN GROEN

We observed the Jewish workweek. We normally celebrated Passover, for example. I remember very well that my mother had special kitchen utensils for Passover. So that *was* kosher. She would save them especially for Passover, and they were never used for anything but Passover. So she actually had two sets.

She wasn't devout, but that was so much a part of her. She kept it up.

◆ LOE LAP

It was Grandma who ran the show in those days, because I remember that when my father was forty-five, my grandmother still had the authority over us. She was more or less devout. And she was adamant about one thing. She wanted to see her grandson be a cantor someday. It made no difference whether I could sing well or not. That was her ideal, and I simply had to resign myself to it. My father, who was liberal and thought it was a bad idea, and who even, when I was born, didn't want me to be circumcised, gave in to his mother because he really wasn't any match for her.

When I turned thirteen, I had to do a bar mitzvah, see. So, my grandma comes along to shul, that was the biggest moment of her life—and I evidently sang very nicely, did it well, and everybody was very proud. That was at the shul on Linnaeusstraat. You had to put on one of those skullcaps. I thought that was really awful. The only thing I thought was nice was that I got a lot of presents. But it was *Shabbes,* it was one o'clock in the afternoon, and we're at my grandma's on Korte Houtstraat, that was the central meeting place, and she had bought me a new suit. Still, I was incredibly bored, so I say to my mother, "I want to go to the Royal Cinema." A movie that I really wanted to see was playing there. So my mother says, "You can't *do* that. Soon the rabbi will be here and then some teacher, so you can't leave."

I kept on whining about it, though, so my mother said, "You're not getting any money from me."

My grandma hears this. So she says, "What is it, dear?"
I say, "Grandma, I want to leave for an hour."
So she says, "What do you want, to leave for an hour?"
I say, "And then I need to have some money."
So she says, "Well, how much do you need?"
So I say, "A quarter. I want to go to the Royal Cinema."

So, what do you think she did, the schlemiel, on *Shabbes,* when she wasn't allowed to spend money? She was blind, so she says, "Look, is that a quarter? Here, here's another one. You go on down to the Royal Cinema."

And that's how I happened to be at the Royal Cinema on Shabbes on the day of my bar mitzvah. I was back at four.

◆ SIMON GOSSELAAR

Friday evenings were far from religious. They were social occasions, see. That social element always played a very important role for Amsterdam Jews, although maybe in its origins it had certain religious roots.

On Friday evenings, the white cloth was spread on the table. There was soup and really delicious food. Jewish children in elementary school whose parents thought it important were allowed to go home early, because on Fridays in the winter the concept of "night" often started as early as three in the afternoon, three—thirty sometimes, the closer we got to summer—that depended on the time of year. We just thought it was fun not being at school and our parents not objecting. Almost all the Jewish kids in the neighborhood did that.

I went to shul once for the wedding of relatives who were absolute non-believers. It was that added social element. They had their *chasseneh,* and that was part of it all, of course. They'd never gone to shul before the *chasseneh,* and they never went after that either, but you were supposed to have one—a sine qua non, you might say.

I remember one family had a wedding on Rapenburgerstraat, at the little *volks*-shul. It was a real working-class shul.

◆ KAREL POLAK

At the Linaeusstraat shul, Mr. De Jong was the cantor, and he presided over my wedding. The chief rabbi at the time was Sarlouis. At a marriage ceremony, it is always the cantor who sings the benedictions and the rabbi who gives the sermon, reads the marriage certificate, and has it signed.

This didn't always take place at a synagogue. Marriage ceremonies were often held in banquet halls, and the banquet and the reception would start right after. We were married at Atlanta, the cafe-restaurant on Westeinde, with the reception directly afterward. There was music, with a piano player and a violinist. That was background music so that people could still talk. Things used to be a lot quieter then than now, with just a few strings playing. It was much more intimate then, which, of course, is also because there were a lot more Jewish relatives. Who can you invite these days? Lots of good friends and acquaintances, but you've hardly got any family left, because they were all thinned out by the war. Extended family ties used to be very strong.

◆ MAX EMMERIK

Mine was a synagogue wedding. You did that for your parents. That's how it was. They cared about those kinds of things even though they weren't religious. Sitting *shivah,* sitting in mourning, I didn't do that either. When my father passed away, though, my mother said, "You would do me a great service if you sat the days of mourning." Well, we had never done a thing by way of our faith, but we did it for my mother. If you were poor, it was the custom that neighbors paying their condolences brought all kinds of things to eat, sausage, say, or glazed gingerbread balls. We were in a neighborhood where poverty was the norm, so we—we were five brothers—arranged that among the five of us we would secretly send things, just as if they had come from this or that person, meaning without a return address. So, one day a big flounder arrived, another day gingerbread balls, and one time we sent a piece of meat. My mother fell for it, because she said to me, "What kind people they are. I don't know where all those acquaintances came from." Later, we told her, and then she had to laugh.

◆ SAL WAAS

I was an official in the Jewish funeral business. I had to collect the contributions. There were about seven funeral associations here once, two for those who were well-off and the others were the *menachem avelim* (comforter of the bereaved) associations. These were for run-of-the-mill people.

I applied for a job at the social *chevra.* That was a society of very modern people, on average. They were almost all socialists. I was selected from at least three hundred people to be a courier for the association. You had to know how to do everything, be able to read Hebrew and lead the prayers during the Jewish days of mourning, the so-called days of *shivah,* for seven days.

My district was Nieuwe Achtergracht, Weesperstraat, Kerkstraat, Jodenbreestraat, and Sint Antoniesbreestraat. That's where I went to collect my contributions. If people were destitute, they couldn't always contribute regularly, so the usual reply was, "Courier, double next week!" The market people paid double during the summer because they didn't have much income during the winter.

You were just part of the family. You went over there if there was a death, a birth, or a marriage. You were one of them because you went over every week. They knew me, not my association. They said, "I'm a member of Waas, of Simons, of Polak." "What *chevra* are you a member of?" "Chevra Waas, chevra Gobitz."

They asked you for advice about everything. You were an instant sage.

There was an awful lot of poverty. Every six months they paid five guilders and seventy-two cents in contributions. Then, at the end of the year, a couple of weeks before Passover, you would go door to door to settle up with them, and they could get three guilders back, or they could get matzo. That would be ten pounds of "eights," eight pounds of "tens," or else handmade matzos, one and a half pounds of matzo per person. There were people with lots and lots of debt, though, and they wouldn't get any matzo at all. They could go to the Jewish Board for the Poor and ask for matzo, which they would usually get. Then, there were people who had quite a bit of self-respect, and they didn't want to do that, so I'd say, "I'll make sure you have some wine and matzo for Passover." There was an association named Betsalel, and I would go there and say, "Listen, I need matzo" or "I need wine for the so-and-sos." I would get a coupon for that, a voucher for those people—they were the "quiet" poor—and that way they would be able to do Passover.

Everybody was a member of the funeral fund here. *Levaya,* that's a funeral. Some people would be carried from their home through the Jewish Quarter to Jonas Daniël Meijerplein. That's where the hearse would be—back then it was usually a carriage—and we'd go to Muiderberg or to Diemen. Usually these people had been members of the Society of Gravediggers, or they'd have been cantors or rabbis. They would be specially carried through the city by men wearing long black capes.

The cemetery in Muiderberg was for those who had "matriculated" (enrolled) and bought into Muiderberg. Before they were married, they would have to pay extra: matriculation was forty guilders. The run-of-the-mill person went to Diemen.

Overveen was a separate community.[3] The rabbi there was not Jewish by origin. The Graanboom family—they came from Sweden, I believe—converted to Judaism. Isaac Graanboom became the rabbi in Overveen. The kind of people who were buried there were, for instance, Visser, the attorney and president of the Supreme Court, the Wertheims, Asser, the attorney, and all those well-known men of culture. That was the elite, see. They felt themselves to be very modern. That "Yiddish" stuff didn't appeal to them; "we" are Dutch.

Now, the cemetery's all overgrown with weeds. Anyway, they were orthodox Jews. Before the war, the Society of Gravediggers would go over to Overveen every year to say prayers for the deceased. That's still done at the cemeteries in Diemen and Muiderberg, but they don't go to Overveen anymore.

◆ NATHAN STODEL

I would say that ninety percent of Amsterdam Jews were nonreligious. Myself, I went to a Jewish school for seven years, but my father went to the barber on *Shabbes!* Still, he would go listen to Rabbi De Hond on *Shabbes* afternoon. He did that in honor of a brother-in-law who had passed away and who had founded the chevra where Rabbi De Hond taught.[4]

For seven years, I was taught by Jo Melkman's father. He was one of those "modern" teachers, certainly for that time. That was on Meijerplein, beside the shul. I had a bar mitzvah, too. My father went to shul twice a year, on Rosh Hashanah and Yom Kippur. He would go to Beth Hamidrash on Rapenburgerstraat. Special services were organized there. To think, my father was considered the most religious one in his family!

On Friday evenings, there was a white tablecloth, although my father did not recite the *Kiddush.* We ate chicken soup, of course—whenever it was possible! On Shabbes morning, he polished his shoes—and that is *not* a *Shabbes* task, you know!—and then he would take a bath, go to the barber for a shave, then listen at his leisure to De Hond on *Shabbes* afternoon.

We did not eat kosher, although my mother used different pans to cook dairy foods and meats. She did do that, even though the meat came from a Jewish butcher who was not under the supervision of a rabbi. When my father was a young man, he had been trained as a butcher out east, in the Achterhoek region

---

[3]The cemetery in Overveen originally belonged to the Adath Jessurun community, founded in 1797, which consisted mostly of notable proponents of the Enlightenment. In 1808, this so-called "new" community was reunited with the "old" High German or Ashkenazic community under pressure from King Louis Bonaparte.

[4]Rabbi Meyer De Hond (1882–1943), was loved by the poor for his advocacy on their behalf. Religiously orthodox yet socially progressive, he often clashed with the Jewish establishment. He was a prolific writer and essayist. He was deported by the Nazis and died at Sobibor.

near the German border, and he thought that you couldn't get good meat from kosher butchers. For good meat, you had to go to Isaac's on Muiderstraat, but that was not kosher meat. My parents' circle of acquaintances certainly didn't keep kosher either.

◆ ELIZABETH VAN DE KAR-STODEL
My father was a market salesman at Nieuwmarkt, the best market in Amsterdam at the time. He had a stand there for years selling silks. My grandfather and grandmother *were* orthodox. My grandfather died when I was eleven. He was on the board of trustees of a small *chevra* shul that mostly working-class people attended. It was on Sint Antoniesbreestraat, number thirty-four if I remember right. All of that's gone, of course.

◆ LEEN RIMINI
I was the manager of one of the Cooperative's stores, the one on Jodenbreestraat. One Yom Kippur I closed up shop, but these Jewish people kept coming to the door for groceries. I lived in back of the shop, so you didn't dare say no, because the customer was king. So, what good did it do me having to run to the door every other minute?! At a certain point, I got so angry, I said, "Well, for my part they can all go jump in a lake, but I'm not closing on Yom Kippur anymore."

Well, you should have heard what they were saying in the neighborhood! But anyway, the Yom Kippur I was open, I sure was busy! All those people who were ranting and raving, they certainly weren't going to the synagogue. If you went to the Rembrandt Theater or to the Tuschinski Theater, it would be chock-a-block full that day with those same Jewish people.

◆ HUBERTUS PETRUS HAUSER
We lived in the Jewish Quarter, and sometimes they would come by asking if I could help out on Friday evenings, on *Shabbes* eve, see. I'd be asked if I could light the lamps or stoke the heater, because Jews weren't allowed to do anything after sundown on *Shabbes* eve. Only the strict Jews, see, not the so-called bacon eaters—the ones that didn't do much by way of their faith. The strict Jews still stuck pretty close to those things. For the most part, these were the ones who were more affluent, but sometimes they were the everyday poor Jews, people who had stands at the market and such. They went to shul on *Shabbes* and everything, see, and wore a skullcap.

The term *"Shabbes* goy" actually was used sometimes, but they wouldn't go around shouting something like "Hey, goy," or anything like that. They just knew me by my first name, and it would be, "Bob, would you mind doing this, would you mind doing that?" Well, if I was home, I just did it. Mostly it was lighting lamps and stoking heaters in the winter, taking the food off the stove, lighting the gas. They'd even ask, "Could you come back in an hour or so?" Well, what do you want? You went back. In those days, if you earned a dime doing these things, it was worth the effort, see.

◆ CAREL REIJNDERS

Sometimes, on the way to school on the Sabbath, I'd be stopped on the street, and they'd ask, "Could you ring the doorbell for me, son?" or "Could you light the gas for me?" These would be orthodox Jews, who weren't allowed to light a fire on the Sabbath. An electric doorbell makes little sparks jump, and if you want to live by the letter of the law, you can't use an electric doorbell. I used to think it was typical that there were two doorbells on Jewish doors, one you pulled and one you pushed: the one you pulled being for the Sabbath, and the one you pushed being for during the week. If there wasn't a doorbell you could pull on, though, they would have to ask a non-Jew, a *Shabbes* goy, to ring it.

When we walked to school through the Jewish Quarter, it was really crowded every day, and back then Weesperstraat was just as narrow as Utrechtsestraat is now.

On the Sabbath, a number of men always wore top hats when they went to the synagogue. One person who very faithfully went to the synagogue was the market hawker Kokadorus, famous for his entertaining oratory. His real name was Meijer Linnewiel, but hardly anybody knew that. My father would always nudge me when we were on our way to the office and school in the morning, and he'd say, "Look, there goes Professor Kokadorus!" He'd be walking home down Weesperstraat.

On the Sabbath, you'd also see people coming from the baker's where they'd left their *tsholent* pots to be kept warm. These were pots that had Saturday's midday meal in them. They would be brought down to the baker's on Friday and the baker would warm them up. Otherwise the Jews wouldn't have anything warm to eat on Saturday since they weren't allowed to heat food. So you'd see them lugging these things down the street. Some pious Jews had a box lined with hay or paper, and on Friday they'd put food in it to keep warm so they could eat it on Saturday. I liked that.

There were also all kinds of activities among the Jews that involved fire. I thought that was pretty weird when I was a kid. All cigar shops used to have a little flame burning all the time so you could light your cigar or cigarette. The Jews, on the other hand, had a little flame at the pastry shop for their glazed gingerbread balls. These came in a can and would be warmed up. I thought they were a delicious bakery treat. And there used to be plenty of Jewish carts with burning braziers on them for roasting chestnuts, or *kastengen* as they were called.

It always had something to do with fire. Before Easter, when I crossed Jonas Daniël Meijerplein, Jewish boys would be standing out there shouting, *"Chametz bateln, chametz bateln!"* and burning pieces of old bread at the curbside. They even got money for that. It was only much later that I understood the meaning behind burning the old leavened bread.

Friday evenings in particular were nosh evenings, when Jews would be nosh-ing. At home, we always spoke in terms of noshing, too. My mother always went out on Fridays and bought fruit, and we always had some kind of tasty treat then. We probably copied that from our Jewish neighbors, who used a white tablecloth when they set the table on Friday evenings. Those people weren't religious, but they still set everything out and got things ready just to eat well on Fridays.

I still love nuts, peanuts and such, which they sold lots of at the Jewish shops. Starting when I was a boy, I learned to eat raisins, dried currants, and figs, and so on, and also a lot of fresh fruit.

◈ JACOB SOETENDORP

If there's one thing that had to do with prewar Jewry, it was that at least you knew exactly what you were going to eat for dinner, because that was always set. Thursday evening was fish and Friday evening was of course your Sabbath meal. The leftovers were kept for Saturday evening. The Friday evening meal was always the same, though. One of the most curious things, however, was that my grandmother would always ask my mother, "Yans, what are you having for *Shabbes?*" And then my mother would recite the menu even though there was never anything different on it! The question was pointless and the answer was pointless. Monday evening was hotchpotch stew, Tuesday and Wednesday evenings, pea soup or beans.

There was another curious thing in connection with food. Socialist Jews didn't eat ritually slaughtered meat, but they would go to this Jewish butcher who even had those three Hebrew letters out in front of his door that spell *kasher* (kosher). The rabbinate had to warn people about this, that it didn't explicitly mean "Under Rabbinical Supervision," because this butcher wasn't. To him it meant no pork, since ninety percent of these Jews—who were socialist and yet so extremely attached to their non-orthodox Jewishness—still ate absolutely no pork.

If you said to a girl, "Come on, we're going out Friday night," she would say, "No, I'm staying home Friday night," because that was always the way it was. Then, if you said, "Sure, sure, Friday night at home, probably eating *kesause mangelen!"* ("Curaçaoan almonds," which were peanuts), she would say, "What? Are you attacking my faith?"

It sounds ludicrous, but it meant that they had kept the physical formalities to retain a sense of unity.

◈ RUBEN GROEN

When I went home with my father Friday afternoons, we first went over to Waterlooplein and looked around the market, especially the fruit market. My father was in the habit of buying anything and everything in the way of fruit that they were selling that day: a melon, bananas, oranges, tangerines. There was a boy he'd hire there who was probably the fruit vendor's son, and this boy would always take the fruit to our home. So, we would walk to the Valkenweg ferryboat and that boy would come along and he would carry the fruit my father had bought in a wooden crate on his head. You still see that in India sometimes. He carried it like that to North Amsterdam on the other side of the IJ harbor. Then my mother would always say, *"Shabbesy's* here again," because that's when she knew that *Shabbes* had started. My father would be home then, on Fridays and Saturdays that is.

◈ JOOP EMMERIK

Friday evenings we always ate well. During the week, though, sometimes nothing, but on Friday evenings it was always nice. Sometimes we'd have veal headcheese or sliced heart. That was cheap back then. But we'd have meat *and* soup.

On Simchas Torah (Rejoicing in the Law), every child that went to shul got a packet of wedding candies. Well, we never missed out on those. We'd be there in less than no time. But once I had that candy, I was gone.

◈ EMMANUEL AALSVEL

My parents grew up terribly poor. The best story my father ever told me was about the *tsholent*. The Jews used to bring a sweet bread or cake to the baker. In Amsterdam they call it a *tsholent*. Well, there were plain *tsholents* and rich *tsholents*. The rich ones had dried currants, raisins, ginger, and everything in them, but the plain ones were just made with flour. The baker would put those *tsholents* in the oven Thursday evening or Friday morning. My father must've told me this story at least a hundred times. He would always say, "Manuel, we picked up our *tsholent* one Friday evening, and when we got home, we feasted on it, because the baker had made a mistake. He'd given us one of those rich Jew's *tsholents*, so we feasted on all those raisins and currants and ginger."

◈ GERRIT BRUGMANS

In a kosher bakery, there's a *shomer,* a supervisor, who just checks to see that people wash their hands before they begin working or after using the toilet or whatever. Now, that's *kashrut*.

At Theeboom's, we always had to have challa during the week, but particularly on *Shabbes*. Challa is a braided bread. Well, at Theeboom's on Thursday, I must've had fifteen hundred malt challas ready for the prayer. Before you start eating, you take a piece of bread, right, and you dip it in salt and say, "This is the bread that thou shalt eat." Before the war, there was supposed to be a little dough braid on it. It looked nicer that way. They don't do that anymore. They have no time for that; it costs too much.

Jews were used to their bread being thoroughly baked. That kosher bread was bread made with water. You can bake it harder that way. Jews don't want spongy bread. They have to be able to sink their teeth into it. Milk, there's no milk in it, that always softens bread, see, plus those fats they put in there. Milk can't go into the bread, just water; that's neutral—you can eat it with everything. Milk contains animal fat.

◆ BAREND DRUKARCH

At a handmade matzo bakery, the matzos were obviously made by hand, which in itself was a work of art. You should have seen those people flattening it, rolling out the dough. The matzo has to be kept moving constantly to keep it from rising. And because the bakers stood pretty close to the ovens, they constantly had to tend to the dough until it could go into the oven. They would have a couple of those kneaded matzos draped over their arms, and they would throw them up in the air, just juggling them around, until at a certain point the matzos could go into the oven. I tried doing that, too, a few times, but the whole business would just gob together. They would catch those pieces of dough in the open palm of their hand, and then the dough would go straight into the oven.

Out on Joden Houttuinen, you had one of those handmade matzo bakeries. It was located between Uilenburgerstraat and Valkenburgerstraat. There was a little alley you'd have to walk down—one of those narrow alleys there were so many of in those days—and the handmade bakery was back there. Those matzos were of course a lot thicker than De Haan's machine-made matzos.

That was forty-seven years ago. I was ten years old at the time. That was in 1925, 1926. That's when they baked them, and for still a few years after that.

◆ EDUARD CHARLES KEIZER

We have the written teachings, the Torah, the fundamental law of the Jews, and then we have the oral teachings, both of which are acknowledged by the Jewish people. The oral teachings are in keeping with what is written in the Torah. In Deuteronomy 12:21 it is written: "Thou shalt kill of thy herd and of thy flock . . . as I have commanded thee." In the oral teachings, this would be explained in greater detail. In Genesis 9:4, it is written: "Only flesh with the life thereof, which is the blood thereof, shall ye not eat." And in Leviticus 3:17: "It shall be a perpetual statute throughout your generations, in all your dwellings, that ye shall eat neither fat nor blood."

These dietary laws are closely followed in every Jewish community. In Amsterdam, with its roughly seventy-five thousand Jewish residents, there were six *shochetim,* kosher butchers, working there, who, under the supervision of the rabbis, made sure that the meat intended for Jews satisfied the laws I just mentioned. In addition, there were twenty-six "authorized" butchers back then. There were also a dozen kosher poulterers. Until about 1920, those twenty-six kosher butchers were all housed in two meat halls, an Ashkenazic one on Nieuwe Amstelstraat and a Sephardic one on Nieuwe Kerkstraat. Each butcher had his own "bench" there, a separate space where he operated his business. There was a supervisor in both of the halls. After that time, these butchers were allowed to locate their businesses elsewhere in the city. They spread out and set themselves up in Central, East, and South Amsterdam. The poulterers had businesses on either Jodenbreestraat or Weesperstraat or Nieuwe Amstelstraat.

A kosher butcher has to be able to *porshen,* devein the meat. By deveining and removing the sinews, the blood that is still in the meat is removed. This requires skill, because the meat has to remain salable and that's only possible if the *porsher* is an expert. When the blood is removed from the meat, the meat can be kept longer, since blood is the first thing that spoils. Before the war, a lot of non-kosher butchers liked to buy those shanks of ritually slaughtered meat. They themselves said it kept a lot longer.

When the meat has been *porshed,* it still has to be "made kosher": a half hour "in water" and an hour "in salt." Then, once it has been well rinsed, the meat or poultry satisfies the requirements and is suitable for the Jewish kitchen. Liver has to be "roasted."

Before 1940, every kosher butcher had to prove that he lived strictly according to Jewish laws. Once that had been determined by the rabbinate, the congregation's board of trustees could acknowledge him as a kosher butcher.

Aside from kosher butchers and poulterers, there were the so-called "meat-roll shops," where out-of-town Jews in particular could satisfy their appetites. Nevertheless, Amsterdam Jews also liked their "salted beef rolls" or "half-and-half rolls," half salted beef, half liver. The Prins and Meijer delicatessens on Jodenbreestraat were very popular, as well as Frits Content's on Utrechtsestraat. You could find the young Orthodox crowd there, especially on Saturday and Sunday evenings. They would head over after their *"lernen"* at the Totseos Chayim or Zichron Jakov, with many a Jewish marriage as a result!

All in all, there was a lot of work involved in making sure that each Jew could live in a kosher way.

Large livestock was slaughtered at the Amsterdam slaughterhouse. There the *shochetim* had private rooms available to them and they could go back there to take a break after a large number of killings. Also, back then they still had meat wagons that were allowed to transport only meat slaughtered in a kosher way to kosher butcher shops. After all, the other wagons transported pork as well! For poultry, there was a separate slaughtering place right behind the Uilenburger shul.

The "authorized" butchers and poulterers had to pay a fee to the congregation's trustees for the *shochetim's* work. For beef, that was about seven cents per kilo, for poultry, five to thirteen cents per bird. Only the front legs of slaughtered cattle are permitted for consumption. The hind legs are forbidden, among other things because of the dislocated hip or "sinew of the thigh-vein" (Genesis 32:33), a term that was correctly translated by Dr. Dasberg as "wrenched vascular bundle."

The Meat Inspection Decree stated in Article 10a that the slaughter of an animal had to be preceded by anesthesia. Article 10b stated: "with the exception of meat slaughtered according to Israelite ritual." In kosher slaughtering, the cow is laid down in fetters. Three legs are fettered and one leg remains free. Within a few seconds, the cow lies still, and then the *shochet* comes in. He stands ready with his knife, which may not have any *pegime,* no nicks or flaws. If there is anything wrong with his knife, he is not allowed to cut the cow's throat, because then there's the problem that a little barb might cause the cut to snag, even for just an instant, and the animal might experience pain. The man who performs the cut is a perfect master. It happens in a split second. He does this superbly! At that same moment, the blood spurts out of the brains and consequently there is no feeling of pain anymore.

So, what people sometimes say, "Oh, how the animal must suffer!" actually isn't true!

◆ ABEL JACOB HERZBERG

There is a famous story about Yokev (Jacob) Content. As you know, you're not allowed to eat before you've said your morning prayers. Now, Yokev Content always had to go down Jodenbreestraat to go to shul, and he just couldn't pass Snattager's (the Jewish pastry shop) without eating one of those chewy, sticky-sweet gingerbread balls. He was hooked on those things. No matter what he did, he couldn't resist his daily gingerbread ball. Finally one day, he gathered all his forces, and it worked. He passed Snattager's *without* eating a gingerbread ball! Then, he said to himself, "Yokev, Yokev, seeing as you were so strong that you went by without having any gingerbread, you may go back and buy one!"

Of course, the question is whether there is any truth to the story, but it's a typical bit of Jewish gossip.

Music

◆ EDUARD CHARLES KEIZER

Friday evenings at the New Shul were an event. The shul would be packed all the way out to the entrance of the building. The *chazzan* or cantor was Wolf Reisel, a good tenor, one of Sirota's students. There was a "mixed choir," which means to say a choir of men and boys.[5] This choir was under the direction of Herman Italie, who was the headmaster of the Talmud Torah School. He had "plenty to choose from" among his students. The best of them went into his choir. I remember the two LeGrand brothers, Heiman and Abraham. Heiman later became cantor in The Hague. I believe that of all those choir members, only Maurits Brilleslijper is still alive. During the time I'm talking about now, he was eleven or twelve years old. He had a beautiful "boy's voice," high and true. His solos were famous. I can *still* hear them, just like those beautiful *chazones* of *Chazzan* Reisel. Brilleslijper later became a cantor too. He served as second *chazzan* at the Obrecht Shul, now the Rav Aron Schuster Shul.

Cantors who sang at the Great Shul were *Chazzan* Katz, *Chazzan* Stoutsker, and of course *Chazzan* Maroko, a little man with a beautiful voice. At the first sounds I heard him make when he was trying out, I said to the person sitting next to me, "He's going to be the one!" His voice was gentle but still powerful.

Then, Sam Englander's double men's quartet, was famous—father and son Gobets, Jo Rabbie, and Louis Nieweg, who was a choirboy at first and later sang baritone. He's the only one from that double men's quartet who is still alive.

At Rapenburgerstraat, first there was *Chazzan* Schlesinger and later Jacob Veldman; at the Uilenburgerstraat shul, *Chazzan* Drukker, at the Lange Houtstraat shul, *Chazzan* Poons, and at the Obbene Shul, there was *Chazzan* Jacobson. This was a time when, on religious holidays, the mounted police had to restrain the crowd in front of the Great Shul.

◆ BAREND DRUKARCH

It's not the rabbi who leads the service in the shul, but the *chazzan*. The rabbi does, in fact, supervise the service, but the *chazzan* is the central figure. It's because of this that great demands were always placed on him, since he also had

---

[5]Women are never included, as it is a longstanding tradition that men and women must be separated in the shul.

to be proficient in halakic literature. He had to know exactly what was allowed and what wasn't. And he had to comport himself according to the Jewish norms in every way, of course, both at home as well as in public. According to these rules, a cantor has to be a person who is accepted by the majority of the congregation or of those who attend the shul where he will be performing his services, but preferably by all of them. It is also for this reason that the *chazzan* is always elected. When elections take place, there should always be several candidates, otherwise you wouldn't have to choose. One person will like tenors better, another baritones. As a result, the candidates always found supporters, one group preferring one candidate, and another preferring another.

In the musical presentation of the prayers, there are two kinds of performer: the *chazzan* and the *baal tefillah* (the person who recites the prayer) and the latter you can't expect much of musically.

Jewish music as we know it originated largely from secular music, from which a motif, such as a piece from Bizet's opera *The Pearl Fishers,* would be adapted and elaborated on. The *chazzan* was free, more or less, to choose his melodies and to improvise them. For the Portuguese, the Sephardic Jews, these melodies practically always derived from the melodies they already had.

There were different kinds of *chazzanim.* At one time, there was a chief cantor, a cantor, a first cantor, and a reader, in descending order, as it were. These were titles for persons who all did precisely the same thing. I recall the case of Chazzan Veldman of the shul on Rapenburgerstraat, who at a certain point felt very shortchanged in his salary because there was a huge gap between his salary and that of the chief cantor and the cantor. So he went over to Dr. Sluis on Meijerplein, who was called "The Dictator of Meijerplein" because he was the congregation's secretary, and whatever he said was law.

So, this Veldman said, "Listen here, what's going on, my salary is so much less than. . . ."

But then Sluis said, "You're only a reader."

At which Veldman gets angry and says, "Then I *will* read!"

So then he actually had the nerve to read the afternoon and evening prayers in seven minutes. He said, "Well, as long as I'm the reader, I'll read."

I knew Sam Englander personally. I was there during the period when the choir was still in the choir loft of the Great Shul. Later on, the choir moved downstairs because the rapport between *chazzan* and choir was better when the choir stood behind the *chazzan* rather than in the loft above him.

I was always impressed with what they offered. Englander, I might add, was internationally renowned as a choir director of both Jewish as well as secular music, even of socialist songs. This wasn't as strange as it may seem, since a shul choir director's salary was so low the man couldn't live on it.

◆ ARON DE PAAUW

When I was a boy between, say, eleven and fifteen, my uncle would take me by the hand, and we'd go to the shul, where a chief cantor would sing with a beautiful Jewish choir led by Englander. Well, those Friday evenings were a delight for me, despite the fact that I wasn't orthodox and never became orthodox. That music appealed to me tremendously. I also knew all the melodies. I could sing them in my sleep. I knew the words, too, after a while. A lot of non-Jews as well came in during the last part of the service to listen. It was just like a concert.

◆ MAX REISEL

My father, Wolf Reisel, was *chazzan* at the New Synagogue, the so-called *Neie Shul* in Amsterdam. He was from Lithuania and had lived in Russia and Berlin for years. He came to the Netherlands in 1909. In those days, there were very few trained *chazzanim*, and so they would look for candidates in other countries. This is how my father was tracked down in Berlin.

He was born in Shaki (Sakiai), a little village in Lithuania, and he took lessons in Vilno (Vilnius) from the famous *chazzan,* Sirota. After that, he studied at the conservatory in Berlin. Then the position opened up in Amsterdam. There were good candidates in the group, including Victor Schlesinger, and it was a pretty fierce election contest. They chose him over Schlesinger, though.

Try-out services were of such great interest, that sometimes a window would be broken so people outside could follow it too! That's how intensely interested people were in *chazzanut* back then. Chazzan Schlesinger was appointed to another synagogue in Amsterdam shortly after that. Now, there were three specialized *chazzanim* in this capital city that was so important to the Jews: Chazzan Katz, Chazzan Schlesinger, and Chazzan Reisel. All three were admired, and it was noted that the first letters in Hebrew of their last names together formed the Hebrew word *kasher* (kosher). People experienced religious and musical fulfillment during the synagogue services these men led. Their exquisite compositions of new synagogal songs were admired, too.

My father's predecessor was Chazzan Heymann, who was called the "Gnezer *chazzan*" because he came from the Polish village of Gnesen (Gniezno). This man had led services for fifty years, and he had trained his children in music as well.

One of them had become a liberal Jew, and on the day of the election he said to my father, "I put on the tefillin this morning.[6] It's been years since I did that."

---

[6]This is a religious procedure prior to morning prayers, when a hollow wooden box containing four texts from the Torah is strapped around the left arm and another little box of texts is strapped onto the forehead.

"Why did you decide to do that all of a sudden?" My father asked him.

And his reply was, "I would like my father to have a worthy successor!"

Musically, a *chazzan* has two possibilities. First of all, singing the recitatives, whereby he primarily transmits the traditional formal elements. Secondly he has the task of performing established, composed music. Now, particularly in the recitatives, there is a lot of room for originality, since along with the traditional motifs, improvisation on those motifs is allowed. Herein lies the freedom, which my father always exercised discreetly.

My father was assisted by a choir that was initially mixed: men and boys. My father derived inspiration from his religious feeling and his Eastern European background. He built his *chazzanut* up in such a way that a relatively simple prayer was given a different coloring. The performance gained even more dimension due to a choir accompaniment of four voices. Part of it was the contrast between the bass and the tenor, the man's voice and the boy's voice, that made it a richly nuanced whole, which in itself already gave one a feeling of well-being. Anyway, the inspiration behind it turned it into something distinctive that left an impression. My father was not a Chassid, but he had the passion of a Chassid.

The conductors who worked with my father were, chronologically, Herman Italie, Barend Muller, Emanuel Plukker, and occasionally Sam Englander. They all performed a lot. Englander's choir was good. That man had a real feeling for good *chazzanut*. "He has Russian ears!" my father used to say. That was a compliment, by which my father meant that Englander had an intuitive understanding of that unique atmosphere. A *chazzan* who improvised made it hard for the accompanying choir to follow. So, anybody who was so attuned that he could follow the improvisation of the *chazzan* obviously *had* to have a special feeling for it!

The mixed choir was eventually replaced by an all-men's choir. It was a relatively small choir of eight people that was supplemented now and then by a young solo singer. Whatever Englander offered by way of his choir was always tastefully selected and performed. He won a prize for Jewish choirs in an international competition in London once. He also gave an absolutely beautiful performance of Ernest Bloch's *Avodat Hakodesh* at the Concertgebouw here in Amsterdam. And the solo was sung by the former *chazzan*, Hermann Schey!

Whenever a *chazzan* of superior talent was visiting Amsterdam, the Jewish community would deny him the opportunity of leading a service because it was against the rules. The man was forced either to ask for hospitality from the Russian shul, or to have a number of friends rent a hall and then give a performance that way. This happened several times with Sirota, who led a few Sabbath services at the Diamond Exchange, at the Building of the Working Class, and at the Concertgebouw, because the Jewish community would not make a shul available.

◆ HIJMAN (BOB) SCHOLTE

Victor Schlesinger had a beautiful voice and was also extremely talented as a composer. Every *chazzan* had his own melody, his own compositions. I don't think it sounds like opera. It's just always precisely those solemn melodies, see. And you have to retain that, adding on the necessary little frills as you go. That can't be taught, you know. Even if you have a beautiful voice, you still have to have the feeling.

At the time I sang at the Rapenburgerstraat shul, Sam Englander's choir was at the Great Shul. It was a beautiful men's choir. Michel Gobets and his father were in that choir. They were its two main strengths. Michel Gobets later became an opera and "lieder" singer as well, a great concert singer. I'm afraid he didn't return after the war, either, Michel Gobets. . . .

◆ MEIJER MOSSEL

I tried out at the Gerard Doustraat shul. It was a very intense election contest. People were picked up and brought by car especially to vote for you. Fliers about the candidate you were supposed to vote for or about his opponent were distributed.

I got a lot of help at that time from the director of The Jewish Invalid, Mr. Gans, *zichrono li-verachah,* bless his soul. I know the Jewish Invalid office went all out to help me. On the morning of the election—it's not the trustees but the members of the congregation who vote—they even stuffed leaflets in members' mailboxes urging them to elect me as *chazzan!* They had stenciled the flier the night before. That's how I won the appointment.

Synagogues and Rabbis

◆ EDUARD CHARLES KEIZER

The atmosphere in shul was very different then than it is now. Everybody went to shul neatly dressed—wore top hats on *shabbes* and *yontif*. Every married man, regardless of his rank or station, wore a top hat. I recall that there was a Mr. Groente who went to the New Shul. He was a cesspit cleaner, but when he went to shul on *shabbes* or the holidays, he would be wearing a very proper black suit and a top hat—and he was accepted like anyone else. The services were long, sometimes very long. Seven to twelve hours on *shabbes* was really not unusual! Well, all the seats in the shul were rented out to "occupants." An occupant had a right to a seat. This meant that the young men and boys had to stand through the entire service—which they did, too, because it was the normal, expected thing. The well-off occupants rented seats for their children as well, but sometimes men who hadn't rented a seat would sit there. Then there would be a disagreement that the synagogue caretakers had to manage to resolve very tactfully.

There were six in our family going to the New Shul, my father, four brothers, and myself. I can still remember very clearly my father pulling me up on his lap when I was very little. I could stand, but not yet for *that* long.

In the Great Shul, the chief rabbi, the trustees, and most of the members of the council stood—the "rich Jews" as well.

I liked to go to the Portuguese shul, or *Snoge* as it was called. I thought it was a beautiful building, and the service impressed me. I was a "High German" or Ashkenazic Jew, not a "Portuguese" or Sephardic Jew, though, so I wasn't allowed into the main part of the interior of the *Snoge*. I had to stand in back.

One day, we were walking out of shul with a couple of Portuguese Jews, and I said by way of a joke, "There were quite a few Ashkenazim in shul today. Did you notice?" After which I said, "Well, it won't be long now before that *Snoge* is ours!"

At which point, one of those people who knew me well came over to me and said, "What's your name, sir? Who are you?"

And I said, very calmly, because I sensed that he had been slightly offended, "Keizer."

Then he exclaimed, "It's not a pleasure meeting you, sir! Not a pleasure! It would be better to put a match to it than for you people to get it!"

◆ DAVID RICARDO

Those proud Portuguese Jews did *not* like to move in the same circles as the Eastern Jews.[7] They set up a special society to support the refugees from Eastern Europe. They helped them get housing, helped them get jobs, but sitting down at the same table? That was obviously a lot less likely. It was even less likely that they would give their daughter in marriage to the son of one of those people. For, if a Portuguese Jew had to be married off to a *todisko* (Ashkenazic male), it was a shameful accident in the family. Portuguese men would sooner marry a Christian woman than a *todiskeh*. There was also a well-known saying among those old Portuguese, pronounced in that special dialect, with that heavy accent, about a man who said to his wife, "Give the blessed child a cookie and that *todiskish* child half of one."

I was a conductor at the Portuguese synagogue. We did everything for free, though. We did have a few good singers, including one very good tenor, but Mr. Englander got him—for money, because over *there* they paid. We had a few other tenors, and they also wanted to go over there. So, I was left without people. One of the ones who ended up singing for Mr. Englander was Duque, who later became *chazzan* of the Portuguese Israelite Congregation. He was also taken away, *nebech,* during the war. But I got to hear him sing at the Great Shul. I conducted the Santo Servicio, which means "Holy Service" and which was the name of our choir. And one fine day these gentlemen said, "We absolutely refuse to sing anymore. We're not doing it anymore. We want to be paid, too." But that was impossible. Maybe the Portuguese Congregation could have managed it, but then we would have been on the slippery slope, because the High German Congregation was much, much wealthier. So, if we were to give them ten guilders, they would give twelve, and if we could give them twelve, they would give fifteen, and we couldn't compete with that. So, one fine day they're saying, "Santo Servicio is quitting. We're going to stop singing!" Well, I thought that was absolutely terrible.

At that point, I single-handedly gathered a group of men and boys and trained them in the entire repertoire, in my room, where I had a harmonium. People thought that the *Snoge* would be without a choir during the holidays, but we brightened the services with our singing.

---

[7]Eastern Jews were descendants of the so-called High German or Ashkenazic Jews from Germany and Eastern Europe who emigrated to Amsterdam during the seventeenth and eighteenth centuries.

◆ LOE LAP

The High German Jews, as Ashkenazic Jews were called, were the common Jews, and the Portuguese were Sephardic Jews from Southern Europe. You could tell by the way they pronounced their Hebrew.

They used to yell at each other, the Portuguese and the non-Portuguese, when I was young. Because, sure, if a boy happened to be called Cardozo, you knew he was Portuguese. And if he said something, you'd say, "Go away, meshuggener Portuguese," because Portuguese means meshugge. Maybe some Portuguese person did something crazy once, so all the Portuguese became meshugge.

◆ AARON VAZ DIAS

Back then, if a Portuguese Jew wanted to marry a High German girl, he was marrying beneath him! It was said that the Portuguese thought highly of themselves. It's a well-known fact that the Portuguese came to Holland with lots of money and connections. Many legacies were bequeathed for special purposes. For instance, there was the "Sortes" or Drawing, where only girls could draw the lots for bequeathed marriage contributions.

There were prizes of twenty-five thousand guilders, twenty thousand guilders, eight thousand guilders, and so on. A long time ago, if a girl drew something and wanted to marry a High German boy, she got nothing. Later, that was changed to half of the amount she drew, and even later, other changes were instituted. The Drawing at the Portuguese synagogue still takes place on the morning of Purim. This happens very formally, with everybody in full dress and the lots on silver plates.

There are also bequests for orphan girls, for poor relatives, contributions to the expenses of the week of Passover, and so forth.

◆ EDUARD VAN AMERONGEN

That congregation wasn't really very democratic, because the most elementary concept we have, the popular right to vote, didn't even exist. In order to vote or be elected, you had to pay a certain amount. That was called matriculation. Then you could vote and be elected to the council, and then you could also be buried at Muiderberg. If you didn't pay, you ended up in a lower class. Then you couldn't vote, couldn't be elected, and you had to go to Diemen to be buried. So, until 1940, there were strange stipulations like that, which you look at now and think: how is it possible that such things still existed? Obviously everything changed after the war.

◆ SIMON GOSSELAAR

You were a member of a congregation because you didn't bother to leave. That may sound a little strange, but there were many people with no ties at all to the faith or to the congregation, either. Congregations expected their members to make contributions, and rightly so. It was called a tax. Administratively, though, it was a real mess, and the majority of the really poor people didn't pay. They'd run into problems, though, getting a marriage solemnized or being buried in a Jewish cemetery, because all those things ran through the administration of the Ashkenazic Congregation of Amsterdam or the Portuguese. They controlled everything.

◈ MAX VAN SAXEN

There was a little shul on Commelinstraat, a *chevra* shul, a little neighborhood shul where people in the neighborhood got together to stay in touch. It had no rabbi. It was pretty close to Linnaeusstraat. I would go there on Saturdays and on Jewish holidays. The *chazzan* was a teacher who gave singing lessons at the seminary. For such a little shul, we had a very good *chazzan*. A little old man, who was distantly related to me, also came, and he would function as the rabbi. There was also a man who had a hat business on Dapperstraat—his daughter is still alive—and there was a member of a chocolate firm, Dünner and De Jong, who was very well educated in things Jewish as well. But there was also a ragman who lived somewhere in the neighborhood who came.

People were allowed to do things in the shul, and it was curious that these privileges were auctioned off beforehand in Yiddish. The *shamash*, the shul caretaker, would say, "Who'll pay three nickels to be allowed to lift the Torah scroll?" And a voice from somewhere in the shul would call out, "Four!" An uncle of mine was a trustee. He had to keep close track of what people had to pay since they weren't allowed to do so on that day. He had a parchment book with little holes for this, with the names of the members in it and the amounts at the top. And he would string a lace through the hole beside the name of the man who had bought one of these privileges and who'd have to pay for it later. In the larger, official shuls, it wasn't done this way.

◈ BAREND LUZA

The Jewish Quarter was one of the poorest sections of Amsterdam. I started out as an acting medical official for the city of Amsterdam, which in those days had an institute that gave free medical help. That help was intended for policemen and firemen and also Amsterdam's poorest residents, who couldn't afford to pay for any health insurance. So, I was also a little bit of a doctor for the poor. Well, one of the poorest areas of the Jewish Quarter was the Jewish Corner, which was still referred to back then as Uilenburg and Vlooienburg.

Rabbi Meyer De Hond was an esteemed figure there because through his views he was able to bring everyday people to a higher level emotionally if not spiritually. There were lots and lots of devout Jews living in those neighborhoods.

De Hond, who at that time already thought very differently than I did, had such powers of persuasion and such a wonderful rhetorical talent, that he got to everybody. In any case, he has always had an influence on me, not in the sense of my becoming religious again or truly pious, but in the sense that I thought about everything he said, which wasn't the case with the speeches of the orthodox rabbis whom I also very much valued and respected, but who didn't have that much of an influence on me.

In my view, he was not antisocialist. He wasn't a member of the SDAP, obviously, but he was a real tribune of the people, and in his sermons, I would say, he was a man of the people. As rabbi, he would often be the spokesperson at both celebrations as well as sorrowful occasions. He was actually called the rabbi of the people. This may also be why he didn't have an easy time of it where official orthodoxy was concerned. He was, in the sense in which I'm imagining it, what a socialist should be and what a believer should be. I didn't get the idea that he had anything in particular against the Socialist Party, but he was so religiously oriented that he didn't think it was necessary. I think De Hond's reasoning went like this, "As long as they think of God, honor God, and follow God's laws, we don't need any socialism!"

◆ JACOB SOETENDORP

I went to the Jewish youth association, Betsalel, and I was personally taught by Rabbi De Hond, who was a fervent opponent of socialism. At Betsalel, the main thing was to learn.

The association consisted of classes where you would meet people and get an extra portion of Jewish teaching. Betsalel also did a lot for culture, theater, and singing. It was a one-man show. It was totally dominated by Rabbi De Hond. He wrote the plays. He also wrote the pieces that had to be read aloud. And when it became necessary to publish a Jewish children's paper that was to be distributed all over the Netherlands, including Drachten and Lemmer, in order to reach those children who no longer had a Jewish congregation in their villages or towns, he was the one who set it up. That's a unique phenomenon in the history of education, that Jewish children's paper. He managed to come up with translations of prayers, of the Torah, word for word, every week another piece, so that those children could learn at home with their parents. It was simply a miracle! That newspaper existed for years, and he did it almost without running any ads.

There was a youth choir at Betsalel that performed at aubades and such.

At the time, I don't believe I knew anything about Chassidism, but if I think back about him now, the impression he made on me as a child was of a Chassidic *rebbe*. He was the perfect example of what you should and shouldn't do. I will always remember the things he said.

For example, we went up to see a bar mitzvah boy, and I said to him, "Mr. De Hond, may we eat here?"

And he said, "Where I go, people may eat, otherwise they should not expect me."

That has stuck with me as a particularly liberal comment, acknowledging another's trust.

His little neighborhood synagogue was on Korte Houtstraat. Sometimes I'd go there in the mornings and the two of us would get the coal stove going. I talked about the people who just passed by, who had no desire whatsoever to belong to the quorum of ten men, to make a *minyan,* and he said, "Maybe they need what they earn more." That man taught me what it means to sanctify life. He was a man who went straight to the heart of everything, who probably offended many people, but who had idealistic ideas about everything that needed to be done.

He was very negative about Zionism, for instance. Anybody who had anything to do with the House of Orange, which the Dutch royal family belonged to, had a special tie to the Jews, in De Hond's mind. He would also talk about William the Silent's "little skullcap." Cultural history teaches us that different people wear caps without its having any bearing on their religious convictions. For De Hond, though, that wasn't true. And that the map of the Netherlands resembles that of the Holy Land—for him, Holland was Canaan. He was, in effect, a Dutch nationalist based on what the Netherlands had meant to the Jews. Imagine if the Jews had had a community as large as the Christian community. De Hond would have been the Abraham Kuyper of the Jews and set up a Jewish Antirevolutionary Party of the poor, poorer Orthodox Jews in his case.[8] Kuyper's and De Hond's point of departure was the same: We don't need socialism. We've got the *Tenach,* don't we? You want to have more socialism than you already get from that? On this point, he doesn't stand entirely alone, either as a rabbi or as a cleric. You could go back a step farther and say that the thoughts that move the socialists really come from the same prophets whom De Hond quoted *against* the socialists.

We were very poor, and that poverty determined the whole rhythm of life, really. Nevertheless, in the middle of all that, Judaism still offered some joy. I only realized later that that idea of philanthropy, of the wealthier people helping the poorer ones, was inadvertently also directed against the struggle to improve one's lot. You were brought up, though, thinking that it was just supposed to be that way and that if you understood Judaism correctly it would bring you to a different lot in life. And a man like De Hond had a certain influence on this. He did

---

[8]Abraham Kuyper was the founder of the Antirevolutionary Party whose followers were mostly lower middle-class orthodox Calvinists.

attack the rich, injustice, and social wrongs as phenomena, but he didn't opt for the socialist solution.

He made an attempt to set up a Jewish housing association. He had a couple of streets in mind for this, what was later called Nieuwe Uilenburgerstraat. And he wanted orthodox Jews to live there. In those days, there was, you see, a definite tendency to stick to one's own kind, in Christian housing as well. Later, socialist housing associations flourished. He may also have thought that the Jewry would become diluted because of these housing associations. Naturally he was very afraid of this, and he always wanted to show that you could do all these things in an orthodox way, too.

He would never, I might add, have used the word "orthodox." For him, there was only such a thing as being Jewish. Well, and if a Jew didn't live up to everything, he was still living according to all the laws, except . . . he was in violation, and that, *nebech*, De Hond couldn't really do very much about.

You knew that there was one view of the ghetto, and that was put forward by De Hond, and there was another view of the ghetto, and it was put forward by the Jewish socialist playwright Heijermans, but Heijermans' view was wrong.[9]

---

[9]Herman Heijermans (1864–1924) was an internationally renowned socialist playwright and novelist. His popular play, *The Good Hope* is still available in its English translation.

Education

◆ JULIA HEERTJES-VAN SAXEN

I came to Amsterdam in 1931. We came from Den Bosch. My father was a chief rabbi, and I had the chance to get into teaching, even though there were lots of teachers. They placed great demands on you, much more so than nowadays. Now they're happy if they can even get a teacher, but back then, you had to fight to be one. You had to teach a trial class first.

So, I ended up at Talmud Torah on Second Boerhaavestraat, and I started with a class of fifty-four students, a real crowd. I thought the kids here were a lot more boisterous than in Den Bosch, but they were also much sweeter and friendlier. When they came in in the morning, they would group around your table right away to tell you all kinds of things about home, and if they saw that you were paying attention to them, they really idolized you, as did their parents. The teacher-student relationship was much more spontaneous than it is now. They needed you. The classes were much longer.

In general, I felt that the Jews in Amsterdam all stuck together. In Den Bosch, a reverend lived next door to us. Well, you just had a civil relationship with him. Of course you had to, though, or else you'd be living in complete isolation. You might have a non-Jewish girlfriend because there wasn't a Jewish girl exactly your age. And on the Sabbath, after shul, your non-Jewish girlfriend might come over after school, and if you were having dinner, she simply sat at the table. You couldn't imagine that in Amsterdam. A Jewish family did *not* sit down to dinner with a goy. I only started consciously associating with Jews here, in Amsterdam.

The Jewish school day lasted longer than the public school day—we taught religion for about an hour and a half every day. The parents thought that was great, because their children were off the streets and warm—and people didn't have to burn coal at home during the day—Sunday mornings and Wednesday afternoons, too.[10] Well, you might teach for an hour and a half, but you didn't get too many results. You still achieved too little. The kids were tired, too, in the end. Usually during the afternoon I'd already be saying, "Children, just fold your arms on your desks, put your head down, and take a nap." Some kids actually did fall

---

[10]Children going to public schools traditionally went six days a week, Monday through Saturday, with a half-day on Wednesdays and Saturdays. Today's children still get Wednesday afternoons off, but go to school five days a week.

asleep. You really had to do that for the little ones. And we *davened*, which means prayed. Well, they all did, but you don't learn anything from that. It lent a certain atmosphere to the class, though. They thought it was especially nice when you talked about Jewish history.

◆ Max Van Saxen

I was a young teacher at the Talmud Torah School. It was a slightly chaotic bunch over there, and I demanded more of them than they were used to at home. They roamed the streets a lot, were often made to leave their house, and were troublemakers. If you went into that neighborhood around ten at night, you'd see quite a lot of children from the lower grades still running around!

There were a lot of things you had to get involved in—hygiene, for instance. The Municipal Health Service came around regularly to check for head lice. Every morning, I would start class with, "Hands on your desks. Your hands are dirty. Your nails aren't clean. Go scrub your hands." We didn't look as closely in the afternoon. The principal would stand by the door, "Why aren't your shoes polished?"

As a student teacher, I had also worked at the public school in that neighborhood, but I didn't see that kind of thing there. Once you had gained the children's confidence, though, you were able to work together very productively. All the parents got together and made our school the gift of a stage you could fold out. I don't know how they managed it, since the money they had to collect was a huge amount for them.

There were also parents who sent their children to us for reasons that were not materially oriented—to keep them in a Jewish environment and to enable a more harmonious education.

One of the material reasons was that at our religious school, the congregation also aided the many working-class Jews who lived in extreme poverty at that time. We did lots of extra things. This was during the Depression of the 1930s.

We served a warm noonday meal, for instance. They did this at the public schools, too, but not kosher, of course. Extra clothing was provided for those who needed it, which came down to a lot of people. Often, children couldn't go to school because their shoes were worn through. At the public schools, they would hand out wooden clogs, so you were marked right away, "He's wearing clogs, so he must have gotten them as a handout." We provided real shoes so the fact that they came from charity wouldn't be noticeable. At certain times of year, the children all received decent-looking clothes, new underwear, a blouse or shirt, trousers for the boys, socks. These things could, of course, have been a material draw for our school.

◆ Loe Lap

I went to the Jewish school Talmud Torah on Boerhaavestraat. That Jewish school was a riot all by itself, because the relationships were very different than at public schools. Jewish teachers had no authority at all over Jewish students. Jews don't regard each other as authority figures anyway, right? No little boys were going to look up to those teachers. A teacher was just another member of the home team, right? A lot of students had family ties with the teachers. They were all a close-knit bunch!

You had to be at the public schools from nine to twelve and from two to four, but at *this* school, you had to be there from nine to twelve-thirty and again from two to five. You had school on Wednesday afternoons and Sunday mornings, and on *Shabbes* you had to be in shul! They checked up on that on Sundays. They'd ask, "Where were you yesterday during shul?" We skipped shul lots of times, and one time we were cleverly caught by our own lies! There were two or three of us, so you had witnesses if you lied. So we're sitting in class.

"What shul were you all at yesterday?"

And we—a Lessing boy, a Verdoner boy, and I—said, "Yesterday, we were in shul at Uilenburg."

And the teacher looked at us and said, "Are you sure?"

"Yes. He was there, and he was too."

"Well," said the teacher, "that seems very odd to me, because that shul burned down Friday night!"

What a riot. Naturally you were punished.

In history class at the normal school, they'd be taught, "Fifty years before Christ, a hundred years before Christ," but we learned, "Fifty years before the Common Era, a hundred years before the Common Era," so the atmosphere was very different.

At nine in the morning, you started off with Hebrew for an hour and a half. We learned from the Torah and we read *tefillim,* and we read Rashi[11] and a few rabbis who had written special books about the faith. You really had to learn the stuff, though. It was drummed into your head, but it had no meaning for you whatsoever. I think it had a counter effect. I started to hate it.

◆ BAREND DRUKARCH

The seminary, in fact, offered a grammar school education, besides providing the youngsters with a purely religious and spiritual preparation. We also had Dr. De Jong, who taught Latin and Greek along with mythology and the like. Life went on in a Jewish environment, of course, because those youngsters were being educated for spiritual occupations and positions. They ended up either in the Jewish congregation or at a Jewish school.

Poverty was pretty prevalent. Dr. De Jong, who was the rector of the seminary, was really far ahead of his generation, though, because he made sure that such

---

[11]Rashi, an acronym for Rabbi Salomon Ben Isaac, was a rabbi in the French city of Troyes during the eleventh century. He wrote a popular commentary on the Old Testament.

poverty could not be noticed by appearances or clothing. If he saw that a boy was unable to afford good clothes, he would call the boy over and say, "Go on over to such-and-such place and buy a suit. Just tell them that you were sent by us." Or else he would give the boy a note to take along, and the matter would be settled. Not a soul ever knew about it, not even fellow students.

When the boys at the seminary had to perform their duties, they preferred smaller shuls because each had its own atmosphere, much more so than the bigger shuls. I myself often went to a little shul that at first was located above Stein's wine cellar, and later next door to the seminary on Rapenburgerstraat.

There was a cabalistic atmosphere there. On Tisha Bov, the day of fasting that commemorates the destruction of the Temple and the end of the national independence of the Jewish people, and which is therefore a day of mourning, we had lots of fun. All the lights would be turned off. The *shamash,* the caretaker, would pass out candles and everybody would sit on the floor. Some youngsters crawled under the benches over to the place where they noticed the *shamash* kept the leftover candle stubs. These were promptly taken out of the cupboard and melted into little balls. Then we tried to pelt people with them from under the benches. At one point, an older man, Shmul Kohn—he was a baker on Zwanenburgerstraat and he belonged to this little shul—was hit on the head by one of those little balls, and he exclaimed, "Now they're even *vershteren* my Tisha Bov here!"

◆ EDUARD CHARLES KEIZER

When I look back, I can see before me the Herman Elte School on Nieuwe Keizersgracht over sixty years ago. Twenty houses down from there on the same canal was Norden's Jewish school.

The orthodox children went to Elte. They received a secular as well as a religious education there. The other Jewish schools were separate religious schools to which students went after their normal classes were over. On Mondays, Tuesdays, and Thursdays from four to five o'clock, on Sundays from nine to twelve and from two to four, and on Wednesdays from two to four. There really wasn't a lot of time left over to play!

The children in my family went to the public school and also went to Mr. Norden's at the times I just mentioned. The public school was the Hendrik Wester School on Weesperplein, where the *Doodkist,* the "Coffin,"[12] is now, between Stadstimmertuinen and Sarphatistraat. The headmaster was the well-known biologist Eli Heimans, also a Jew. There were some non-Jewish teachers, men as well as women, but the school was closed on Saturdays. Only a few dozen students

[12]The *Doodskist* or Coffin is the nickname Amsterdam residents gave the university's psychology lab, built during the 1960s, due to its black glass façade.

went there. A large majority of the students went to shul on *Shabbes*. Mr. Heimans taught us respect for everything that lives, in all of its facets.

My father sent us to public school on purpose. He said, "You're living in a society of Jews and Christians. You need to learn to get along with everyone and not isolate yourself." And I have to say I'm very happy that I learned to get along with others who thought differently and to respect them.

Now things are different. Just a tiny core group of Jews remains, and Jewish life is entirely focused on Israel. That's why I think it's right for Jewish people to send their children to specifically Jewish schools where they can learn what it is to be Jewish and what Israel means to us in the world.

◆ JACOB SOETENDORP

My parents were fervent opponents of specifically Jewish education. My mother was one of the fiercest proponents of the public education of the day. So, I received my Jewish education at a Jewish school. That meant that you went to the public school from nine in the morning until noon. Then you'd be at the Jewish school at half past. You could get there as early as quarter past twelve for a kind of soup kitchen meal. From twelve-thirty until one-thirty, you received Jewish education, and at two o'clock you'd be back at the public school. At four-thirty you left the public school, and at five you'd be back at the Jewish school to start on a good dose of Jewish education, lasting this time until six-thirty. The public school was on what was later called Valkenburgerstraat, but we always called it Marken. That was the famous "number two school," located next to a neighborhood synagogue. Jewish education was taught at the large Jewish school on Rapenburgerstraat that had over twelve hundred students. That was right across from what was later the seminary.

We lived in the mainly non-Jewish Kattenburg neighborhood on the east side of the harbor. Maybe "Jew" was shouted occasionally, but I don't recall that. We were totally integrated there socially, except we didn't go to school there. Even for public elementary school, you went to school in the Jewish Quarter. So, we ended up on Valkenburgerstraat, because there were plenty of schools around there on the Islands. Going from one school to the next was very easy because Valkenburgerstraat to Rapenburgerstraat is only one street over. I think this was purely for reasons of efficiency. The Jewish school times were set up in such a way that in order to be able to get into the pattern as a whole, you had to be going to a public school nearby.

◆ BEN SAJET

Other kids were free on Sundays and on Wednesday afternoons, but we'd have to go to the Jewish school. I went to a public school, but you still had to learn all kinds of things, like Hebrew. We lived in a very Jewish community, after all. The

schools we went to, including the public schools, were attended almost exclusively by Jewish kids.

I had Jewish friends, but then that was obviously going to be the case. I lived
in a neighborhood where practically nobody but Jews lived. At school, there was
nothing but Jewish boys, just about. When I reached high school, though, I made
some non-Jewish friends, some of whom became very close friends. One of those
boys was the son of a police chief. His father thought pretty highly of himself. . . .
It was an event when that boy came to our house for the first time, that Christian
boy. And maybe when I went to his house, too! Seeing a goy over at our house,
though, that was unusual. You accepted it, but it was still strange. Later on it got
to be very normal.

Philanthropy

◆ NATHAN STODEL

There was an association, the Bar Mitzvah Association, a *chevra,* whose members included jewelers and small diamond dealers, for instance, with an orthodox background. That association held a drawing three or four times a year for a boy's bar mitzvah suit. They would have one made by some second-rate tailor, who, in any case, was happy enough to have the opportunity to sew it. Along with that suit came a coupon to buy some underwear for a young boy of thirteen at a particular dry goods business, plus a little money to organize some sort of small reception.

There was a building on Muiderstraat, the Pigol, the Portuguese Israelite Home for the Elderly, which rented out rooms. This is also where the board of that chevra met for the donors and the members, who had made a contribution of about two and a half guilders per year, to draw lots. Those bar mitzvah-boys-to-be, though, they had to stand in the corridor with their parents. If someone who didn't have a son won, these parents would try to approach that particular donor or *chevra* member through relatives to help their son get the bar mitzvah suit.

So, at a certain point, I was also almost a bar mitzvah boy, and there was going to be another drawing. I can't remember anymore what her name was, but let's say Mrs. Kulker won, and my father, with me in tow, raced over to her, "Mrs. Kulker, *mazel tov!* You won. May my son be the bar mitzvah boy?"

My father, a street vendor, pushed his cart through what people back then called the "well-heeled" neighborhood, the Plantage Franschelaan, now the Dr. Henri Polaklaan, where various small and mid-sized diamond dealers and such lived.

Well, it frequently happened that someone like Mrs. Kulker would have promised the bar mitzvah suit to one of her husband's employees a long time before, in case she won. Sometimes not, though. So, that's how I got my bar mitzvah suit. My perception of the way I got that bar mitzvah suit was that it was extremely demeaning, because of course they called out your name in shul.

◆ KAREL POLAK

My father died when I was nine. I was the youngest of five children, and age-wise I was just old enough to be taken in by the Dutch Israelite Boys' Orphanage. This

65

was on the Amstel River near the Blue Bridge. The back door of the building was on Zwanenburgerstraat (Swanburg Street), which we orphans called Swineburg Street instead because it bordered on the Waterlooplein market. After four o'clock, lots of people with rag carts would go there to get rid of their goods, so in the afternoons it was a pigsty. But, by the entrance, which was facing the Amstel River, it was always quiet and clean and free of rubbish.

Back then there were no social-service laws yet. Everything had to be done through philanthropy. The Dutch Israelite Board for the Poor is a very unfortunate name. Nowadays, it's called the NIISA, the Dutch Israelite Institute for Social Work. They helped the poor as much as possible, giving them interest-free advances to buy goods to sell, for example, or if there was no food or heat, they'd contribute money for food or coal for the stove. And yet, those were the days when the trustees of the charities ruled.

At the orphanage, it was one big family of eighty children split into three groups: the youngest, the middle group, and the oldest ones. The oldest were naturally the boys who went to high school or trade school, or who went to work at a firm.

When a boy left elementary school, which was at the orphanage, he would be invited along with his guardian to go to the trade commission where he would be asked what he wanted to be. If it was possible, it was done. We even had boys at the orphanage who wanted to be doctors, accountants, and teachers. So, they made the most of what the boys had to offer.

An awful lot was done to stimulate intellectual and cultural development, but also to provide a Jewish education. Synagogue three times a day, prayer in the morning, prayer in the afternoon, prayer at night.

◆ JACOB SOETENDORP

The seminary is one of the oddest schools you can imagine. It's a school where children received a secondary school education when their parents really didn't have the income for it. A large number of seminarians decided against becoming rabbis, and they began a social career by way of the university. However, that rabbinical education did get you to the state exam for admission to the university. It was an unusual way of getting a well-rounded education.

I myself was a "people eater." This concept was also known at the Talmud schools in Eastern Europe, meaning that the poor students had to go eat midday meals at the homes of those who were better off. My father had died, and I had to work very hard outside of school to earn a little extra for the family. I tutored a few less gifted boys, and I trained bar mitzvah boys. On top of this, I stood watch over corpses, which I already started doing when I was sixteen or seventeen.

During that time, I fainted once. The vice-rector of the seminary found me and decided that I should go eat at people's homes three days a week from then on. Of course, when you were a boy, there were people about whom you thought, "They're giving me the food I hate on purpose the day I eat here." Or you had to be good and offer your paw like a good little poodle. The underlying thought, though, is that the study of the Torah is reinforced by helping people. It still really was the old way of doing things, though, and I believe it was a typically Jewish idea. Our perception of it was that it was still demeaning, though. On top of this, I had a hard time with the fact that although I got to go eat, back home my brothers and sisters hadn't had enough, and they'd say, "You got to stuff yourself." One of my brothers was in the orphanage. He had a terribly hard time dealing with the humiliation inherent in organized charity.

I felt that way, too. One time I got a coat from somebody, a nice coat. When I arrived at the home of one of those people where I ate, the man took the coat over his arm and said, "Nice coat you have there," giving you the impression that you'd stolen the coat. Yes, I rebelled a lot against organized charity when I was young, and I think most of the boys did, really.

◆ MOZES HEIMAN GANS

In a radio speech, it was once said of The Jewish Invalid, "It's for crippled and broken people who can't work anymore." And it was considered very normal that people donated money. You have to remember that the circumstances back then were very different from what they are now. Those people in The Jewish Invalid largely came from slums, from the ghetto of Amsterdam. Some were on the verge of starvation.

The Jewish Invalid relied on private initiative, and this is what made it so popular. Back then, there was no question of the city or the state or even the Jewish congregation providing support. It was private individuals who collected the money. This happened through coin collection points, and later on through drawings and musical revues as well.

The Jewish Invalid was founded in 1911, I believe. The odd thing is that The Jewish Invalid really flourished during the Depression. Just when things were the hardest financially and poverty in Amsterdam was at its height, The Jewish Invalid became *the* example. It was, for instance, a very unusual thing for the two "anti-lottery" ministers, Colijn and Oud, to be speaking out in favor of The Jewish Invalid on the radio. This was before the days of television, so it was significant in itself that radio devoted evenings to the facility. Newspapers contained extra inserts to advertise The Jewish Invalid.

Of course, there was a lot of talk about the revues and about the lottery drawings and about all kinds of possible money campaigns, but in the Netherlands my father ranked as the major *shnorrer,* the major beggar. He didn't feel that way himself, though. He thought of himself first and foremost as the institution's director.

He got into that work thanks to my mother. He was a diamond polisher for about ten years, hated the trade, thought it was terrible. My mother wrote the boss a letter at a certain point giving notice. My father had all kinds of jobs after that and finally became the fund-raiser for The Jewish Invalid. Five or six years later, he became its director. He was a totally self-made, self-educated man. That was very common among the diamond workers, though.

My father was very good with Henri Polak. I remember that Polak and his wife were at our house one evening and that an intense discussion arose between Polak and my father. My father was saying, "You all may have principles, but in the meantime so many people are going down the drain. We try to help people, first, and because of this, we often forget the principles." He knew that in several decades, the national or the municipal government would take these things over because there would be a much more socialist society then. "But," he said, "we have to make sure it's here *now,* because that's how we can help these people."

They did everything imaginable. For instance, every Friday evening a group of young people would sing Sabbath songs. We would go around the place from ward to ward and sing everywhere we went.

There was a large auditorium, and I recall Fritz Hirsch or Louis Davids or somebody performing. Henri Polak would come to speak about Old Amsterdam, say, and he would show lantern slides. I recall that he was at his wits' end once because evidently during his talk he mentioned how scandalous it was that people shut little birds up in cages and whatnot. Those creatures needed their freedom, too, didn't they? And at this point, some woman burst into tears because the little canary above her bed happened to be her life, and Henri Polak didn't know how he could make it up to her.

The great violinist Sam Swaap would also come to play. And when Jack Hilton was in Amsterdam with his band from England, he would play at The Jewish Invalid. This was something everyone took for granted. There was some kind of dwarf theater troupe, too, from Austria, and it came to The Jewish Invalid.

On Seder evening, according to ancient Jewish tradition, anyone who was hungry was allowed to come have dinner. Four hundred people could come to celebrate the Seder. A couple of days before the Seder, one woman said to us, "It's a shame they'll be tromping all over my nice clean floors!"

I said to my father, "She's only been here a couple of months herself. What kind of circumstances does she come from?"

To which my father responded, "Isn't it beautiful the way she already feels at home here?"

In 1937, 1938, Princess Juliana was to go to Germany, and she wanted to show that she did not in any way sympathize with German anti-Semitism. At that time, the best way to do this was to pay a visit to The Jewish Invalid. So, a few days before she came, The Jewish Invalid was informed that Princess Juliana wanted to visit the facility. She had just married Prince Bernhard. So, she toured the building, and suddenly she asks, "What's in that room?"

So my father said, "There's a dying man in isolation there."

And she said, "I'd like to visit him."

So, they went in, and my father said, "Mr. Green, this is the Princess. This is the Princess, Mr. Green."

At which point the man suddenly sat up, placed his hand on his head, and recited the eulogy appropriate for seeing a royal personage. Those were the last words he ever uttered.

III

THE OLD JEWISH QUARTER

Around 1900, the large majority of Amsterdam Jews were still living in what was called the Old Jewish Quarter, a city district located approximately between Nieuwmarkt and Sarphatistraat. As early as 1800, affluent Jews gradually began spreading out to other parts of the city of that time, into an area that roughly corresponds to the district called Amsterdam Center today.

Between 1870 and 1900, new residential districts arose in West, South, and East Amsterdam, some of them intended for the wealthy, others for the "lower" classes. The first category included the Plantage (the Plantation) and Sarphatistraat, to which mainly distinguished Jewish families relocated. The tree-lined lanes of the Plantage bordered on the original Jewish Quarter, as did the Sarphatistraat, and so were incorporated into the Jewish Quarter, as it were.

Jewish families also moved into the new, chic districts around the equally new Vondelpark as well as around the Concertgebouw, but not as many by far as moved into the Plantage area. Of the new workers' neighborhoods of three-story brick apartment buildings that were constructed during the final quarter of the nineteenth century, those in West (the Kinkerstraat neighborhood, etc.) housed practically no Jews. A few went to live in De Pijp (The Pipe) in South Amsterdam. In contrast, many Jewish workers, particularly the diamond workers, settled in the new workers' neighborhoods in East Amsterdam (Vrolikstraat, Swammerdamstraat, Blasiusstraat), streets that joined up directly with the Old Jewish Quarter.

Originally, poor Jews and wealthy Jews lived at a stone's throw from each other in the Old Jewish Quarter. There were, however, streets for the poor in this neighborhood, such as Valkenburgerstraat and Batavierstraat, along with the passageways in between them. For the wealthy, there were thoroughfares along canals such as the Nieuwe Herengracht and the Nieuwe Keizersgracht. As the city expanded after 1870, when modern capitalism was introduced to Amsterdam, class distinctions became much clearer, geographically as well. Rich and poor spread out into separate neighborhoods, regardless of whether these neighborhoods had a specifically Jewish character or not.

The great exodus after World War I of Jews of all social classes to new areas of the city in East and South Amsterdam—including the Transvaal neighborhood, what was called plan-Zuid or "South Plan," and Betondorp or "Concrete Village"[1]—will be the subject of the next chapter. One of the consequences for the Old Jewish Quarter of this shift was that more Christians went there to live.

---

[1]The Transvaal neighborhood is in East Amsterdam. The South Plan was urban architect H. P. Berlage's 1915 plan for what is now Nieuw Zuid/New South and the Rivierenbuurt/River District; Betondorp is a southern subdivision of Watergraafsmeer and the second early 1920s building experiment in concrete.

Living and Housing Conditions

◆ KAREL POLAK

Rapenburgerstraat was an unusual street, the center for Amsterdam's Jewry, in fact. There was the seminary, the rabbinate, then the Jewish nursery school and kindergarten, and Stein's kosher wine shop. On Rapenburgerstraat, there was the Dutch Israelite Girls' Orphanage and also Beth Ha Midrash, a place where everybody who wanted to learn could go.

◆ CAREL REIJNDERS

When I was a boy, a saying at home was, "That Delmonte or Vleeschhouwer or Daniels family is 'the Nation kind.'" I had absolutely no idea at the time that it meant anything like "High German or Portuguese Jewish Nation." It was just the same, though, saying, "He's the Nation kind," about a Jew as saying about a Catholic, "He's the wooden T kind," meaning of the faith, referring to the crucifix.

Only later, when I was a student, I understood that there was a historical origin and that until the days when the French were in the Netherlands, the Jews belonged to the "Hebrew Nation," which clearly meant: were *not* citizens. They had no part in anything. I used all these Jewish expressions without knowing it. We'd talk about "gein" (fun). You had "pech" (bad luck) and "mazel" (good luck) playing marbles. We'd refer to "ponum" or "porum" (face, look). And "attenoyelehaineh" was really a Jewish curse, but you used it simply as an expletive. It means *Adonai Elohainu,* "My Lord and my God." I found that in a little book by Beem.[2] "Addenom," another bastardization, was also sometimes used. In Amsterdam's non-Jewish popular parlance, though, it was bastardized into "attenoye," and that was used all the time.

My mother's from old Amsterdam, from the Groenburgwal neighborhood, and that fell under the Moses and Aaron Church. The peculiar thing is that that Catholic church, whose real name is "Holy Anthony of Padua," is commonly called the "Moses and Aaron" Church. But then, this has to do with the old secret underground church that was behind the current one, and it used to have two lin-

---

[2]Hartog Beem wrote dictionaries containing Yiddish terms and expressions used in the Netherlands.

tels with "Moses" and "Aaron" inscribed on them.[3] They used to joke about the priest of that old church being "the rabbi of the Catholic synagogue."

On Christmas night, the church would be full of Jews, and the church always made sure there was a policeman inside, which was strange because there was never any trouble. The Jews just went on Christmas night because there was beautiful singing and an orchestra to go with it. They would go to listen and often stood in the back.

My mother was around, though, when it was rumored that a Jewish girl who'd become Catholic was going to be married in that same church. So, all the pious "fruit Jews"[4] ganged up on the wedding guests and wanted to have at them—until they managed to make it clear that the girl wasn't Jewish after all.

◆ MAURITS ALLEGRO
The Old Jewish Quarter before the war consisted of Valkenburgerstraat area, desperate poverty and misery, one-room tenements in tiny courtyards. I can still recall how wretched it was on that little canal, the Boltensgracht (currently Anne Frankstraat), roughly where the police station is now. In the three-story tenement houses, there were two sets of stairs, and you had to pull yourself up the third one because the third set was just so incredibly steep. A thick rope hung along the side—God only knows how old that thing was—and you really had to do some climbing. And I remember a family with eight or ten children living up there, and they didn't have so much as bread to eat. The kids got four tickets at school for what was called the "soup canteen." So, they were able to get soup there, and then they'd toss in some water so the whole family could eat. Those kids wore socks donated by the city that were trimmed in black and red, the city colors, so you could tell they were from city charity. It was terribly poverty-stricken in the Jewish Quarter, simply indescribable. Of course, there were a few people who were a little better off. But still, the majority was dirt poor. Really, with pushcarts full of rags.

◆ HARTOG GOUBITZ
We lived thirteen people to one room on Marken. That's the Valkenburgerstraat, the street that runs along the ramp going down to the IJ Tunnel now. That used

[3]After the Alteration of 1578, when Amsterdam was in the hands of a Protestant administration, the Catholic religion was officially banned. Secret underground churches were built behind normal housefronts. If these were discovered, the Catholics had to pay a fine, in effect paying a tax to continue practicing their religion away from the public eye. The existing Moses and Aaron Church was built in the nineteenth century to replace the underground church.

[4]This term derives from the fact that many poor Jews were fruit vendors.

to be Marken. One side, which is where we lived, was torn down. There used to be a canal in between, and Rapenburgerstraat ran along that. But Marken was a street as wide as this room.

Those apartments had no kitchens. They were just rooms with a built-in-the-wall bed, and a lot of them had a cubbyhole over that recessed bed that you could reach with a ladder. It had a door to it, and you could sleep in there, too.

There was water, but no flush toilet, just a commode, a stool with a bucket. In the evening, right before dusk, the city sanitation people would come by with carts that were ironically called "Boldoot" carts, after the popular eau de cologne, because of that nice stink they left in the air. The slop buckets would be placed outside the front door, and those "Boldoot" carts would empty them.

When I think of my grandmother, who lived to be a hundred and one and a half, I still see her in front of me on Marken, behind Valkenburgerstraat, where she lived in the Red Lion Passageway in a slum dwelling on the first floor, the way those places were in those days. I still see her sitting with a foot stove under her feet, the way people warmed themselves back then. And my father, who visited her on Friday evenings, as was the custom among Jews, noticed that that foot stove was a fire hazard because it was full of holes, and he said, "Memmeh, I'm going to get you a new foot stove."

My father had a foot stove delivered to her that week, and that same week, her husband, my grandfather, died. He was a shoe-shine man. He'd have his bench out in front of what was then The Bishop Cafe. That was on the corner of the little Marken Square and Jodenbreestraat. And when my father went to see her that week, she said to him, "Maupie, you've gone and given me that stove, so now I can sit *shivah* on it."

You can see the photograph of my grandmother's hundredth birthday at the Jewish Historical Museum. In the picture, she's sitting between chief rabbi Onderwijzer and Mayor Tellegen.

◆ ALEXANDRE JOSEPH GOUDSMIT

Valkenburgerstraat, that was downright poor, you know. There was a passageway under those houses, and in the courtyard behind them it got a bit wider, about eight or nine feet wide. There were four row houses on both sides, and that's where the poorest of the poor lived. It was called the Red Lion Passageway. I can remember a story about Henri Polak. He recounted once in *Het Weekblad*, that was the diamond workers' weekly paper, that he had received a letter from Samuel Gompers in America. Gompers was the founder of the AFL, the American Federation of Labor, the largest labor federation in America. He was one of the groundbreakers. He was born in Red Lion Passageway and emigrated to America with his parents when he was a baby, and now he just wanted to see where he'd been born.[5] He spoke no Dutch and referred to "Red Lion's Court," so Henri Polak, chairman of the Dutch Diamond Workers Union, was worrying himself sick about what that might be. But, because Gompers had said that it was in the center of the Jewish Quarter, Henri Polak understood that it must have been Red Lion Passageway. So, when Gompers came to Amsterdam, that's where Polak took him. It's gone, now, though, because that side was completely torn down.

◆ BAREND DE HOND

In those days, you had only Jewish friends and acquaintances because you really didn't get outside the Jewish community. You also lived in a kind of ghetto, and there were very few Christians living there. If you lived on Nieuwegrachtje, like we did, there was still Uilenburg and "Vlooienburg" ("Fleaburg"—that was Lange Houtstraat) and Batavierstraat and Rapenburgerstraat. And then there was also Valkenburgerstraat. That was the circle, see, and when you crossed the bridge, you came to Foeliestraat, where there were Christians. A few Jewish people were scattered in there. It wasn't hostile, but it was right on the edge of the Old Quarter, see.

I was born at number one Nieuwegrachtje, on the third floor. Our rent was one seventy-five, give or take, per week, and Mr. Roodenburg, the landlord, always came to pick up the rent on Sundays. My father worked at Nijkerk's, a hardware business. They had to haul metal onto ships, which is all done by crane nowadays; 175 to 200 pounds on their shoulders, all day, from six in the morning till five at night.

My parents had ten kids, and my father earned only sixteen guilders a week. So, you can see why my mother had to fib a little now and then. "Mr. Roodenburg, could you come back next week?" she'd say, because she didn't have that one seventy-five.

And those apartments were built so that if you didn't have any rugs on the floor, you could see the neighbors walking around downstairs. All there was were beams and floorboards with cracks in between, so you could hear every word the neighbors said.

In our family, there were ten kids and three beds. Four boys slept in one bed, the three girls in another, and my father and mother slept together in a third bed. Later, we were forced to put a bed up in the attic too.

---

[5]Gompers was actually born in London, the son of a Dutch cigar maker, who probably had lived in the Red Lion Passageway. This passageway, like the others, ran underneath the apartments lining a street, so that it was extremely narrow, leading to small tenements behind.

We were used to cooking up a pot of soup on Fridays. One Friday, though, my mother had no money for soup, even though she had some self-respect. So, what did she do? She puts a pot of water on the stove.

In the afternoon, the neighbor lady comes upstairs and says, "Aunt Diek, what kind of soup are you making?"

And my mother says, "Well, I'll tell you, tonight I'm going to have a delicious pot of soup, don't you worry."

"You don't say," says the neighbor lady, "Well, I'm going to take a peek anyway." So, she lifts the lid and sees that it's just a pot of water.

That neighbor lady went downstairs, and for two-fifty she got soup meat and vegetables and potatoes, and she gave my mother five guilders besides and said to her, "Now you can have *Shabbes*."

There was a little old man, and there were these boys and older people who used to tease him. The man was very devout, but he called down a curse on them. That's called a *cholilleh* in Yiddish. He said, "You will fall in love with a woman and never be able to win her." That was Japie Schapendief. He only went around begging, along with a couple of other fellows, whenever there was a *chasseneh* on Rapenburgerstraat.

◆ JOOP EMMERIK

I used to live in the poor part of town, on Kerkstraat, between the Amstel River and Weesperstraat. That was a *very* poor neighborhood. Now and then there were a couple of people who could say that things were going pretty good— maybe a couple of shopkeepers who had shops there.

A "prodder" would come by at night to wake people. His name was Brammetje Lelie. I was a boy of four or five, see, and I'd be so scared I'd crawl under the blankets. He'd rattle at the door upstairs. There weren't any doorbells on the doors, so he'd have to walk up. And he'd call out, "Betje, aren't you up yet? It's four o'clock, you know!" because Lamme Betje had to go to the market early every morning.

There was Japie Schapendief too. I can still see him walking along with his cane. Whenever people got married, he would stand there begging. We called it mooching. If he got something, he would say, *"Mazel, and a bracha* for all of your *mishpocheh,"* meaning lots of luck and a prayer for your entire family, right? But if he didn't get anything, he would start to curse. That got pretty unpleasant.

Then there was this man called Joost Melhado. They nicknamed him Joost Canal because he used to piss out on the street a lot.

Then there was this man who lived above the little Russian shul. They called him Hemeltje, heavens, because he was always looking up at the sky. He was a devout Jew. If you were a little kid and you shouted "Hemeltje!" he would chase you.

Later on, a boat trip association was organized on Kerkstraat. It was called "Our Delight," I believe. They'd hire a boat once a year to go down the Amstel. They'd come back in the evening, the marching band blaring, and march off the boat right down Kerkstraat, led by the band. The whole street would turn out. Everybody would walk behind them in this long parade. That was fantastic. My father was one of the people who started the event, along with Benjamins and Brammetje Lelie. Everybody had a ball. My father would play records on this gramophone with one of those big horns. He'd play dance music. You'd have to wind the thing up, and he'd play it out the window, and people would start dancing in the street. There was also a family by the name of Swaab. Their son Barend could play piano really well. That boy often played with the window open, and people would enjoy listening in the street below.

◈ LEEN RIMINI

First, there's the Rembrandt House, then there was De Vries van Buuren, then a poulterer and De Raap's tobacco shop, Kaats's cheese shop, Van der Woude's butter and cheese shop, and then there was my shop, which was part of the Cooperative.

The Tip Top movie theater was on the corner of Uilenburg Alley and Jodenbreestraat. For the Cooperative's shops in Amsterdam, closing was at eight o'clock. They set the example. Later it was seven, but I couldn't do that because Tip Top opened at eight, and I was too busy between seven and eight what with the candy and all—because lots and lots of candy got sold. The customers, Jewish people, came to get peanuts and chocolate creams and chocolates to go to the Tip Top. So, I was allowed to close from six to seven and then open up again from seven to eight.

Oh, if you only knew how those people shopped. . . ! Two ounces of butter was hardly anything, but if they could have gotten half that much, they'd have bought it. They did eat good butter, though! They had no notion of a pound of sugar. No, they had to have four ounces. I sold it myself, so I know: a penny's worth of vinegar, a penny's worth of powdered bleach, two pennies' worth of powdered bleach, a third of a cup of salad oil, one penny's worth of pepper, two ounces of raisins, a spiced honey bread worth three cents—it was a really decent little loaf, you know.

In those days, where the "Dockworker" monument now stands, was the Handwerkers Vriendenkring (Craftsmen's Fellowship) bathhouse.[6] It was the only

---

[6]The Dockworker is a monument in memory of the Amsterdam workers who went on strike in February 1941 to protest the first big Nazi raid in the Old Jewish Quarter. The February Strike is still commemorated there every year.

bathhouse in the whole ghetto. It cost five cents, and if you got a ticket in the morning, you'd get your turn that evening. This was the work of the Handwerkers Vriendenkring. Sometime after that, the city put a bathhouse on Uilenburg, and then they built another bathhouse and laundry on Valkenburgerstraat.

◆ BEN SAJET

It was a terribly poor neighborhood, to which I often had to go because I helped deliver babies when I was a medical student. You'd head out with a midwife, and the midwife I was assigned to worked on Uilenburgerstraat and Batavierenstraat. What can I say? You couldn't imagine worse living conditions. One-room places with ten or twelve kids, and every year there'd always be another one. Imagine how they slept in a room like that: a couple on the floor, six in a bed—three little heads going one way, three little heads the other.

Together with a friend named Van Gelderen, a statistician, I wrote up some studies in social medicine on measles and whooping cough and so on, in which we showed that disadvantaged children died of those illnesses although affluent children hardly ever did. Because of the poor housing and terrible conditions, though, the disadvantaged children would get tuberculosis and die. They got those illnesses when they were a lot younger, too, because there were a lot more children crowded together on Uilenburg and places like that.

In the poverty-stricken Jewish Quarter of Amsterdam, trachoma—that's an eye condition where granulations occur on the conjunctival membranes—was very prevalent. Those granulations grow and they can invade the eye itself, the cornea, so that serious damage to vision can occur, as well as blindness. In backward countries, like Egypt, for instance, is where you get a lot of trachoma. In Amsterdam, though, there was what we call an "endemic infection." It affects a particular population group, whereas an "epidemic infection" is widespread. So, trachoma was what we call "endemic" among the Jewish poor in the slum. I conducted a house-by-house investigation of trachoma, which is actually the first "social medicine" work I did. It turned out that almost everyone had trachoma or had had it—you could tell by the scars. It was that prevalent.

◆ LOE LAP

My *oma* on my mother's side had a candy shop on Uilenburgerstraat where she sold sweets for children. Well, I had it lucky since I was sitting on a pot of gold, see, because I could grab as much as I wanted. Later, it turned into a really big store with a grocery and all that. It was called Aunt Pinnie's, next to the little Van Rosenthal school. All those schoolchildren would stop by my *oma's* shop in the morning to buy a little nosh for half a penny or a penny.

I can still see that little candy shop in my mind, you know. It was around until I was something like ten or eleven. You had shoestring licorice, gumdrops, cinnamon sticks, candy canes, salty salmiac licorice, and nougat squares. And on the

Queen's birthday, she sold cap-gun caps and fireworks. She was a strapping woman. She had twenty-two children, and my grandfather was an alcoholic. He drank like a fish. It's too bad, but those cigar makers, they all drank. There really were Jews who drank, you know. That's another one of those myths: "Jews don't drink." Well, if only that had been true. There wasn't a campaign to combat alcoholism for nothing though. It was a social problem.

The Jewish Quarter and the Jordaan were really very closely related. Both these parts of town had their own way of talking, and the people in these two neighborhoods used to get together all the time. If you were Jewish and had a stand at a market in some country town, you noticed you were Jewish a *lot* more out there than in Amsterdam.

◆ NATHAN STODEL

When talking about the good old days, the way, for instance, the journalist and historical writer Meyer Sluyser does, he paints a good picture, but he still poeticized it too much. The poverty was horrible. Imagine, on the Sluice and all over the Jewish Quarter you could get three or four herring for a dime, but people just couldn't afford that!

My parents had a grocery on Lazarussteeg. They needed ten guilders a week for operating expenses, which they didn't have. The way they had to borrow in order to be able to do business is unbelievable! They were decent people through and through. I was an only child, but oftentimes my parents had no money to get my shoes fixed, so I'd get pieces of cardboard instead of new soles.

I helped by running errands, but they sent me to middle school when I was eleven. You were already allowed to work when you were thirteen, and they could really have used the money, but they sent me to school instead: "Nathan, go to school. Nathan, learn your lessons." My father certainly didn't have much education, but it was something they took for granted: Nathan had to learn. He had to get out of poverty. As for them, they went to the wholesale produce market at five in the morning.

◆ MOZES DE LEEUW

There were also prominent people in the Jewish Quarter, such as De Beer with his wine shop. De Beer himself manned the shop in his twill trousers and beret. He lived somewhere on Plantage Parklaan, though, in the rich neighborhood. That's where Jews who were both financially as well as culturally prominent lived. They were a whole different breed from the Jewish Quarter. The devout Jews were members of Artis, the zoo with the scenic park and all the old trees. On Saturdays they'd stroll around the grounds, since as members they didn't have to pay. All of Jewish cultural life went on over there. That's the area where the rabbis lived, too.

◆ MAURIUS GUSTAAF LEVENBACH

Every summer we all went to Artis, the entire family. We were members. Membership was for the well-to-do, of course, the ones who were somewhat better off. After all, a year's membership for the whole family cost twenty guilders or something. On Sundays during the summer, there would be concerts in a pavilion at Artis. It was usually Zaagmans who gave those concerts—out on the grounds during the summer and in the big hall during the winter. Later, this hall housed the public records office.

◆ EDUARD VAN AMERONGEN

Artis is just a zoo, of course, but back then it was really the special park for Amsterdam's Jewry. Every Saturday afternoon they would go there. They would sit out on the terrace or in the cafe, order something, and not have to pay because they'd settle up the following week. They had absolutely no interest in animals. They didn't go there to see the animals.

They would sometimes go when the sea lions were being fed. Then they'd look, but they wouldn't bother with the rest. It was their park, though. Frans Van Diepenbeek would do concerts back then. He conducted there during the 1920s. After him came Van Beinum with the Haarlem Orchestra Association.[7] Several concerts were given, on Wednesday evenings and on Sunday afternoons. But that atmosphere at Artis on a Saturday afternoon. . . . There were only Jews at the park. It was theirs, and it was part of their life.

◆ DAVID RICARDO

Every Sunday Frans Van Diepenbeek of the Fifth Army Regiment would give concerts at Artis, outside in summer and inside in the big hall in the winter. It was a wind orchestra. They played operas.

I would almost say that only Jews went. It would be really crowded. It was something very festive.

This is where the rudiments of my conducting skills were crafted—copied from Frans Van Diepenbeek!

---

[7]Eduard Van Beinum was the successor to the brilliant conductor Willem Mengelberg who had been discharged from his position with the Concertgebouw Orchestra due to controversy over his association with the Nazis.

IV

EMANCIPATION

The emancipation of the Jewish proletariat in Amsterdam, meaning the economic, social, and cultural betterment of skilled workers, diamond workers, cigar makers, and so on, occurred within a Dutch framework. Ties to the SDAP, the ANDB, and later the NVV and the AJC promoted a certain amount of integration of the Jewish and non-Jewish proletariat. This integration was never complete, though, as is revealed, for instance, by the fact that at the beginning of the twentieth century, the Amsterdam branch of the SDAP balked at using Jewish campaigners in the western workers' neighborhoods during elections. This objection did not apply to voting District 3, however, predominantly the diamond workers' district, where non-Jews were more familiar with Jews and therefore less prejudiced against them.

What was particularly unique was what the ANDB did to educate workers. People like Henri Polak considered the union to be not only an organization to stand up for higher wages and better social services, but also one that encouraged workers to gain a knowledge and love of art and nature.

Of course the ANDB did not have a monopoly in this department. The HWV or Handwerkers Vriendenkring (Craftmen's Fellowship), an organization whose members were workers of various political stripes, had fostered cultural engagement among Jewish workers starting in the 1870s and 1880s. In fact, Heiman Barnstein, a staunch Liberal Democrat and president of the HWV for many years, significantly contributed to the founding of the ANDB in 1894.[1]

After 1909, a number of major and minor parties split off from the SDAP because the party appeared to be neglecting the revolutionary ideal, and Jews were well represented in all of them. The fact that Jews became communist, Trotskyist, OSP members, or anarchists, had no bearing on their Jewish origin as such.[2] The struggle between Jewish social democrats of the SDAP and Jewish

---

[1] In 1901, progressive liberals and radicals merged to form the Liberal Democratic Union which found itself between the Liberal Party and the SDAP in the Dutch political spectrum.

[2] In 1932, a group of radical Social Democrats split from the SDAP and formed the Independent Socialist Party (OSP) because they thought the SDAP had lost its revolutionary zeal.

communists in Amsterdam was particularly fierce, no doubt largely because they were very often personally acquainted. This controversy over principles sometimes even took on the character of a family quarrel.

In this chapter, in the section that deals with the new neighborhoods, considerable attention has been paid to what was known as the Transvaal neighborhood. This neighborhood actually consisted of various core groups, each with a different social makeup. The Pretoriusstraat neighborhood, for instance, was somewhat tonier than the Retiefstraat neighborhood.

Politics and the Labor Movement

◆ HARTOG GOUBITZ
Cigar makers worked together in the factories. Issues and conditions were hotly debated while people were hard at work. The cigar makers promoted the life of their organization because they were physically together. Typographers were the most proficient workers. The diamond workers are an entirely different story, although they also worked together in factories, which also led to discussions and ultimately different schools of thought.

Wages were very low for a long, long time. The Cigar Makers Union was practically the first organization that was able to successfully negotiate a collective labor agreement, an employment contract with better provisions regarding wages and relationships within the company.

The Cigar Makers Union was one of the oldest labor organizations. The Typographers Union was the first union in Amsterdam. Back then the ANDB hadn't been founded yet, although you did have a small diamond workers association. The ANDB, which the majority of the 10,000 Amsterdam diamond workers joined, was founded by Henri Polak after that huge strike. I think it was in 1894. The cigar makers were having a strike at the same time.

My father was a cigar maker. In 1898, we had that big cigar makers' strike here in Amsterdam, and my father was a striker. He was all for improving living conditions for the working class. After the strike was over, the people who'd gone on strike were considered agitators. They were blacklisted and couldn't get work anywhere. That was common practice at that time.

The union set up a cooperative factory for the victims of the cigar makers' strike to give those people work. Harry Eichelsheim, the future president of the Cigar Makers Union, for one, worked there. After the cooperative had been set up, small new factories came into being, including one small Jewish cigar factory, the Leuvenberg factory on Binnenkant, which is where my father ended up working. Leuvenberg's father taught Jewish religion on Rapenburgerstraat, so at his son's factory they worked on Sundays, but not Saturdays.

Later, my father was on the Cigar Makers Union board. At that time, if you were sick, you had to figure out for yourself how to get some kind of income. There were no sickness or disability benefits back then. So, my father set up a health insurance fund. People paid a quarter a week, I think, and if they got sick, they could get maybe three or four guilders a week. At thirty-five, my father went to work one morning, and we never saw him again. He had to go from Utrechtsedwarsstraat to Binnenkant. It was February 22, 1902, and well below freezing. I was thirteen. His heart gave out.

My mother was left with nine children and no income. If a family was left with no income, it was the custom, particularly on the part of the directors of the Cigar Makers Union, to sponsor a benefit of some kind. These benefits would be put on at the d'Geelvinck building on the Singel canal, where Amsterdam City Savings is now. At that time, it was a building for common workers and their families. That's where the various union directors deposited the dues. A drawing or something would be tied in with it. That's how they could raise a modest sum. Remember, a hundred guilders was a fortune back then, enough to live on for a couple of months. Anyway, that's what they did for us, too.

◆ GERRIT BRUGMANS

In those days, people still worked at night. People who went around during the day with a pushcart of fruit would be at the bakery at night, earning four fifty a week plus forty cents' worth of bread every night.

So, I ended up on Lepelstraat, at Koppens's, a Jewish bakery. That was around 1903. I was at Koppens's when the big strike, the general railroad strike, happened in 1903. It was a strike across the board and resulted in a lot of misery for those people. All those railroad officials fired. Still, it provided the first push, because after 1903, at least people's awareness was starting to grow. I really witnessed the rise of socialism.

I used to be a member of the bakers' union. Still am by the way. I always said that I'd be a member till the day I died. In those days, we went on a number of strikes, and I was always involved. I was also locked out a few times. I was working at Snapper's on Jodenbreestraat. I used to work at Snattager's, the big pastry bakery next to Joachimsthal. There was a strike there, and I was involved in it. But after that, there weren't any bosses left who wanted to have me work for them. That's sixty-six years ago now. Blacklisted me. So, I worked in Germany for a time, as a mine worker, too. A friend of mine, Japie Grishaver, worked in the mines. We called him Japie Bokkie because his mother, who went around with the chevra book collecting contributions, married a second time to a man by the name of Van der Bokke.

◆ BERNARD VAN TIJN

Weesperstraat was the Red street. If I'm not mistaken, Troelstra was elected in 1913 at the first election. They always said, "In District 3," meaning the Weesperstraat neighborhood, "you could run a red street lamp, and it would probably get elected!" After things went wrong for Oudegeest, there was a cartoon in the *Telegraaf*. There sits Oudegeest—his name, of course, means "old spirit" or "old ghost"—leaning against a street lamp, and the caption below the cartoon read: "If only I'd been a street lamp and given up the ghost." I can still see that drawing in front of me.[3]

◆ JO JUDA
My father wanted to be a musician, but his parents didn't know how to go about it. And besides, they didn't have the money. He had to learn a trade, and the quicker the better. He learned lots of trades, as it turned out, but nothing appealed to him—until he finally ended up at the diamond polishing plant.

He was a socialist, because socialism had a big hold on Jewish workers. My father told me that when he was about sixteen, he went into the factory at six in the morning and came out again at six at night. Thanks to the ANDB, the diamond workers union, this changed in 1911 when the eight-hour workday was instituted. That was a huge improvement.

◆ SALOMON DIAMANT
The ANDB was strongly antisyndicalist and against the NAS (National Workers Secretariat): those were the anarchists, the syndicalists. They didn't set up strike funds, for instance, like the ANDB did. There was even a ditty about that in those days:

> *Henri Polak, yes, he's my cousin,*
> *We'd have no money in the strike fund if he wasn't.*

This was directed at the anarchists. The anarchists depended on the solidarity of other fellow workers to rescue them financially if they went on strike or were locked out. The anarchist movement was important for a long time, until about 1908. Then it died down a little because the SDAP gained the upper hand, and its standpoint was the "parliamentary approach," that is, you had to use the parliament as a forum for the interests of the working class, not revolution.

◆ ARON DE PAAUW
It was a whole world in itself. People didn't say, "I'm at a diamond polishing plant." No, they said, "I'm in the trade." And they'd say, "I'm a member of the

---

[3]Jan Oudegeest was, after Henri Polak, the most important socialist union leader in the Netherlands. He was also an SDAP parliamentary representative in the Lower House several times.

Pieter Jelles Troelstra (1860–1930), originally from the northern city of Leeuwarden, was a lawyer and a Friesian poet. In 1894, he was one of the founders of the SDAP, and for over thirty years he was the leader of the SDAP. His popularity, his immense eloquence, his chairmanship of the SDAP in the House of Representatives, and his position as editor of the party paper *Het Volk* (The People) gave him an almost unassailable position.

Union," instead of "I'm a member of the ANDB." There was a *trade* and there was a *union*.

You couldn't work at a factory without being a member of the ANDB because no diamond worker would want to work with you. People were very orthodoxly socialist about that. You didn't do anything behind the organization's back. Say an important stone, a diamond, was being worked. If it happened to be break time, the stone had to be finished, first. If that was going to take up fifteen minutes of break, they'd call the Union to make sure it was OK.

◆ KAREL POLAK

You had to take an exam to become a member of the ANDB. Besides the ANDB, you also had a Jewish diamond workers union, and it was called Betsalel, I think. I wasn't a member of it, though. My future father-in-law had a lot of faith in the SDAP. He was consciously Jewish, but not religious. They used to talk a lot at my in-laws about the rise of the SDAP, and they were very active in that movement.

◆ SALOMON DIAMANT

When I was something like fourteen years old, I became a member of the ANDB because I'd become a diamond worker. They made sure that the youngsters who hadn't had any middle school or high school education were still able to learn something.

In 1917, the October Revolution took place in Russia. This was a major turning point not only in the Dutch workers' movement, but also internationally. There was a wave of enthusiasm. I was a member of the SDAP at the time. At that moment, people realized that socialism was being instituted in a country for the first time in the history of the world.

When the First World War broke out, I was twenty-three. I recall the solidarity between Jews and non-Jews, thanks to the modern workers' movement and the aspirations of the SDAP. Its platform stated that it was a party whose standpoint was the class struggle. This couldn't be said of the other movements, which accepted the status quo as "God-given."

I was around when the ANDB was still on Binnen-Amstel as well as when the building on Franschelaan was opened. There are tiles there with an appeal written on them: "Workers of the world, unite!" This slogan was the basis of the modern socialist movement. It brought with it the reasoning, "There are no Jews or Christians, there are only the exploiters and the exploited."

◆ LEEN RIMINI

If somebody asked for a glass of water in the Jewish Quarter, they called him a "Little David Wijnkoop." I heard that from an old cigar maker who was talking about November 1918, when the Dutch communists, led by Henriette Roland

Holst and David Wijnkoop, marched to the Alexander Garrison to free some of their comrades. The demonstrators were shot at, and David Wijnkoop got so nervous that the first thing he said when he got there was, "Could I trouble you for a glass of water?"[4]

◆ JAN DE RONDE

I lived in the Kinkerstraat neighborhood. I went into the service in 1918. In the middle of October, Secretary Ruys De Beerenbrouck cancelled all leaves due to the danger of foreign troops crossing the border when the western front collapsed. The military men who were not allowed leave were extremely disappointed.

At that time, I was friends with a young army doctor who also hated the military. He asked me if I could bring his laundry to his wife on Willemsparkweg in Amsterdam. He gave me a guilder. That was almost as much as my pay was!

I started walking from the Central Station toward the Kinkerstraat neighborhood: Kalverstraat, Elandsgracht . . . but when I got to Elandsgracht there was a huge revolutionary action committee demonstration going on. Wijnkoop, Mrs. Van den Berg-Van Zelle, and Kitsz from the NAS were there. The three of them had decided to continue the revolutionary fight in Amsterdam and to organize a demonstration.[5]

I thought, "Hey, I should join them!"

Then Wijnkoop started talking, "Comrades! We demand that military supplies be divided among the suffering population! The revolution has already started in Russia, but your enemy is here at home!"

That made a deep impression on me. I was standing there in my uniform and suddenly a policeman with a helmet and all those copper buttons grabs me by the collar and says, "You! Keep on walking!"

I say, "Did we go to school together or something?"
He says, "No military personnel are permitted at demonstrations!"

---

[4]In 1909, a number of intellectual revolutionary socialist members split from the SDAP and founded the SDP (Social Democratic Party) whose name changed to Communist Party of Holland (CPH) in November 1918. The most important SDP leaders were initially David Wijnkoop, son of a well-known Amsterdam rabbi, and Herman Gorter, one of the Netherlands most important poets, later joined by the poet Henriette Roland Holst.

[5]Immediately after the armistice in November 1918, Troelstra announced in the House of Representatives that the Dutch proletariat was going to take over and overthrow the bourgeoisie. Other SDAP leaders, however, disclaimed this, judging the move undemocratic. The rather small SDP nevertheless tried to convince soldiers garrisoned on Sarphatistraat to join the revolutionary action committee demonstration, which ended in a tragic bloodbath initiated by the military.

I say, "Well, you're wrong, pal, because I have to know what I'm supposed to defend!"

But Wijnkoop, too, told me, "Just keep walking. They're looking for a reason to beat our brains in." So, I went home. They shot at those demonstrators, and that night I went to my first Communist Party meeting. It was at Waterlooplein. Seegers and Henriette Roland Holst spoke there, and I signed up as a member. That was on November 7, 1918. I'm one of the oldest party members!

Starting early in the century, Wijnkoop consistently defended Marxism against the Revisionist trend, from within the SDAP.[6] Then, in 1909, at the Deventer Convention, the split became a fact. They published a pamphlet called *Eruit!* (Get Out!), by which they meant that the Marxists were being thrown out of the SDAP. That convention was very important and people like Wijnkoop, Van Ravesteijn, Gorter, and Henriette Roland Holst played major roles in it. So the orthodox Marxist SDP was set up after that convention in 1909, although there had already been a leftward trend starting in 1905.

When the Great War of 1914 threatened, there were socialists who kept their mouths shut because they wanted to maintain what they called "God's peace" at home. But others, like Jean Jaurès, Karl Liebknecht, and Rosa Luxemburg, said, "If war breaks out, workers will have to announce a general strike!" Jaurès was shot dead a few days before the war broke out.

It did come to war. My father was disillusioned. He said, "The socialists are so strong in Germany, in France; we have so much power in the Netherlands with the labor organizations! And now we're all running over to the bourgeois side, and it's going to be mass slaughter!" But when the Revolution of 1917 broke out in Russia, he was ecstatic and shouted, "That's the beginning of the end of capitalism!"

I was eighteen and a member of the youth alliance "De Zaaier." Wijnkoop's son was a member too. A number of communists came from the diamond workers union, but most Jewish communists could be found among tailors. I was a tailor, and I know that there were lots of Jewish tailors, particularly those working at home, who thought along communist lines or, in any event, were on the left. They didn't make it through the War. They were killed by the Germans during the February Strike of 1941.[7] Seven or eight Jewish tailors had distrib-

---

[6]The Revisionists were followers of German socialist Eduard Bernstein, who believed that society could change by evolutionary (not revolutionary) means.

[7]In February 1941, Amsterdam communists staged a general strike protesting the German raid in the Old Jewish Quarter. Five hundred Jewish men were arrested during the raid and taken to the Mauthausen concentration camp in Germany where within six months they had all been killed.

uted manifestos. They were proletarian and had experienced what capitalism meant first-hand.

The majority of the Jews, being diamond workers, came under the influence of the SDAP. Tailors worked at home by themselves, though, and that situation produced lots of people who were progressive and active. I think it's because they had the opportunity to think about things quietly while they worked, not hearing any machines or anything. That's probably one of the reasons you can find first-rate amateur philosophers among tailors! Old Gerhard, the first socialist in the Netherlands, he was a tailor. I knew a couple of tailors here who could give wonderful talks on the philosophy of Spinoza! Plain, ordinary tailors, who sat at the sewing table all day and had no contact with anybody, could talk beautifully!

There were so many Jewish tailors because it was a free trade you could do at home. Certain factories didn't want any Jews, but in the clothing industry, tailors could work at home.

Culture and Upbringing

◆ BERTHA BARNSTEIN-KOSTER

Heiman Barnstein, my uncle, was born in Hoorn on the northern coast. He originally went to Amsterdam to become a rabbi by going to seminary, just like his grandfather, who performed the office of *rebbe* in Hoorn for many years. My uncle went to seminary for a year, but the education conflicted with both his political as well as his religious sentiments.

The diamond industry in those days was known to be an especially favorable trade for Jewish employees—it was shortly after the Cape times[8]—and he applied as an apprentice. When he mentioned it at home, the news didn't get a very friendly reception, because his father wanted him to become a rabbi. But, he received training and then practiced the trade, too. Early on, he proved to be a real organization man, and as such he also came into contact with Handwerkers Vriendenkring (Craftsmen's Fellowship). It wasn't long before he was president of the organization. Handwerkers Vriendenkring was intended to increase the intellectual development of workers and to raise their cultural awareness. The organization's building was on Nieuwe Achtergracht in the Jewish Quarter. It had a lot of Jewish members, mostly diamond workers.

My uncle also made sure there were a couple of musical or theatrical performances every year in order to offer the women some entertainment as well, which they particularly appreciated. There was also a monthly magazine, *De Handwerksman* (The Craftsman), that always carried a pretty good story. My father often translated stories. Handwerkers Vriendenkring, by the way, had a very good library from which members could borrow books every week for a small fee. The leaders took turns lending out those books and receiving returned books. At the organization's headquarters on Nieuwe Achtergracht, you could also spend an afternoon playing games.

The building was enlarged when a couple of houses became vacant on Roetersstraat. As you can tell from the auditorium of what is Kriterion now—

---

[8]Following the discovery in South Africa in 1869 of unheard of quantities of rough diamonds, the diamond industry in Amsterdam flourished for a number of years. Wages were high because there were not enough workers to handle the demand for cut diamonds after the American Civil War. This period of prosperity is referred to as the Cape times.

that movie house that's run by students—it's clear the entrance must have been somewhere else.

Handwerkers Vriendenkring was active in various areas the government takes care of nowadays, like the bathhouse on Jonas Daniël Meijerplein, which met a great need because there wasn't a single bathhouse in the entire neighborhood! That kind of thing didn't exist at all yet in the Jewish Quarter.

One of the most important things that Handwerkers Vriendenkring brought about is the founding of the Ziekenzorg (Health Care) health insurance fund. As it happens, my uncle was annoyed that the doctors played such a heavy-handed role in the AZA (General Health Insurance Fund of Amsterdam).[9] He thought that the clients, the people who used this fund, had the right to have an equal say. So, that's when Ziekenzorg (ZZ) was founded. He was president until he died. He had very bright board members, like De Casseres who was secretary, and Mr. Kanes, a real SDAP man who made sure that Ziekenzorg was run in a very democratic way.

The Ziekenzorg office was at 719 Keizersgracht , and my uncle lived on the first floor. That certainly shows how closely involved with the organization he was!

Handwerkers Vriendenkring functioned very well at a time when the efforts of the City of Amsterdam were still a dismal failure where the disadvantaged were concerned.

◆ Aron De Paauw

The ANDB was not just a union that worked to improve wages and working conditions. It also worked to raise the level of cultural awareness of its members. That's why the ANDB had a really big library. The library was extremely important not just to me, but to hundreds of other young men and older people as well. That library was run by people who sacrificed an entire evening to help others, doing it all for free. They were diamond workers themselves! The library was actually considered to be a kind of temple, like a temple of knowledge, as much of an overstatement as that may sound.

The great driving force behind the ANDB was Henri Polak, though. The diamond workers got an issue of the union's *Weekblad* (Weekly) at home every week, and every week Henri Polak wrote a feature article in it. He would write in such simple terms that everybody understood them. The directors were very capable on the whole, but they were mostly busy with wage issues and secondary working conditions, so the spirit of the organization bore primarily Henri Polak's stamp.

---

[9]Health insurance funds, and others like them, still exist today in the Netherlands, although they are state subsidized now. They were initially set up to provide money for health care to those who could not afford it.

A monthly paper for young people, *Het Jonge Leven* (Young Life), came out later and it had articles on sports, culture, chess, music, you name it. I read a lot, and that weekly and those articles by Henri Polak motivated me even then to get involved in politics.

Polak always said, "All of you need more education and better education." When I was apprenticing with Stokvis, one of Stokvis's sons was already studying to be a psychiatrist and the other was going to law school to be a lawyer. And that's what they became later. Their father was a very good diamond worker at Asscher's.

Andries Rodenburg, who was a diamond polisher, had his son studying violin with Oskar Back, and the boy was already appearing as a soloist at the Concertgebouw. After a while, though, he decided to study medicine because he wanted to go to Detroit in the U.S. He married one of Professor Snapper's daughters there, and it turned out Professor Snapper's father had also been a diamond worker at Asscher's.

A friend of mine on Lepelstraat, he lived across from me and I played with him every day, was Professor Groen, the psychosomatics specialist. His father also used to be a diamond worker.

Dr. De Vries, the well-known eye doctor, his father was a diamond cutter. Dr. Luza on Apollolaan, his father was a diamond polisher, and the list goes on and on.

◆ MAX EMMERIK
Down there at the union building was old Duinkerk, the librarian, and he'd lay books aside for me that he knew I'd be interested in. I went to the ANDB every Tuesday night. That's when you could look for books. When I was thirty-five, Duinkerk was already in his seventies. He did it all for free. I never had to pay a penny.

Oh, that library! There'd be lines and lines of people waiting to get a book or to reserve one. If you asked Duinkerk to put a book on hold, he'd say, "I'll see if I can get it," and in less than an hour he'd have it in hand. There were thousands of books there in every field.

◆ HARTOG GOUBITZ
I generally read history, and I read a lot on socialism; and good novels, too. Jewish writers like Herman Heijermans, Israël Querido, and M. H. Van Campen were writing at that time. Querido wrote a book specifically about diamond workers called *Levensgang* (The Course of Life). He was a diamond worker himself. One of the first works by Herman Heijermans was *Diamantstad* (Diamond Town). Back then, I got a lot out of them, but now those books seem outdated. A niece of mine was recently able to buy that book, *Diamantstad,* for next to nothing at that store that sells remainder books, De Slegte. So, I read it again, but

it didn't mean anything to me anymore. Back then, though, those books were unnusually realistic because they described the way things were in that part of town.

◆ Leen Rimini

Did you know there's a Jewish symphony? It's Beethoven's Fifth. They called it "The Jewish Symphony." On Thursday nights, Jewish people would go to the so-called public concerts, the less expensive concerts that were open to the general public. At first, it was the diamond polishers that went, although later on they dragged all the other workers along too because Henri Polak wanted all the workers, not just the diamond polishers, to be culturally enriched. And he succeeded. Then there was also the Instituut voor Arbeidersontwikkeling (Institute for the Education of Workers), which did a lot to boost the level of cultural awareness that workers had. That was a success too.

◆ Joop Voet

My father always told me that when he left elementary school and went to the factory, he didn't think that was any way to live. There was a hole in his life. He didn't read, he didn't do any writing—until he got wind of the union, the ANDB. Pretty soon he was elected to be second secretary of some committee or other. He had to take the minutes and had to write. That's when he noticed he almost couldn't write anymore. So, he threw himself into it, and he got to be a very good journalist and stylist. Later on, he became secretary of the ANDB, which he'd joined as a boy of seventeen or eighteen, and which is where, in fact—and this may sound a little odd—he really learned to write.

The ANDB managed to convince people to educate themselves. For example, my mother told me that when she got married, there were two things she didn't know how to do: she didn't know how to mend clothes, which you had to do as a housewife, and she didn't know how to write anymore, she hadn't done any since elementary school. So, she took a course in mending, and she also took writing lessons again, as an adult. The ANDB gave people a very strong incentive to do this kind of thing.

Berlage's Union Building—it was something very special to have a building like that designed for a relatively small union by Berlage, who was *the* leading architect of the day. In the end, it was only half completed.

The diamond workers had their own print shop. They printed their weekly paper themselves. They printed everything themselves. Later, it merged with the Cooperative and became the "Dico," the Diamond Workers and Cooperative Printers. They had a huge lending library. They had many cultural institutions of their own, which no longer exist because nowadays they can be found anywhere.

The fact that it was their own library, though, located in their own Union

Building, induced people to borrow books much more readily. We'd go borrow books every week. They had books for boys, and I'd get books for my mother. It was an abundantly stocked library. The library's acquisitions consultant and cataloguer was the later well-known writer and critic, Michel H. Van Campen, initially a diamond worker as well.

ANDB dues were very high for that time, so they were able do a lot more than other unions.

◆ JOANNES JUDA GROEN

The fact that our fathers were diamond workers means a lot more than that they simply had the same occupation. It meant a certain cultural setting, the more so because they were Jewish. In those days, at the end of the nineteenth and beginning of the twentieth century, workers had the opportunity to emancipate themselves, to have access to the cultural world around them, and the diamond workers were the first ones to take advantage of it.

As a worker, my father earned little for many, many years, but in spite of this he had books. One of the books he placed in my hands, perhaps a little too soon, was Multatuli's *Max Havelaar,* because I was still too young to understand it all.[10]

But I saw all those books in his bookcase: on the history of the workers' movement, a good number of brochures by Troelstra, and particularly the diamond workers union's *Weekly.* The ANDB published a cultural supplement in their paper once a month, which was always written by Henri Polak or his colleagues. It had articles about social development, but also about flowers and plants. Van Laren, one of Henri Polak's friends, was "hortulanus" or botanical supervisor of Hortus Botanicus, the botanical gardens, right near the ANDB building. He also wrote for the paper. I read articles about art history in there too.

This paper here, *Het Jonge Leven* (Young Life), was distributed to all the homes of all the diamond workers, and it was read not just by the workers but by their families as well. I'd go so far as to say that I learned to read *before* I went to elementary school, because I learned how to spell: *Het Volk, Dagblad voor de Arbeiderspartij* (The People: Labor Party Daily). That was the newspaper my parents read.

I recall coming home one day all excited and talking about history class and Jan Pieterszoon Coen and all his victorious voyages in the East Indies. The next Saturday afternoon, my father took me to the Rijksmuseum and took me to the

---

[10]*Max Havelaar* is a critical novel about Dutch rule in the East Indies (Indonesia). Roy Edwards' translation of Multatuli's 1859 classic satire is available as *Max Havelaar or the Coffee Auctions of the Dutch Trading Company* (1995 Penguin Classic reprint). Written under a pseudonym by a former government clerk in Java, this powerful story about corruption was instrumental in effecting change in the region.

place where treasures from Bali and Lombok were displayed. And while I was looking at it all in amazement, he said, "All stolen! None of that belongs to us. Now, I want you to think about this: The Dutch fought for their independence from the Spanish, but they shouldn't have used that freedom right away to do the same thing in the East Indies that the Spanish did in the Netherlands."

I sensed that this wasn't particularly the kind of thing I should tell my teacher at school, but it made a deep impression on me.

My father had educated himself. When he was older, he first taught himself how to play the trombone, then the clarinet, and then he was playing in the Dutch Diamond Workers Union Orchestra. The Union had an excellent brass and woodwind orchestra conducted by a certain Mr. Heijmans, who played in the Concertgebouw Orchestra.

They performed at the Paleis Van Volksvlijt during the summer, out in the garden, and for the rest, of course, they marched along in the May Day demonstrations. That went without saying. And I was very proud, of course, when my father marched along playing.

When I was about thirteen or fourteen, my mother said to my father, "Take that boy to the Public Concerts." So, the first time I went to a public concert was with my father. But once I knew that something like that existed, I went and stood in line myself, because it was hard to get tickets.

Very early on, the ANDB set up an impressive lending library. When I was young, there were small libraries around the city, privately owned by book dealers, where you could borrow books for a fee. The book dealers would select the books, which were usually cheap novels or minimally uplifting literature. Henri Polak, once again, set up a lending library very early on where the diamond workers could borrow books for free. The library committee and Polak would make sure that it had books of a high cultural level. So, it had all the great classic novelists and lots of books about the workers' movement, of course, but also books about flowers, plants, and animals.

That library wasn't just a success with the workers, but with their families as well. It's an absolute fact that Polak was always more concerned about progress for the urban working class here and now than about any beautiful ideals and revolutions to come at some uncertain future time. He distinguished himself from many other socialist leaders by having a great deal of common sense and practical judgment and also remarkably few hateful feelings toward the propertied class. He could be totally uncompromising when he organized strikes, but it was remarkable to see how little enmity the man expressed. This was also typical of his parliamentary activity as a whole. Within a short time after he got a seat in the House, and also when he was on the city council, he enjoyed respect from almost everyone, even his opponents. But then, he did make extensive use of this talent by talking with them personally about his ideas. That same kind of common sense was also shown by the fact that he was never hostile toward the Royal House. At a very early age, he understood that he would merely lose people's sympathy that way, and that it really meant very little to workers.

He was also always ready if you needed his personal help, by going to a government department and talking to people, say, in order to do something for a worker's son. You could always talk to Henri. Any diamond worker could go talk to him. You went to Henri for everything. Henri was the father figure over at the diamond workers' building there on Franschelaan.

I went up those impressive stairs over there, the ones up to Berlage's building, where you could see the Richard Roland Holst murals. Even there, you were already swept up into that spiritual realm of a better humanity, of that nonviolent kind of better humanity where everybody would understand everybody else and where a better world would come into being through discussion and love for one's neighbor. The socialism of those days was still somewhat influenced by a background of religious love for one's neighbor, whether that was Jewish or Christian.

I know for certain that Henri Polak considered it his duty as the representative of labor in parliament to embrace and fight for the interests of workers in every way. And to a certain extent, he also regarded that second generation, to which I belonged, as the people he was proud of, because they were growing up at this particular time and able to get involved in culture. He also had tremendously varied interests, something that was pretty unusual for a labor movement leader. He took private instruction from that same Van Laren fellow at Hortus so he could learn about flowers and plants.

As a child and also often in Israel, I saw Jews who came from the ghettos of Poland start a whole new life the first time they had their own garden.

I was born on a third floor, and those little back courtyards, of course, were nothing. Those workers' apartments hardly had yards to speak of. So, I didn't know what flowers were, or birds. It was the same with Henri, and he was able to make up for that at a later age. That's also why he went to live in Laren, in The Gooi.[11] I heard my father and his brother-in-law talking about it at home, "Henri went to live in Laren. Why? He has to go back and forth by train every day. Why's he doing that?" But later they understood, when my father and my uncle started taking bicycle trips. *The* bicycle trip, of course, was going to The Gooi. Another world opened up for them there.

I also remember what a huge event it was for us the first time my father had a

---

[11]The Gooi is a scenic area of heath and pine forests just southeast of Amsterdam.

week's vacation! That was back in 1913, if I'm not mistaken.[12] My parents rented a cottage, and we all went to stay there.

In that respect, very early on Polak already had the vision to see that the purely Marxist economic road of socialism was too limited. I heard my father and his friends discuss this a lot, and Henri would be referred to as a "right-winger." It was a common fact that from the time the ANDB was founded, Polak saw it not only as an organization to improve working conditions, one that was able to stage a serious strike if necessary, but he also saw human welfare, mental and emotional well-being, as the ideal *alongside* that of material prosperity.

◆ RUBEN GROEN

I remember Henri Polak started up an art grant that a number of diamond workers took advantage of. It applied to both music as well as painting. I remember a friend of mine, Simon Furth, when we were students of the diamond business together. We both played violin, and he was taking lessons from Ferdinand Helman. His father, a cigar maker, was self-employed, an "independent operator." The boy later studied music through funding from the Henri Polak Foundation. Ferdinand Helman was one of the Concertgebouw Orchestra's concertmasters, along with Zimmerman, so Simon Furth was able to find his niche in the orchestra as a violinist. The painter Sal Meyer also studied through funding from the Henri Polak Foundation.

◆ JO JUDA

The ANDB also had an ethical background. It wasn't just that people wanted to be better off materially. No, we were headed toward a better world! All that culture, always available to only a select few—that's how people looked at it— would now be available to everybody. To my feeling, there was a kind of religious ecstasy in this notion, as well as in the ethics it expressed, that in the future, everybody would lead a decent life worth the living.

Take that paper for young workers that they published. I still remember it; very nice paper, that smooth, shiny kind of paper. They must have done that in the spirit of Henri Polak, always getting the best there was for *their* workers.

In my father's bookcase, I still remember books by Karl Kautsky, some by Marx too, but not many, and also by the Dutch socialists, including Vliegen, I believe, *De dageraad der volksbevrijding* (The Dawn of the Liberation of the People). I can still see it on the shelf right there in front of me. Otherwise, my father liked travel accounts. Realist novels, too, like those by Zola, in Dutch

---

[12]Groen is mistaken on this point, since an obligatory week's vacation was instituted in the Amsterdam diamond trade as early as 1910.

translation. Then there was also a book by Bernard Canter entitled *Kalverstraat*. I read all of them, starting from the moment I was able to read.

My father took me to the Concertgebouw. He took me to museums, and he'd try to explain things to me *his* way.

It was a fact, though, that diamond workers' children were largely people who achieved something later in life. In my day, three people were accepted into the Muzieklyceum, the music academy in Amsterdam. All three of them were diamond workers' children: Louis Metz, Alex Baune, and me.

The first time I saw and heard a violin was on one of the Sunday afternoon walks I had to take with my family. It started to thunder and lightning, and we ran out of the downpour into a cafe on Amstelstraat. An orchestra was playing there. Somebody with really long hair was up in front of it. That was Long Freddy, a very famous cafe fiddler. So, I asked my parents if they'd let me learn how to play the violin. Right away they said, sure, we'll try to find a music teacher. That teacher turned out to be a second violinist in the orchestra that played at the Flora Theater. He sat way in the back with the second violins. During the day he was a diamond polisher, like my father, and at night he played at the Flora.

At first I didn't have my own violin. But after about seven or eight lessons, there was a little violin lying on my teacher's table. It was to be my violin.

When my parents came to pick me up from my lesson, my father asked my teacher, "How much is it?"

They talked very quietly, but I could hear what they were saying. "Seven fifty," said my teacher. "For the violin, plus the case and the bow."

And my father pulled out his wallet in that typical way of his and paid the money. I felt sorry for my father because he had to spend so much money on that violin. I couldn't get over it.

My mother said, "Well, as long as you really study, because it cost a lot of money."

No kidding. That's what I was thinking too, and I took a sacred oath to study hard and well, because of course, a violin like that had to pay for itself somehow. That's the feeling I had at the time.

◆ **ARON PEEREBOOM**

In the newspaper, I read that VARA, the Workers' Association of Radio Amateurs, was being founded. Being pretty socialist, I went to a meeting at the Amicitia building on Waterlooplein.[13] There was somebody I knew at the meet-

---

[13]The Amicitia building was used for meetings and festivities. Until 1675, it was home to the Portuguese congregation, Talmud Tora. It was from here that Spinoza was excommunicated from the Jewish Portuguese congregation in 1656.

ing, and he nominated me to be on the board, so I became secretary-treasurer of two really big divisions. I did that for about eight years. Later, that slowed down a little, though, but at the time it was out-and-out idealism because these positions were all unpaid.

And when there was that competition going on between AVRO, which was ideologically neutral, and VARA, there'd be twenty, twenty-five workers at my place. Tuesday nights they always went to the Carré Theatre when AVRO broadcast its "Mixed Bag Night" show from there, and they'd stir things up a bit. I didn't go in for that. I always said, "Guys, just try not to fight. They're going to win anyway." But when they were at my place, we'd go door-to-door to talk with people and recruit members and membership contributions, that kind of thing, and we had lots of success doing that.

I was the only Jew on the VARA board, but I always worked well with everybody.

◆ LEEN RIMINI

I was in the diamond trade for two years to start with. After two and a half years, you went to the vocational school on Albert Cuypstraat and received your diploma there. But then, during the First World War the crisis started.

So, I ended up at De Dageraad (The Dawning of a New Day), a workers' cooperative. That must be some sixty years ago now, 1914 or something. That's right, I started there in 1916, as store help on Jodenbreestraat. That's where I came into contact with the ANDB administrators, since those people got their groceries through the Cooperative. So, when I was a teenager, I had to take those orders and deliver them.

One time I was at Mr. Polak's. I was earning well at De Dageraad, because I got seven guilders a week, and at private stores I could only get two fifty. But I said to Mr. Polak, "What do you think, should I quit this job and become a diamond polisher, or not?"

And he said, "If I might give you some sensible advice, keep what you've got, because the trade will never be set right again."

Henri Polak was one of the founders of De Dageraad Cooperative. The purpose was to pay the surplus that the cooperative was going to make back to its members. The idea came from England. De Dageraad may have flown the nonsectarian rainbow flag, but we were Reds! The original plan was: one for all, all for one.

I actually stood behind the counter thinking: "This is it!" It was an ideal. Later, I learned about the labor movement by way of De Dageraad and the ANDB.

We were among the first hundred members of VARA, fifty years ago. I was the first one in my neighborhood to get a little crystal "breadboard" set, one of those little radio sets. That antenna was something like thirty meters, some ninety feet, long. And at night you'd hear a violin. *That* was an experience!

When we started VARA, we didn't have the money to pay for eight hours of broadcasting time. We didn't even have a studio. The studio was above the Royal Cinema in Amsterdam. That's where our first program was broadcast from. So, if you actually had a radio—there weren't many people who did—you'd hear a piece of music playing in your room, and off in the background you could hear somebody shouting, "Oranges, real beauts!" because the vendors went around Sunday mornings selling oranges in the alley. So, you'd hear that too.

I still remember very well that the people at De Dageraad were the first ones to get vacation pay, for two days of vacation. So, I brought a two-and-a-half guilder coin to Swertbroek, who was later on the wrong side during the war. I said, "Here's a *rijksdaalder* to cover broadcast time."

◆ JOOP VOET

The ideal that the modern labor movement strove for in those days seemed to be realized in the second generation. Besides this, practically immediately after the First World War, the youth movement, the AJC or Workers Youth Federation (Arbeiders Jeugd Centrale), started becoming an important element, at least for me personally. I spent a lot of time on it. My mother always referred to me as, "Joop, my boarder." I went to school, but all my free time went into the AJC after I'd rushed through my homework as fast as I could.[14]

The fun of it was the camaraderie, the idealistic striving, and maybe also being able to play a role in the organization since I already had a certain amount of practical knowledge and education. So I was able to be treasurer and district head and was allowed to collect dues. I did this in the Transvaal neighborhood and was very diligent, at that. I guess I was pretty well known there as a dues collector, because whenever my finger pushed on a doorbell, they'd shout down, "Who's there?" And I'd say, "A. . . ," and they'd automatically finish my sentence, "JC."

Only much later did it become clear to me that the Jewish influence certainly was an important cultural aspect of the Amsterdam AJC. There were, of course, a large number of Jewish AJC members in Amsterdam.

The AJC was divided into groups that corresponded to districts. In the beginning, they were called group one, group two, and so on, but later they used the names of the neighborhoods: Apollo neighborhood, Oosterpark neighborhood, Transvaal neighborhood. As a result, there were largely Jewish AJC members in the districts where lots of Jews lived. Within the framework of the labor movement's strong tendency toward assimilation, this wasn't anything unusual. People

---

[14]The AJC, an organization that positioned itself against modern big-city culture, emphasized a new socialist community. AJC members set themselves apart by wearing wide-wale corduroy trousers or flower-print dresses and sandals.

associated with each other on a completely equal footing and in a comradely way, and so lots of mixed marriages followed too.

Jewish AJC members had a major share in cultural life, especially in music, on the stage, in public speaking, and in literature, areas in which the youth movement did a lot. The people who gave speeches at the Pentecost celebrations included a very high percentage of Jews. The AJC was evidently not aware of this, just as little as people in the Dutch entertainment world in those days were aware that a lot of popular singers were Jews—much, much higher than the percentage of Jews in the population.

But this gave the Amsterdam AJC something of that Jewish liveliness, that Jewish atmosphere, the need to live in a more extravert way.

◈ Simon Gosselaar

I'd say that I received my education in the AJC. I was a member of the AJC from when I was fourteen until I was twenty-one. After that, I wasn't interested in the AJC as much.

In the Transvaal neighborhood, where I lived, there were lots of boys and girls from certain families who were members of the AJC. We didn't have an underlying socialist principle. It was fun, a youth movement. We took long hikes on Sundays, and they'd sing those young people's songs.[15] Once a month all the groups in Amsterdam would get together in a meeting hall, where the Kriterion is now, on Roetersstraat. It belonged to Handwerkers Vriendenkring then. They did that in the winter, and every group, for instance the Transvaal group I was a member of, would take a turn hosting an afternoon. That was really fun.

---

[15]There was an abundance of such songs promoted through the AJC that included camp songs, marching songs, songs of struggle, labor songs, as well as songs of joy, love, and spring.

Socialism and Religion

◆ JOANNES JUDA GROEN
My father was born in 1875, so he was nineteen in 1894 when the SDAP and the ANDB were founded. Not long before that, he had become aware of the tremendous deprivation among workers, and it made him incredibly bitter that the Jewish rabbis did absolutely nothing to convince Jewish employers to have a little more sympathy for their Jewish workers.

There was an extremely patronizing kind of philanthropy at that time. The little pan of soup that protagonist Kniertje gets from the ship owner in the play *Op hoop van zegen* (*The Good Hope*), that's what they got, the workers that is, from the rich Jews.[16] It was not something that would make you feel solidarity with them. My father used to say, "It's written in the Old Testament that you may not leave a worker's wage overnight." That means that you have to pay out a day laborer's wages at the end of the day because he's so poor he can't wait until the next day. He has to bring that pay back to feed his wife and children.

Even my father went through that as a young man when he had to bang his fist on his employer's desk on Friday afternoon to get his pay.

When he was about eighteen, he consciously broke away from the synagogue. After that, he literally never set foot in there again. He learned to read Hebrew very well there, still knew exactly how the prayers went. But since he broke with the synagogue, he ridiculed all faiths, and Multatuli's work only reinforced that. He didn't care for Jewish holidays and customs and so on anymore. On the contrary, he took a very dim view of all that.

My mother came from a middle-class family. Her father was not a diamond worker (like my father's father was), but had a store, a grocery store. Not only that, my mother came from a very good, conventional, and loving family. So, for her the Jewish faith and customs were closely connected with hospitality, extended family ties, and patriarchal concern, a father who was interested in his children. When my father and my mother married, there was an immediate conflict in that respect between them. My mother more or less resigned herself to the fact that my father was not going to go to the synagogue on Saturday and that the synagogue was going to be talked about with disrespect and so forth. She

---

[16]*Op hoop van zegen (The Good Hope)* was Herman Heijermans' most popular play.

never had trouble supporting him when he went on strike or whatever, and never had trouble with his always going to meetings or with whatever they involved. Still, on Friday evenings, we would eat something special. She made sure there was chicken if at all possible. Our family was poor, so we often didn't eat meat during the week. We'd have that on Friday night, or we'd have something else that was out of the ordinary, like apricot compote. Very simple things, but they were always served and eaten with a certain joy, and my father wasn't unappreciative of that. It really was a peculiar situation. On the one hand, my father would get together with his friends or brothers-in-law, who were also in the diamond trade, and they would carry on deep, insightful discussions about the content of *Het Volk* (The People), which was the labor party's paper, or about what Henri Polak had written in the diamond workers' *Het Weekblad*. On the other hand, though, at home with their families, they lived like Jews, due to their strong family ties, even if they'd broken away from the synagogue.

In 1890 and 1900, when the material circumstances were really awful for the working class, the infant mortality rate in the back streets of the Jewish Quarter was just as low as in the best neighborhoods of Amsterdam. That was because of the wonderful care these Jews took of their children, that strong family tie.

◆ Hartog Goubitz

I'm from a socialist family. When my father was forced to start working on *Shabbes,* thereby cutting his ties with his religion, he was known in the neighborhood, which was the Valkenburgerstraat, as "the socialist guy." And when he went to work on *Shabbes* or when he came home, they sometimes threw rocks at him. They'd be waiting for him with rocks. That's how things were.

He had to work on Saturdays. Otherwise he couldn't get any work. There weren't any openings at any of the Jewish factories. That was also the main reason why he left that neighborhood, see. He could do no right there. He'd been a *chazzan* at a little shul on Marken, and he'd been devout from the day he was born. When he was forced to break with religion, he started organizing. He became a member of the Cigar Makers Union. Later, he became a steward so he was part of the leadership.

There weren't many religious Jews among diamond workers either. They discovered through their organization that only by means of union action could you improve your situation. And then, as people moved away from that specifically Jewish part of town around Jodenbreestraat, Uilenburg, Vlooienburg, and Marken, many of them also broke with their religion.

◆ Barend Luza

I was very religious for a year. That was when I was thirteen, fourteen years old—a consequence of the religious education I was getting. My father, who wasn't religious at all and who smoked and read a lot on Saturdays, didn't light up a cigar on Shabbes that year, and the lights weren't turned on until Shabbes was over and he could read again. When I was at the New Shul, I had my seat at the synagogue as a devout Jew. I said my prayers there, too, at least the way a pious Jew is supposed to. I'd fallen under the influence of some of the leading figures at the Jewish school, particularly that of De Hond and also of Van Creveld, the father of the later Professor Van Creveld. My last year there, I also read Rashi, that was a privilege. Rashi used a particular kind of writing, and I was able to read it, too. I can't do that anymore. I can decipher it a little bit, but I don't know anything about it anymore.

One day, though, I went to my father and said, "I've gotten far enough along that I can't go on with it. I don't see religion in the same way anymore."

To which my father said, "Well, my boy, I guess I'll be lighting up a cigar again on *Shabbes.*"

After that, I went to meetings with my father and heard Troelstra and Mendels speak, and I got away from religion altogether. A meeting with Troelstra at the Krasnapolsky Hotel, that was an experience, you know, and on May 1, walking behind the red flag, that was a ritual. I'd become a devout socialist!

◆ ALEXANDER VAN WEEZEL

My father was a member of the Jewish association of diamond workers, Betsalel. Well, it was yet another economic crisis and my father was out of work again. Then, one day he found a job working for a Christian boss, but he'd have to work on Saturdays. So, he was faced with the choice: be out of work and have no food to eat, or "go bad" and work. And that's what he decided. On Saturdays, he simply put on his *Shabbes* suit, but instead of taking his tallith in his tallith bag, he took a worker's frock, supposedly going to shul, although he was secretly going to work because things were just so bad. By doing that, though, everything at home—like being Jewish, orthodoxy—got watered-down.

I still remember where we went to shul. It was on Commelinstraat, near Platanenstraat. The tallith would be brought along, and on Yom Kippur, the Day of Atonement, we had to fast. I was thirteen and I had to fast too. My father and his brother would sit next to each other in front. I can still see it all clear as anything. The tallith would be put in the bag, which would be put in the bench—you could flip up the seats. And then my father and his brother would slip out and go to The Crown on Rembrandtplein and have something to eat. Honest. When we were kids, we caught on to that, so we left too.

At a certain point, it was Yom Kippur again, and we were supposed to fast. My mother was an extremely wise person, and she said, "There isn't a God in the world who said that we still have to do penance for something that happened so many thousands of years ago. We fasted *then,* but as long as there's food now, we're going to eat. It's bad enough when there isn't any food."

So, that's how we abandoned the faith. People were kept quiet through faith, whether they were Jews or Christians, and by gaining awareness, something Henri Polak contributed to the most, people started thinking differently.

My grandfather was also in the diamond trade. It was a "closed shop," which is why my father was able to be in it, I think. I know that my father wasn't allowed to go back to his parents' house because he'd become a Red.

My father was a student at the rabbinical seminary, but after taking just the first class, he said he didn't want to continue. He thought it was out-dated. He'd been moved to other convictions and become a member of the SDAP, which is why he wasn't allowed to go back to his parents' house. Later, my grandparents definitely voted SDAP, too, but back then it was still a terrible thing to do.

◆ Ali Voorzanger-Suurhoff

My father was a diamond worker and as much an atheist as the day is long. He didn't want to hear the word "synagogue" at home. But then, we weren't allowed to say "God" either. That was hurtful to others. I thought at the time, and still do, that this was exceptionally broad-minded on my father's part!

My parents felt that "faith," meaning any faith, produced an element of rigidity. Socialism was their "faith" and ours too, really; our children were also infected by it. My husband was two years older than I, born in 1905. When the diamond workers union celebrated their twenty-fifth anniversary, my father-in-law, who was a painter by trade, took his son along. He felt the boy really had to go see that!

So then the boy asked, "Who is that man they're all cheering for?"

And my father-in-law said, "That's Henri Polak. That man has done absolutely fantastic work!"

My grandparents weren't religious. Well, I guess they did set aside Friday evenings. We'd go over there for dinner then sometimes. My parents were married in a shul, under pressure from the family—especially the family on my father's side—because for their part my parents didn't want to. And my mother did tell me that this had been a real drama, since it took its toll on both of them. But they had the support of all my mother's brothers (she came from a family with ten children). My parents told them, "We're getting married in Zaandam. It's cheap there." What's more, Rabbi De Haan, the rabbi in Zaandam, had a daughter, Carry Van Bruggen, who was a well-known novelist, and she had turned away from the faith.[17] My father sent two of his brothers-in-law to De Haan to tell him that he could marry them as long as he didn't tell them how they had to live their lives as Jews, because he'd walk out of the shul. De Haan accepted this. Those brothers-in-law were evidently convincing enough that he did it.

My parents felt they had made a concession by marrying in a shul, and that was that. They also wrote to remove themselves from the Jewish congregation rolls.

My grandparents lived on Groenburgwal, my parents moved to Van Ostadestraat. They were conscious Jews, but they didn't want to be lumped together with all other Jews. Not that they looked down on being Jewish. It was more that they felt they were "people" who could associate with anyone—what they now call "citizens of the world."

When their first child, my brother, was born, my grandfather came by and asked, "What is the baby's name going to be?"

"With your permission, he will be named after you!" His name was Mozes.

"And is the baby going to be circumcised?"

"No!"

And my grandfather stood on the threshold and said, "No uncircumcised Jew will go through life with the name Mozes Voorzanger! And if I ever have to beg, I'll walk past your house!"

I was born in 1907 and my brother in 1906. Where else did such things happen!? Even in families that weren't orthodox, the boys were circumcised! I'll never forget that story, because my mother told it to us so many times. After that, they didn't see one another for eight years because my parents moved to Antwerp.

When we came back from Belgium in 1914, there was already a lot of unemployment in the Netherlands. So, we had to go to the refugee committee, which housed us in a school. I was seven years old then and my sister three years younger.

My mother thought, "Well, I should just go and see how things are on Groenburgwal!" That was at six o'clock in the morning.

My grandmother said, "I was wondering where all of you were staying."

"Well, in the school."

"What an outrage! Go get them. The soup's already on."

That was their reconciliation. My grandmother must have been very quick, because by the time my mother had picked us up, everything had already been arranged. And there was never any more talk about the uncircumcised boy.

---

[17]Caroline Lea De Haan became known under her married name as the feminist prose writer Carry Van Bruggen (1881–1937). She was the third of sixteen children, and her brother Jacob Israël De Haan, later renowned as a poet, was the fourth. Both suffered severely from depression.

◆ Jacob Soetendorp

Six months after my bar mitzvah—I'd been at the seminary just over a year—my father died. We were faced with utter destitution. I slowly started breaking away from De Hond's influence. You understood that the situation was just too serious to be remedied by predications. I went through a time that we had absolutely nothing to eat, and then, of course, you start wondering: Is that possible? Can something like that be tolerated? That one person has so much and the other so little? That's when you start reading the prophets more and getting more and more outspoken. And I did become outspoken at the seminary, but in the direction of socialism. You did that kind of thing by means of simple demonstrations, like walking around with a broken gun or putting an AJC handout on the teacher's desk, who then suddenly thinks that the revolution's going to break out tomorrow, and there you go![18] That's how you try to bring forward that Judaism does teach something different from what goes on in practice. In your own family, there were boys who were in the AJC, and sometimes you went to meetings. I went to a Pentecost gathering once or twice, and I've marched in one or two May Day parades. That's when you slowly start to see that you can be a devout Jew *and* be part of that, and you see that not everybody who's part of a socialist movement automatically has to be a freethinker.

Those people said, "Everything we learned about Judaism was only to keep us quiet, and in socialism you see the manifestation of what Judaism once was." So, it wasn't necessary to be part of it anymore, which is not to say that they were ready to step out of the Jewish community—God forbid.

The people around me were all people who were convinced that boys should have bar mitzvahs and that kids should go to the Jewish school, meaning public school *and* Jewish school. After all, they thought: What you learn is never wasted. You never know. It's not necessary to pretend beforehand that you don't want to learn, is it? No. On the contrary, if you want to be against schooling, you have to have learned it all first. That's typical Jewish reasoning.

The people around Henri Polak, and my uncles were among his close followers, always prided themselves on the fact that they had learned so much and that they could list by heart and in order the sections of the Torah that are read aloud every week. And they prided themselves on the fact that they knew everything about Old Testament history. They flaunted their knowledge of Judaism, those Jewish socialists. You shouldn't think that they came to socialism out of stupidity, not at all.

---

[18]Carrying a nonfunctional "broken" gun in one's breast pocket was the insignia of members of the antimilitaristic movement, which grew after the First World War. The movement was particularly against the planned extensive expansion of the Dutch naval fleet for the defense of the colonies.

I recall being very little, and I was at the home of family friends on Marken one Friday night, and at a certain point the focus shifted and everybody was singing Jewish songs. They alternated Jewish songs with socialist rally songs. They'd always sing Psalm 126, Shir Hamaalot, that's the psalm introducing the prayer of thanks, and then they'd also sing songs of socialist struggle.

◆ ELIZABETH VAN DE KAR-STODEL
When I was getting to know my husband, I was orthodox, and we had a kosher home. However, my husband wore a loden coat in those days, a "Social Democrat" coat. The way boys walk around with long hair or whatever.

I was "going" with my husband—he still hadn't come to our house—and there was this uncle of mine who told my father, "Your daughter's going with somebody from the AJC." He wasn't with the AJC, but for them he was, wearing a loden coat like that. Well, he was a Jewish boy anyway.

That mixture of his Jewish foundation with his socialist bent plus the things he picked up from our family made him what he is now. We had very deep discussions back then as we walked along the canals at night. On my twentieth birthday, the first gift my husband ever gave me—he came up the stairs with quite an armful, there was a party going on, I can still see him standing there—were four large volumes tied up with thick twine: Troelstra's memoirs.

Liberals and Liberal Democrats

◆ SIMON GOSSELAAR
Rich liberal Jews were very dismissive of the socialist ideas that were adhered to by the Amsterdam Jewish proletariat. There used to be and still is, although it's now a very different paper, the *Nieuw-Israëlitisch Weekblad* (New-Israelite Weekly), a paper for the orthodox, because liberals, like Soetendorp's Liberal Jewish Congregation, didn't exist then.

It was largely an advertising outlet, and it gave the middle class extensive coverage—births and deaths, that kind of thing. It's what people found interesting because everybody knew everybody else. There was somewhat of a political slant to that paper, though, and it was antisocialist.

My mother had a subscription. Crazy, all those Jewish people who read that paper only for the "mishpochology." Well, it's how you stayed up to date on things. During elections, though, it really revealed itself to be a nasty little paper. It played on feelings of Jewishness. There was also a liberal party at that time, the Liberal Union, later called the Freedom Union *(Vrijheidsbond)*. The top candidate was Boissevain—you had a lot of those former Hugenots or refugees from France at that time. Second man on the ticket was Dr. Vos, a well-known doctor in Amsterdam. The latter was pushed especially in the Jewish Quarter, and it was pointed out particularly to proletarian Jews, who made up the bulk of the subscribers, even though it was a conservative, orthodox paper, what ties were not in their interest. So, according to the paper, they were supposed to vote for Dr. Vos, a Jew. Politically, of course, that was a little unsavory. Consequently the Jewish element in the socialist movement strongly opposed this.

The Liberal Union convened its last campaign meeting on Monday night in the Jewish Quarter at the Diamond Exchange, which is still there. The following Wednesday the elections were to take place, as even now elections are always on a Wednesday.

The chairman, Asscher—the famous diamond man and Jewish Council man—a well-known Liberal, was also a Freedom Union candidate, but for the Provincial Council, and he was to speak along with Boissevain and Vos. At first, the meeting was going to be held somewhere else, namely at the Concordia building across from the Diamond Exchange on Weesper Square. It had probably been built by the same architect as the Diamond Exchange because it had the same form, except it was much smaller. That's where the Liberals were originally going to meet.

The socialist Jews from the SDAP, including Sam De Wolff, had come too, and he wanted to debate at all costs, because he wasn't going to accept that Jewish sentiment was being manipulated in such a heavy-handed way just to get them to vote Liberal.[19] As a result, the audience for the meeting got to be so large that it was impossible to have the meeting at Concordia. So, everybody moved to the large meeting hall on the other side of the street.

The atmosphere was tremendously charged and emotions were running high between the Liberals and the socialist Jews, particularly on the part of the latter. And then that whole crowd crossing Weesper Square . . . . There was no chance for a debate. They wouldn't stand for it. It deteriorated into bickering and wrangling that got pretty loud. This was in 1929, I think. My wife, a teenage girl then, was there.

At a certain point, mounted police suddenly rode into the hall—very strange when you know that this hall was on the first floor and you had to go up marble stairs to get there. One of the police stations must have gotten a report that there was a political ruckus going on, and those horses came in from various sides of the auditorium. My wife was really scared, but I said, "Don't worry, they're all Jews here. They only fight with their mouths. Nothing's going to happen." And that's exactly how it turned out. In the end, they still had a chance to debate, and so it was Sam De Wolff who took the floor, they trusted him with that.

Sam De Wolff made a joke, a comparison I thought was very funny. He always talked very emotionally and deliberately. He said, "Meeting members, this reminds me of the vendor who sold winter radishes"—that used to be a favorite Jewish treat; Friday nights you dipped them in salt—"and in front of the Blue Bridge that vendor would shout, '*Shayner retish!*'" (nice radishes) because he was still in the Jewish Quarter. But on the other side of the Blue Bridge, his cry became 'Nice radishes!'" That was, of course, a comparison with the way Dr. Vos's campaign had been launched. And the whole place roared with laughter.

◆ LEEN RIMINI

Well, you had the Freedom Union, which was led by Boissevain. Jews were not allowed in the Big Club (Grote Club) on Kalverstraat, on the corner of the Dam Square. So, what did they do during the election campaign? They promoted Dr.

---

[19]Salomon (Sam) De Wolff (1878–1960) was a Marxist economist and lecturer at the University of Amsterdam. He was active throughout his life in socialist and Zionist causes, gaining attention with his publication of *Het economisch getij* (The Economic Tide) in 1929.

Vos, the second candidate, in the Jewish Quarter and they kept Boissevain, an active member of the Big Club, in the background on account of the club's anti-Semitism!

◆ MAX EMMERIK
Boissevain, by the way, made a bad name for himself later. The socialists submitted a proposal to give people public shower facilities, because there was no such thing in the workers' neighborhoods. And then Boissevain said, "Well, they'll just have to wash themselves in a washtub."

◆ ALEXANDRE JOSEPH GOUDSMIT
We went to Liberal meetings just to let our voices be heard. Then there was Professor De Vries, he was an economist and a Liberal as well. One time at the Bellevue, he was talking about how much the Liberal Union had done for the workers. Walraven Boissevain was the top candidate at that time, and Monne De Miranda, he was the bathhouse fellow, right? And Boissevain had said, "No, there's no need for that. Workers can just wash themselves in a wash-basin. They've always done that." So, when De Vries brings up the bathhouse there at the Bellevue, I shouted out from the audience, "Sir, you've forgotten Walraven Boissevain's washbasin!" And everybody knew what I was talking about.

That was an absolutely wonderful election campaign, by the way, with debates going on out in the streets. All kinds of slogans were painted on the wood fence around the empty lot where the Cultural Palace for Worker Industry stood before it burned down, like the one about Dr. Vos: "If you let a fox (*vos*) into the chicken coop. . . ." There were so many people who were out of work. They'd get their unemployment cards stamped at the nearest municipal social assistance office every morning, so they'd stand in line out on the street and debate.

◆ BERTHA BARNSTEIN-KOSTER
My uncle, Heiman Barnstein, was a staunch Liberal Democrat and also a member of the party. But we were still surprised, though, when we heard that he had been asked to run as a candidate in Amsterdam's Election District 4, which had to elect a new member to the Provincial Council. That seat had been held before by the Liberal, Boissevain.

My uncle, as president of Handwerkers Vriendenkring, stepped forward because people were saying, "If anybody in this neighborhood has a chance to beat Boissevain, you do, because Handwerkers Vriendenkring is so important for so many people in this part of town." They had a bathhouse, and the organization had its own building there, plus the library, and the fact that they frequently helped the kids of impoverished members to go to college.

Well, of course we were there at the end of Election Day. The polling places closed at four o'clock, and we were in the Golconda building on Nieuwe Herengracht. We were waiting there, and we'd keep hearing about how many votes had been tallied. Close to five o'clock, a young woman shouted that somebody with a little flag on his bike was coming. It turned out that my uncle, a representative of the Liberal Democratic Party, had been elected by a decent majority in that neighborhood, which had always been the stronghold of the more conservative Liberals. This must have been in 1910.

New Neighborhoods

◆ HARTOG GOUBITZ

We moved to Vrolikstraat in 1904. It was a relatively new street in East Amsterdam. If you're on the Amsterdam-Utrecht train, you go from Central Station through the City Wetlands (Stads-Rietlanden), then you go through the Muiderpoort Station area and the East Indies neighborhood, and finally you get to a bend right along the houses on Vrolikstraat. Now it's been raised up, but then it was at street level.

It was a Jewish neighborhood because lots of Jews went there to live, especially a lot of diamond workers, because the houses were new and in those days you could get a beautiful apartment for three or four guilders a week.

It was a huge improvement for us. As a little boy, I thought it was great to get out of the cramped quarters of the old neighborhood. On Valkenburgerstraat, we'd been living eleven to a room, so it was a huge improvement, having your own room.

◆ LIESBETH VAN WEEZEL

In 1911, when I was twelve and a half, we moved to Pretorius Square, only two or three sides of which had been built yet. The other side got built between 1914 and 1918. There's a lintel there showing two canons, that dates back to the First World War. When we moved there, though, there was an exceptionally big sand flat, and it was lots of fun to play there on the wood pilings.

East Amsterdam—meaning in the Transvaal neighborhood and in a part of Watergraafsmeer—was where a good number of intellectuals, socialists, and people who played a role in the Zionist movement lived, like A. B. Kleerekoper and Sam De Wolff.

The politics of the party, the SDAP, were discussed a lot, so much so that when I was a girl of eight, I would talk about *our* party, much to my parents' amusement. There were little stamp booklets all over the house, so I started pasting the stamps into these booklets, and then I'd write "this is our party" in them.[20]

---

[20]In the Netherlands before World War II, contributions to organizations and parties were often paid to couriers who provided receipts in the form of stamps that would be pasted into the appropriate booklet. The reference here is to the SDAP stamps and booklets.

When we moved out to Pretorius Square, only a few Jews lived there, and our landlord's tactic was to put the few Jews who applied for apartments together along the same stairway. So, the Doozeman family was on the first floor, we were on second, and the third was David Wijnkoop. Later, when Uilenburg and Marken were cleared and torn down, Handwerkers Vriendenkring added big blocks of apartments here. The result was that Jewish working-class life was transplanted to our neighborhood. All of this happened on Retiefstraat and on the small side streets behind the "gold rim"—which became Pretorius Square. The chicken farmers would be there on Fridays, and we'd hang around those carts. That's where we picked up our Amsterdam Yiddish.

◆ Bertha Barnstein-Koster

Handwerkers Vriendenkring had no choice but to request a subsidy from the city, since part of what they did was building apartments. I still remember my uncle grinning from ear to ear and telling my father that he was going to build apartments and wouldn't have to pay a penny himself.

But in reality, though, Handwerkers Vriendenkring put up a thousand guilders, or else they wouldn't have had a hand in construction at all anymore. The City provided the rest. Mayor Tellegen, who was a Liberal Democrat like my father, was happy to back him up in this.

When Mayor Tellegen laid the cornerstone for the apartment block, he praised Handwerkers Vriendenkring for their initiative. The second, third, and fourth apartment blocks, along Tugelaweg and Retiefstraat, were also built with support from Handwerkers Vriendenkring. It was a totally new thing, the City letting them build like that. They started building in 1917.

◆ Ben Sijes

In order to say anything about Retiefstraat, you have to understand what used to be Uilenburgerstraat and Valkenburgerstraat. In old photographs, you can see how narrow those streets were. Uilenburgerstraat and Valkenburgerstraat were demolished and were replaced by wide streets. The people who lived there had to move out, though—out of those densely packed neighborhoods, out of the little courtyards, the alleyways, the basements, and the "passageways." The SDAP's influence was significant in the city of Amsterdam at that time, and it was particularly when they were in power that new housing was built—not just in the Jewish Quarter, but in other areas, too, like Retiefstraat and Krüger Square in the Transvaal neighborhood.

Retiefstraat was a street with apartment buildings only on one side at first. They looked out over the railroad tracks. Across the way is where the new buildings that would house poor Jews were built. The people who were already living on Retiefstraat were more or less "emancipated" when they moved from the

Jewish Quarter: they earned more, they had better homes, their street was clean, the knobs on their front doors were shiny, something you wouldn't ever dream of on Uilenburgerstraat. I saw that because I went to live "on my own" and moved in with my sister and brother-in-law on Krüger Square.

On the "old" side, the doors were neatly shut, the way they're supposed to be, so no cats could get in or out. The new people from the Jewish Quarter, though, well, they had all their doors wide open. Their kids played in the street, and people were pretty nonchalant about where they threw their rubbish—it wasn't neatly put in bins or anything. Not all the stairs would be kept clean, and all of this annoyed the "old side" people. That was all in the very beginning though. Later on the new people "adjusted."

◆ HIJMAN (BOB) SCHOLTE
The Retief neighborhood was really a Jewish neighborhood, because people coming from Uilenburg or Batavierstraat, coming from the Jewish Quarter, got a new apartment in the Retief neighborhood. They even made a little joke about it: A hundred years before Christ, the Romans enter our country; fifty years before Christ and the Batavians (the Germanic tribe the Romans stationed in Holland) enter our country. In 1920, all the Batavians go to Retiefstraat. This was in reference to all the people from Batavierstraat that the government moved to Retiefstraat.

◆ GERRIT BRUGMANS
You could call the move to East Amsterdam a true mass migration. A lot of people had to *learn* to live properly, because they were getting decent rooms and flush toilets when they used to have "quiet ones," or commodes—something that looked like a toilet with a seat but with a bucket under it. They were used to the "Boldoot carts" coming by every night to empty the buckets. First, a guy would come by with a rattle, and then the women would come down with those buckets. Sometimes troublemaking boys would tie a string to a bucket so it would spill all over the stairs.

Those people would have preferred to stay in their old neighborhood because they were so attached to Waterlooplein, and what they called the Alley, the Jodenbreestraat. But the slums had to be cleared, and that was a good thing. Later on, though, they were happy that they had decent apartments, although they still actually had to learn to live decently.

The new buildings were very differently equipped, and there was a decent toilet that you could flush, so everything could be flushed down. They thought that was the strangest thing, a contraption like that. They'd do their wash on the stairs because they thought it was a shame to get the kitchen all wet.

◆ JOOP VOET

The people in the Transvaal neighborhood had strong socialist leanings, particularly those living on and around Transvaal Square. A socialist housing association had built three-story apartment buildings there with a standard of living that was ahead of the times. They had communal back yards, a decent square, a little park.

Then there were more typical streets, too, not unlike other streets being built in Amsterdam at the time, where a lot of "modern" workers, as they were called, went to live. A high percentage was Jewish. The diamond workers were very modern and mostly Jewish.

Organized labor and particularly the diamond workers took advantage of social opportunities available at the time. Others were able to do this as well. There was a Catholic housing association in the Pretoriusstraat neighborhood, called Patrimony.

Three or four years later, families from the Old Jewish Quarter started moving into the Retiefstraat neighborhood. That area was a lot more Jewish. The residents were poorer too. Generally speaking, the workers who lived in the Transvaal neighborhood or on Pretoriusstraat and adjacent streets made a good living, because the rents weren't *that* low. The Retiefstraat, which lay behind them, was definitely poorer, though, because the people had more or less been forced to move there, which is why the apartments were cheaper than on Pretoriusstraat.

In the beginning, there was a lot of resentment against having to leave the old familiar neighborhood, even though people were now living much better. It wasn't as serious as in *some* European cities where the police had to evacuate the slums by force. But there was still a lot of resistance, and adjusting to the new apartments wasn't all that easy.

There was a distinct split between the "new" people in the Retief neighborhood and the "old" people on the slightly tonier Pretoriusstraat and the Patrimony housing association people. We Jewish boys—totally oblivious to being Jewish since no traditions were observed at home-preferred to play in the Transvaal neighborhood.

In retrospect, I do realize that there were probably a lot of Jews among those boys, but I'm not sure about that because even though about thirty, forty, fifty percent of the Transvaal neighborhood was Jewish, that wasn't everybody by a long shot. At school, for instance, it was completely mixed. Very good friends of mine weren't Jewish.

◆ NATHAN STODEL

In 1926, when I was fifteen, we moved to the Transvaalstraat, the "Red Village," a real SDAP neighborhood. We had to move out of Lazarussteeg because our building had been condemned. The bedbugs just about fell into your soup. We got an apartment through the General Housing Association (Algemene Woningbouw Vereniging), which you couldn't move into until the lice had been removed from your bedding.

My parents lost their store though, their quote unquote livelihood. My mother got very sick at that time. She got terrible eczema from nerves and was going through the change of life and suffered through all that for quite a few years. My father still went door-to-door down Plantage Middenlaan, Plantage Franschelaan, and Plantage Badlaan with his produce cart.

In elections, the Transvaal neighborhood voted ninety-eight percent SDAP and De Miranda, as you probably know.[21] I recall my parents getting a visit at a certain point from Elie Smalhout, a leading SDAP man, and he railed about my being with the OSP. "I don't understand how your son can run off with those left-wing OSP radicals!"

◆ EMMANUEL AALSVEL

I had a very pleasant childhood in the Transvaal neighborhood. We saw poor Jews from the Jewish Quarter move in when the Quarter got torn down. I was about seven then, so it must have been 1922.

I won't ever forget the courtyard behind Tugelaweg. It was a large garden with benches. My father had slightly socialist leanings, and he talked to those people from our balcony about how they should behave and that they shouldn't hang their dirty laundry in public.

They also organized afternoons for all the disadvantaged Jewish kids, for St. Nicolas Day and so on. And donated clothing so those people would start adjusting a little after all that time. I recall somebody from the Handwerkers Vriendenkring Housing Association calling for how bedding shouldn't be hung outside on the street side, but out back on the courtyard side.

There was no difference between Jews and Christians. We simply lived together. Smitstraat was different, though, because Catholics lived there. We played them in soccer lots of times, our Transvaal Square team did, not as Jews but as socialists.

◆ ALI VOORZANGER-SUURHOFF

Henri Polak went to live outside of Amsterdam pretty early on because of the natural beauty around the town of Laren in The Gooi. Whenever we were at Mie's cabin in Laren, my husband would say, "That's where Henri Polak lives." That

---

[21]Salomon ("Monne") Rodrigues De Miranda was a former ANDB leader who became a progressive city commissioner, serving from 1919–1939 with a brief interruption.

example sank in pretty deep, particularly among Amsterdammers. My parents
moved to Betondorp (Concrete Village).[22]

Lots of people said, "That Voorzanger family must be absolutely out of their
minds to move over there!" because it was so far away from the center of the city.
A bus ran from Leidseplein out to the Eastern Cemetery and they called it the
"Crow Catcher," because there were always people in funeral garb on the bus
who'd ride it to the end of the line. There was a little ditty about it, too:

> *Roundtrip for just a dime*
> *On the Crow Catcher,*
> *The Crow Catcher!*

The Gooise tram, the tram going north to The Gooi, was too expensive, of
course. So you biked or walked. I even bought a rent-to-buy bike!

Lots of diamond workers lived in Betondorp. Who *didn't* live there? My father
and mother would take a look in the evenings to see how construction was coming along, and they'd walk through Betondorp.

◆ LODEWIJK ASSCHER

A lot of diamond workers lived here, on and around Tolstraat in De Pijp (The
Pipe area of South Amsterdam). This little street over here is called Diamantstraat
(Diamond Street). Those small apartment buildings used to be ours, and that's
where our people lived, in those low buildings. This is the gemstone neighborhood. There's a Ruby Street, an Emerald Street, and a Sapphire Street. Before the
Second World War, there were three hundred sixty people working here. There
were twelve survivors after the war, which says enough.

◆ ARON DE PAAUW

The importance of De Miranda was actually not so much his work as an ANDB
official, as much as the fact that without any education he worked his way up
from diamond polisher to Amsterdam city commissioner, along with the fact that
he did so much for Amsterdam. He was in charge of the Housing Commission,
and all those new housing blocks in the Stadium neighborhood, all those housing
associations, all that came about under his leadership. In that respect, he did
groundbreaking work for the city of Amsterdam. People from abroad, from
Austria, I believe, even came to see how things had been done here.

---

[22]Despite its name, Betondorp is a garden district built on the southeastern outskirts of
Amsterdam.

◆ MOZES DE LEEUW

In a ghetto, you live largely protected by one another. When we moved, other Jews who were a little better off were moving out at the same time. But as a Jew, you weren't going to go live in a neighborhood where no other Jews lived just because you could afford to.

We moved to what they named Churchilllaan (Churchill Boulevard) after World War II, which was a new development at that time. A solid part of this boulevard, from Waalstraat to Victory Square, was a chic, Jewish street. Jewish doctors had homes there, the whole Plotske family lived there, all my uncles lived there, all the De Leeuwens that is, the entire Kuil family. . . . It became a sheltered, privileged neighborhood. Our family doctor's father owned a butcher's shop out on Vrolikstraat, across the Amstel River in East Amsterdam, but his son lived here on Churchilllaan in South Amsterdam.

Jews were held in pretty high esteem in financial terms, of course, and that's why better stores, butcher shops, fish shops, and so forth sprang up here.

Nieuwmarkt (New Market) with Jewish vendors' stalls at the foot of the Waag, the medieval weigh station. To the right, behind the Waag, is the fish hall. At the back of the fish hall, boats delivered the fresh ocean fish Amsterdam Jews adored. (Photo circa 1920.)

Waterloopleinmarkt (Waterloo Square Market) was the major market in the Old Jewish Quarter. The philosopher Baruch Spinoza was born in a house on this square. (Photo circa 1930.)

Pre-Passover rummage sale on Korte Houtstraat near Waterloopleinmarkt. (Photo circa 1920.)

J. Goudeketting sells herring and pickles on Sint Antoniesluis (Saint Anthony's Sluice) near Jodenbreestraat. Pickling was a Jewish specialty in Amsterdam. (Photo circa 1920.)

Sunday market on Oude Schans near Jodenbreestraat. Many Christians also frequented the markets in the Old Jewish Quarter on Sundays. (Photo circa 1920.)

Jewish pushcarts on Jodenbreestraat, where the Dutch painter Rembrandt van Rijn lived during the seventeenth century. (Photo circa 1910.)

Crowd of working-class Jews on Foeliestraat in the Old Jewish Quarter. (Photo circa 1910.)

Burning leftover bread before Passover (*chametz batteln*) was always a festive occasion for kids in the Old Jewish Quarter. (Photo circa 1920.)

Batavierdwarsstraat was one of the streets on Uilenburg in the Old Jewish Quarter where many lived in lamentable circumstances until 1916.

One of the many decrepit alleys on the island of Uilenburg, whose slum dwellings were torn down at the city's expense starting in 1916. Most of the Jewish residents moved to the newly built apartments in what is called the Transvaal neighborhood of East Amsterdam.

Hachnosas Orchim Association (Association for Visitors/Wayfarers) on Weesperstraat, where, starting at the turn of the twentieth century, East European Jews in particular found temporary shelter on their way to the U.S. (Photo circa 1910.)

„DE BIJENKORF" - AMSTERDAM

GROOTST EN MEEST GESORTEERDE MAGAZIJN VAN NEDERLAND

72 AFDEELINGEN

LUNCHROOM · LEESBIBLIOTHEEK

De Bijenkorf (The Beehive), founded by Jewish entrepreneurs, on Dam Square across from the Royal Palace. Along with its many branches, it is considered to be one of the Netherlands' finest department stores. (Photo circa 1920.)

At the time when seventy percent of all ornamental diamonds were being cut in Amsterdam, I.J. Asscher was the most prominent diamond merchant. His factory, shown here, was on Tolstraat in South Amsterdam. Its tall windows let in the uniform light that was so essential to the diamond worker's craft. (Photo circa 1920.)

Jonas Daniel Meijerplein (Jonas Daniel Meijer Square). The seventeenth-century Great Synagogue, right, the smaller of the two, and the eighteenth-century New Synagogue, left. These two synagogues currently house the Jewish Historical Museum. (Photo circa 1900.)

In 1937, poor, elderly, and ailing Jews were able to receive outstanding care in the new building designed by J. F. Staal for The Jewish Invalid, located on Weesperplein (Weesper Square) across from the Diamond Exchange.

Crown Princess Juliana receives flowers from a Jewish girl in front of the entrance to The Jewish Invalid. (Photo circa 1937.)

Tens of thousands of Jews and Christians followed the funeral procession of the beloved Isaac Gans, who died in November 1938. Here, the procession is shown as it sets off from The Jewish Invalid.

The Sephardic chazzan and composer David Ricardo, who emigrated to Israel, sings one last time on the bimah of his renowned Amsterdam *esnoga* (synagogue, in Portuguese) in 1975.

The interior of the Portuguese Synagogue is still illuminated by candles in the gorgeous chandeliers, as well at the end of each row. (Photo circa 1930.)

The choir of the Great Synagogue directed by Sam Englander during a 1938 recording session for NBC radio in New York.

Chazzan Abraham Katz with the Great Synagogue choir. (Photo circa 1920.)

Diamond polishing hall in 1919, decorated for the ANDB's twenty-fifth anniversary.

Small diamond-working studio in 1930, most likely used by cleavers and cutters.

Portrait by Paul Citroen of David Wijnkoop, renowned Communist leader and son of a rabbi. (Portrait circa 1930.)

Henri Polak (1868–1943) was founder and president of the Dutch Diamond Workers Union (ANDB), the World Federation of Diamond Workers (WD), the Dutch Federation of Unions (NVV), the Social Democratic Labor Party (SDAP), and the Association for the Conservation of Nature Reserves, to name just a few of his activities.

Owners and personnel of Koco on Rijnstraat (Rhine Street) in South Amsterdam. This popular ice cream parlor was owned and operated by A. Kohn and Ernst Cahn, Jewish immigrants from Germany. In May 1939, Dutch Nazis wearing brass knuckles attacked "Jewish-looking" customers in a mini-pogrom, the likes of which had not been seen in Amsterdam since the eighteenth century. (Photo circa 1938.)

The Young Boxer was a predominantly Jewish boxing association located in the Old Jewish Quarter. Boxing, like wrestling, was a favorite sport among the Jewish working class in Amsterdam. Ben Bril (first row, third from right) became a national boxing champion at sixteen and also took part in the Olympic Games in Amsterdam in 1928. He survived the Bergen-Belsen concentration camp with his American wife. (Photo circa 1925.)

Anne Frank (second from left) in 1939 on her tenth birthday, standing with her girlfriends on Merwedeplein (Merwede Square) in South Amsterdam where she lived. Many of the affluent Jews who fled Germany after 1933 settled here.

Three-hundredth-anniversary service of the Amsterdam Ashkenazic congregation at the Great Synagogue on November 14, 1935. (Painting by Martin Monnickendam.)

Sukkoth service at the Portuguese Synagogue in 1929. (Painting by Martin Monnickendam.)

Painting of the socialist diamond merchant Jacobus Batavier by Jacobus Van Looy.

Max De Vries van Buuren, president of a textile wholesale company and member of the Amsterdam City Council. (Painting by Thérèse Schwartze.)

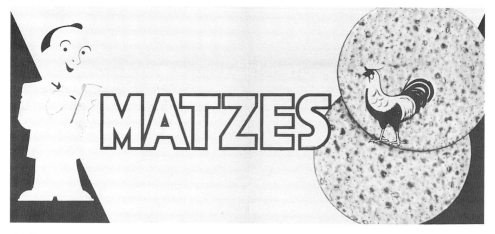

Ad for De Haan ("The Rooster") matzos factory, the largest of its kind in Amsterdam.

Labels from the fashionable Maison Gerzon clothing store.

This poster is an appeal to sign the petition drawn up by Jewish organizations in view of the coming peace urging the Dutch government to take into account the individual and national rights of Jews elsewhere. The petition collected 47,000 signatures, representing more than half of the adult Jewish population in the Netherlands. (February 1918 by Albert Hahn Jr.)

Poster by Mommie Schwarz announces a benefit at the Amsterdam Opera House on May 29, 1933 for Jewish refugees from Nazi Germany.

Poster by Jewish painter Meijer Bleekrode for the Independent Socialist Party (OSP) demanding a total boycott of Nazi Germany.

Social Democratic Labor Party (SDAP) campaign poster urging voters in the province of North Holland to elect Amsterdam City Housing Commissioner Salomon Rodrigues De Miranda, candidate for the Provincial Council (April 17, 1935.)

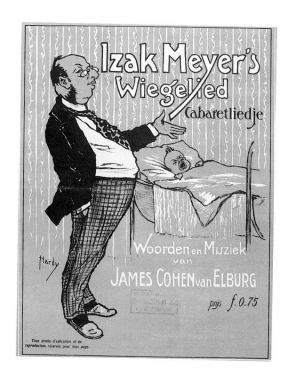

Cover to the sheet music for "Izak Meyer's Lullaby," This popular song was written by James Cohen Van Elburg, one of the Netherlands' many Jewish composers and lyricists. (Circa 1920.)

The Jewish composer, conductor, and violinist Max Tak wrote this popular ode to the city of his birth, "Amsterdam, You're the City of Cities" ("Amsterdam, je bent de stad der steden"). The cover, showing Amsterdam's coat of arms, sports a photograph of the somewhat vain Tak in lieu of the shield's third X. (Circa 1935.)

Upper portion of the stairwell in the Dutch Diamond Workers Union (ANDB) building. The building, now the home of the National Trade Unions Museum, was designed by H. P. Berlage. The spectacular lamp designed by Jan Eisenloeffel was the gift of ANDB members on the occasion of the twenty-fifth anniversary of their union in 1919.

Portion of the recently restored ANDB board of directors' meeting room with the original directors' table and frescos by the socialist artist Richard Roland Holst. Board chairman and president Henri Polak, particularly respected among Jewish diamond workers, was a passionate art lover, and commissioned Berlage, Holst, and other artists so that union workers could gain an appreciation of art.

V

JEWS AND CHRISTIANS

Jews and Christians lived peacefully beside, with, and among one another in Amsterdam until 1933. Through work, community, school, club, union, political party, and mixed marriage, mutual contacts increased and became more intensive. This does not mean to say, however, that there were no prejudices or even hostile feelings on either side. The fact that religious Jews and Christians rejected mixed marriage speaks for itself. Nevertheless, this attitude did not by any means exclude mutual appreciation on the human level. Even among nonreligious Jews and Christians, mixed marriage was still resisted to a certain extent.

The great majority of Amsterdam Jews, whether religious or not, took Dutch citizenship for granted. The fact that they were readily identifiable to others and themselves did not get in the way of integration into Dutch society at all. In Amsterdam, assimilation, in the sense of compulsively hiding forms of behavior considered to be Jewish, such as the use of the hands while speaking, occurred relatively infrequently. There were quite some Jews who were unduly proud of non-Jewish looks, though. As Jews became more educated, differences from non-Jews in look and bearing fell by the wayside. Even Zionists did not avoid this form of natural assimilation. Mixed marriage occurred with some frequency even among Zionists.

Obviously Jews were shaken by the rise of the National Socialist Movement (NSB) after 1933. However, even this party did not seem truly alarming to the Jews. After all, from the moment that the NSB as a party officially began touting anti-Semitic propaganda, the number of votes it received during elections fell dramatically.

Anti-Semitism

◆ HARTOG GOUBITZ

We lived in what was then Commelinstraat, above one of the first little shuls in the neighborhood. That shul had been set up for the few Jews who lived around there. But just by going to shul, those people stood out, and they'd get harassed a lot. So then we realized all the more that we were Jews, due to the anti-Semitism all around us.

They taunted you with "Jew" when you walked down the street. Being a seven- or eight-year-old at a school with all these Christian kids, you stood out because you were Jewish. The people who lived there had never been around Jews before, and they raised their children that way too. Because, don't forget: "The Jews crucified Jesus"—the idea that Jews were therefore bad people, was so widespread. Kids heard that from their parents.

◆ BAREND BRIL

You used to have turf battles. Foeliestraat—that was the "non-Jewish" section, although some Jews lived there—against Valkenburgerstraat, called Marken back then. Fights every day with big, heavy pieces of lumber. One party would stand on one side of the bridge and the other across the bridge on Rapenburg. It was Jew against non-Jew.

But, if you ask me whether they were anti-Semitic, I'd say no, because the same people, those same Kattenburg and Foelie Street people, took the side of the Jews in 1941 during that February Strike.

◆ JOËL COSMAN

Jewish people here in Amsterdam were a minority compared to the rest of the population. I won't say that there was discrimination. They made up about thirteen percent of Amsterdam's population. But as a group they felt more or less inferior. They often expressed this in fights using pieces of lumber against non-Jewish boys.

There were lumberyards on Joden Houttuinen, and at around five or six when those businesses closed, they would come and take pieces of lumber and use them when they fought Foeliestraat or Kattenburg.

Both sides were to blame for the fighting. The Foeliestraat and the Kattenburg people would provoke those Jewish boys, which the Jewish boys wouldn't take, so there were all these battles all the time. Not that people were done in, but sometimes you'd have a hole in your head because they were serious.

On Rapenburgerstraat, there was a Jewish school that Jewish boys went to at four-thirty after their regular school. Now, next to that Jewish school there was a Catholic school, and that was fire and water. The Jewish boys who waited from four to four-thirty for the school doors to open would be out there to welcome all the Catholic boys when they got out of school, so there were regular run-ins and fistfights all the time. In the end, the Catholic school changed its hours so that their school let out at three-thirty instead of four.

◆ GERRIT BRUGMANS
I went to school on Batavierstraat. On the other side of the school was the Oude Schans canal, and we'd go there to fight the "lousy bums." It was a "third-rate" school, which naturally meant it was a school for the rich. So, you'd stash your sticks and clubs on Oude Schans in some basement or other, and at twelve o'clock it would be war against the lousy bums.

◆ SIMON GOSSELAAR
I recall that a couple of Christian boys were fighting, they were maybe ten, twelve years old, and one of them called the other a "dirty filthy Roman papist." I didn't understand that, see, because for me what wasn't Jewish was all the same. You were either Jewish or not Jewish.

◆ JOOP EMMERIK
Sometimes we'd set up something among the boys from school, something like, "Wednesday afternoon we're walking to Muiderberg," or, "We're walking to Sloterdijk." That was far away from Kerkstraat for a boy who was eight or nine years old. Sometimes we'd jump on the back of one of those horse-drawn wagons. The first thing you'd hear would be, "Filthy, stinking Jew, get off my wagon or I'll knock you off." Eight or nine I was. And shouting "Moze" or "Sam" at us a lot. That wasn't just out of the blue. That's why I fought a lot when I was a boy, honest. I couldn't stand that kind of thing. But then, lots of us couldn't take it.

◆ NATHAN STODEL
In the Jewish Quarter of Amsterdam, whenever we played around the corner from the Roman Catholic Church and a priest walked by, we would sing:

Seven nails, seven staples strong
That's what we hung Jesus on!

We sang that little song right in the middle of Waterlooplein, on the corner of Lazarussteeg.

There was also a superstition. If there were Jewish vendors out on the street in the morning and a nun or a priest walked by, they'd call out, "Touch metal!" and they would have to grab a piece of metal. Otherwise, the nun or priest would bring your business bad luck that day.

◆ EMMANUEL AALSVEL

One thing happened to me that I'll never forget. I was twelve and in my first year at the school on Linnaeusstraat along with five or six other Jewish boys. There was a teacher who taught German, and he asked us, "Which of you children are Jewish?" We all raised our hands, and we all failed that first year. The man later became a fascist. That made a deep impression on me. It was the first time I had ever experienced that kind of thing.

My father went to the mayor along with several non-Jewish parents, and that teacher was thrown out of the school. Later, during the German occupation, the man became the principal of the five-year high school on Mauritskade.

It was very typical of Amsterdam in those days for parents to complain to the mayor about an anti-Semitic teacher. And of course it was utterly true to form for Amsterdam when the Strike was on during the war and they said, "Give us back our Jews."[1] That was really typically Amsterdam.

◆ JO JUDA

I was going to a new school right near Oosterpark, a real working-class neighborhood, and it was my second year, I think.

One day, some boys in my class asked me, "Do you believe in God?"

I'd hardly ever heard the term, so I said, "No."

The next thing I know, this one boy runs off and comes back with a bunch of other boys. I noticed that all these boys were looking at me with such curiosity and were so eager to hear what I had to say, that I figured I must have said something wrong.

So, he asked me again, "Do you believe in God?"

And I said, "Yes."

The funny thing was that they weren't satisfied with that.

The same boy said, "You're a liar!" And to the others, he said, "He doesn't believe in God." So, this turned into a fistfight between six or seven boys and me, and there wasn't much I could do against them, of course. This all happened

---

[1]Reference here is to the February Strike, a two-day strike in 1941 on the part of Amsterdam's population to protest the arrest of about 500 Jewish men in the Old Jewish Quarter.

during recess. So then it was time for us to go back in. I stayed behind for a long time, but finally I just went inside.

But from then on, they gave me trouble. Those boys taunted me in the usual way: they did imitations of a Jewish accent, really badly, I thought, but anyway, they really made fun of it. That's how they dealt with me.

I think the whole thing was caused by my name, Juda. I don't know if those boys were Catholic or Protestant, but they did go to Sunday school. They came from a religious mileu.

The teacher at school found out I was color-blind. There were two blackboards, and on one of them the arithmetic problems were written in purple and on the other in blue. And that woman said, "You have to do the purple problems." I kept walking back and forth because I didn't know which of the blackboards had the purple problems, and felt completely at a loss because I couldn't see the color. The whole class started jeering, of course. They thought it was hilarious that I didn't know that. At a certain point the teacher said, "OK, Mozie, I think you'd better sit down." I felt so totally out of place, that I went back to my seat.

I hated being looked at like I was different, which of course happened because I had that name. It spoke volumes. One time, when I was able to figure out when Palestine, which has the region of Juda in it, was going to be taught in geography, I didn't go to school. Those boys would have looked at me funny every time the name was mentioned.

The surprising thing was that when I brought my violin to school one day, their attitude completely changed. To start with, I noticed that the teacher wasn't very musical. I would sit by myself on a bench in the back, and she would always practice her singing lesson right near me. I noticed she sang flat and that she had trouble staying with the beat. She would tap out the beats with a tuning fork. She had all the means, but the only thing that counts, having your own feeling for it, she didn't have. This gave me a tremendous sense of vindication. I thought: That's what she gets for teasing me so much, along with those boys. She simply can't sing in tempo, and on top of that she sings flat. And her voice is shaky to boot.

At some point, she heard that I played violin and said, "Bring in your violin, why don't you." I did, and I had to play along with those songs; she had it easy, then, of course. From then on, she switched to the other extreme, and I was such a nice boy.

I started making a kind of tour through the entire school because I was supposed to play for all the classes, upper and lower grades, like a kind of phenomenon, you know what I mean? And when school let out, those same boys who had teased me so much at first, stood around me and suddenly treated me like one of them. I felt that very keenly. It really took me by surprise. A couple of guys from the other class asked if they could walk part of the way home with me and carry my violin, but then that one boy who had teased me the most lay his hand on my shoulder and said, "No, because Juda's my best friend." I was totally baffled by that.

I didn't understand any of it, either the one situation or the other. What I did get, though, was a sense of how unstable people, children, and circumstances can be. Anything could happen at any moment, and that feeling has never left. On the other hand, it motivates you to try to achieve something so that you can compensate for that sense of inferiority. Study hard so that you prove at least to yourself that you're somebody compared to those who give you the feeling that you don't measure up.

Even with people who had good intentions, you were aware that whenever you said something, a hint of ridicule would creep into the corner of their eye, because of your Jewish accent, of course. You know, sometimes they'd even do a quick imitation. But of course you were terribly sensitive to things like that.

Looking back, I believe many Jews see ghosts when it comes to discrimination, just like I do. I used to be completely crushed if somebody said, "I sold it to that rag-and-bone Jew." Now I see it's just a term. They could just as well have said "ragman," but among those kinds of people, they said "rag-and-bone Jew."

People who are forced into the position of being an exception start becoming unstable. They start perceiving things that sometimes aren't there at all in reality.

◆ JOOP VOET

When I was about seven, I got glasses. I thought they were a little weird, but also something to be proud of. So, I went out on the street wearing my glasses. Boys shouted, "Brillejood" (Jew-boy with the glasses).

So, I went to my mother, and she asked me, "How did you like being out on the street wearing your glasses?"

And I said that I could see everything much better now, but, "Boys are starting to call me 'Brillejoop.' But, that's funny. How do they know my name's Joop?" That's how unaware I was of the fact that I was a Jew.

Now and then we'd make little jokes at school about what the letters in particular words meant, like SDAP: Sort Do Always Pout. So I said, "Amsterdam Taxi has 'BWT' written on the side of their cabs, that means Besholem When Traveling." The teacher didn't get it, so I told him that Besholem meant in peace and that it was a Jewish expression. Then another Jewish boy in my class said to me, "How can you say something like that? What business is it of that goy's?"

◆ BEN SIJES

I was probably about thirteen when I had my first girlfriend. We were in the eighth grade. We took lots of walks, and I'd walk her home. You know how it goes. You walk up and down a bit, and say school lets out at four, you're still saying goodbye to each other at four-thirty.

One day we agreed to go out to the coast, to Zandvoort, on Sunday. At that time, you had to get train tickets ahead of time because in the summer Central Station was always incredibly busy and crowded. Saturday she went to buy tickets—we were going to go Sunday. On her way home from Central Station, she was hit by a car. The next day I went to the station, but I didn't see her. I kept waiting and waiting, but she didn't show up. I couldn't figure out why. Then, I went to her house and heard what had happened. A couple of days later she was buried at the Eastern Cemetery, and of course the whole class went.

After they had all gone, I was still there, heartbroken. One of her relatives came up to me and asked, "What are you doing here?"

"She was such a good friend, and we were going to go away together," I said.

Then that guy looked at me hard, "Are you a Jew?"

And I said, "Yes."

"Well," he said, "We aren't very fond of Jews here, you know. You better get going. You have no business here. Just go on over to the Jewish cemetery."

So, I walked back to the Jewish Quarter like a real shlemiel.

◆ EDUARD CHARLES KEIZER

I had a brother who was a year older than I was, and we always walked to school together. Sometimes we would walk along the Amstel, sometimes down Weesperstraat. I was maybe eight, nine years old, and one day I'm walking along with my brother—he had blond hair—and this little boy comes up to us and says to my brother, "Hey, do you have to walk with a rotten Jew? Didn't you know the Jews killed Jesus?" That boy was no older than seven or eight, so they pumped it in early, a hatred of Jews.

My brother gave him a good wallop.

◆ JEANETTE ALVAREZ VEGA-KEIZER

I remember, I was taking violin lessons from one of my mother's cousins. He lived near Burgerziekenhuis, and I had to walk through Oosterpark to get home. I had my hair cut short, in the so-called pageboy style. Two boys walked by and shouted, "Hey, pagehead, filthy rotten Jew-girl." At which I turned around (I was eight years old) and said, "Was Jesus a rotten Jew too?" I still don't know where I got that, but they just kept walking. I think they were too dumb to come up with a good reply. That would have been too much for them.

I didn't feel hurt though. I thought: You know better. I didn't think it was terrible being a Jew. One person was a Jew, another was a Catholic. In those days, there was great animosity between Protestants and Catholics, which I didn't understand either. I had liberal and orthodox Jewish girlfriends, plus Christian girlfriends. They came over and were treated just like anybody else. If I went over to a Christian girl's house and they served sausage or meat or something, I'd say, "I'm not allowed to eat that because it's not kosher," and I'd get something else. That was it. It wasn't a problem at all.

◆ ELISABETH VAN DE KAR-STODEL

We lived near Nieuwmarkt. That's where my father had his business. It was actually on the edge of the Jewish Quarter, but the area was Jewish. It was an extension of the Jewish Quarter.

Personally I never witnessed any *rishut*.[2] I do recall that sometimes when I was at my father's stand, not so much to help out, but after school or during vacations, there would be some issue or other with a customer. Let's say she felt cheated over the amount of fabric she'd just bought. There would be arguments sometimes, and customers would call you a Jew. And my father had a short fuse. So then if he showed her he was right, he'd want to physically attack the woman. Sometimes a cop from the Nieuwmarkt station came over.

That made a huge impression on me, particularly that the first thing those women who bought at the market would shout was "Jew"—not just at my father, most of the market consisted of Jewish vendors—when in reality they couldn't have been cheated because those vendors had to be out there day after day. They couldn't swindle people because they had calibrated yardsticks that were calibrated every year or every other year. Sure, I still always defend them, you know. I always thought that was awfully unfair. I have never been able to stand injustice.

◆ ROSA COHEN-DE BRUIJN

I went to a night school. I was the only Jewish woman there. A couple of girls were talking with each other about, "Yes, that filthy dirty rotten Jew. . . ." I didn't know what they were talking about because I stumbled into the middle of the conversation. "Well, that man went over behind the trees over there, and he wanted to come up to us, and. . . ."

I said, "So, what did he want?"

"Well, one of those filthy perverts, one of those disgusting Jews. . . ."

At which point I said, "I don't know if you know this, but I'm Jewish myself. And was that man so disgusting and dirty?"

They immediately checked themselves, "Oh, but my mother knows so many Jewish people. . . ."

---

[2]*Rishut* or *rishes* in Dutch Yiddish means anti-Semitic behavior.

Then there came a time when I really started looking for what was positive about the fact that I was Jewish. When I was fifteen or sixteen.

◆ ABEL JACOB HERZBERG

I went to a working-class school on Jacob Van Campenstraat, the school where the music library is now. When I first entered the classroom, the boys sang:

> *One, two, three, and the Jew's in the pot,*
> *mashed up good and put the cover on,*
> *but when it was time to put that Jew on the plates*
> *he was all covered with little fried crusts.*

Still, this doesn't mean to say that I didn't have a lot of non-Jewish friends after that. It was just an experience that stayed with you.

After that you get to grammar school, right? There was this fraternity chapter there called DVS, Disciplina Vitae Scipio. That was written on the front of the building, it's still there, on the front of the Barlaeus Gymnasium on Weteringschans. The chapter had one rule: admit no proles, no girls, no Jews.

◆ CAREL JOSEF EDERSHEIM

As far as I know, Nisita was started as a "class club" with a few Jewish members. Back then, Jews weren't eligible to be in the "chapters" (the groups acknowledged by the Corps).[3] Jews had very little "value" on the student market.

You see, the Amsterdam Student Corps was originally a chic outfit. Over the course of time, proportionately more Jews in the population went on to study. The "more stylish" young men were admitted to chapters. There was a Catholic chapter, and there were chapters that liked to have fun—like Odoleh and Vivat did in my day.

If more than one chapter wanted you, it was important to be a "new pledge" (an incoming freshman). On the "pledge market," a Jew was worthless to Hera, the Catholic chapter.

Quite a few chapters didn't accept Jews. Just Bredero. Unica, for example, referred to itself as a very distinguished chapter. It so happened that Offerhaus, who later became a professor and a judge, was "rushed" (asked to be in a chapter)

---

[3]The Amsterdam Student Corps was a fraternity that acknowledged various chapters. After initiation and acceptance into the Corps, the new members had to join a chapter. Those who weren't invited into a chapter might form one on their own made up of similarly unaffiliated fellow class members, which were called class clubs.

along with a few other boys. Posthumus Meijes was one of them, I think, as well as Cohen, a very proper, correct young man. He was assimilated, later became a lawyer. Those boys had gone to grammar school together. So, Offerhaus said, "We're really good friends, and we'll join Unica only if you take Cohen as well." I'm absolutely sure that that young man was badgered out of there after a year or two.

I used to say, "You can't blame them for not taking those boys. They don't mix with Jews in everyday life either."

In a lawyer's family, there was generally extremely little contact between Jews and non-Jews. Now, of course, things are slightly different. At a certain point, people wanted to do away with the distinction, and contact was allowed, as in the scientific world. Complete equality was practiced there. But as far as I can remember—and obviously that's personal—it was still true that outside the professions, families were strongly Jewish or non-Jewish. Until there were mixed marriages, which had their own problems.

Doctors didn't have much trouble. They all used to have their own practices. They worked on their own. Lawyers had firms together, though, and it was very exceptional for Jews and non-Jews to have firms together.

In lawyers' circles, they would sometimes use the term "proles" in reference to those kinds of lawyers. And if one lawyer were up against another, the first one might say of the other, "When he litigates, he uses Jewish tactics." But then, this happened among non-Jews as well, although then it would be said of a lawyer that he just "split hairs." You have to see these things from more than one perspective.

◆ BAREND LUZA

I recall one incident very well. When I finished medical school, I didn't go into practice right away. I ended up at Professor Saltet's laboratory. There was a colleague there at the time wanting to specialize in the same area I did. This was when the German mark was plummeting. We needed some important books, and I was able to get them cheaply in Germany because the mark had gone down so much. So, this colleague, having looked into these books, said, "I'd like to have copies, too, but I have absolutely no contacts in Germany. Could you order them for me?" So, I did, but it took a little while for those books to get here. In the meantime, the mark had gone up again, causing this man to have to pay more.

Then he demanded that I pay him back the difference. And because I refused, I was made out to be a "filthy kike." That really set things off. I wanted to get my hands on him, but others held me back, see. Then I went to Professor Saltet. I told him what had happened, and I told him that I had written a letter to this colleague which I didn't want to send before he, Professor Saltet, had read it. He read the letter and said he thought it was a very good letter. "It's true. You're very right, but I advise you to hold onto the letter, sleep on it, and then read it again in the morning. If you still want to send it, go ahead and send it." I never sent it.

But that doctor had called me a kike. Things like that happened on more than one occasion, even in the Netherlands.

◆ ARON DE PAAUW

There was a dance hall on Kalverstraat. Sometimes we'd go there to dance on a Friday afternoon. At a certain point we were barred by the doorman. Then we asked to talk to the manager. He poured us a lot of wine just to keep us quiet, but finally it came out anyway, "There are ladies who don't want to be asked to dance by Jewish fellows."

I was twenty-some years old at the time. We were just boys, and our fathers weren't men of consequence, so what were you supposed to do? Resign yourself to it.

Trianon, right near the Hirsch building, also refused to admit Jews in 1912. Lots of Jewish lawyers who used to go there for a drink boycotted them in protest. Later, they allowed Jews back in.

◆ MAX EMMERIK

Before World War I, you had Trianon on Leidseplein. It was an amusement center for upper-middle-class people who all used to get together there. At a certain point, it was off-limits to Jews with long noses. That was just before World War I.

I was personally witness to that. Our boss, Brammetje Asscher, who was one of Amsterdam's notables, demonstratively went in there to see if they would turn him away. They didn't. He was the president of the chamber of commerce.

◆ ARTHUR FRANKFURTHER

Before the war, you couldn't become a member of the Big Club in Amsterdam if you were of Jewish origin. Then there was this incident with Mendes De Leon who was a member of an aristocratic Portuguese Jewish family. He was a doctor and married to a non-Jewish girl, the daughter of Karel Veldman of the Vermeer & Co banking firm.

Mendes De Leon's father-in-law sponsored him to become a member of the Big Club, which turned into a huge uproar in Amsterdam. Everybody who was a member, but who never went, ran over to make sure to vote "yes" to his acceptance. But it didn't work. They took him out of the running.

It happened later on, when Mayor De Vlucht's daughter married Nico

Heijmans, and Henk Van Nierop, the banker, went to the wedding.[4] When I asked him how the wedding had been, he said, "Oh, it was very nice, especially after-wards. Some of the guests went over to the Big Club for a drink, but the groom and most of his guests, *we* had to go to the Leesmuseum" (now the Mak Van Waay antique auction house).

That picture was clear enough. They were just not allowed in.

◆ MOZES HEIMAN GANS

The mayors of a whole slew of places in the province of North Holland had formed a committee, and they came to The Jewish Invalid very courteously to ask what would be the best thing for them to do in the aftermath of a heavy hailstorm that had caused them a lot of damage. First of all, how were they going to get all the money that was needed? And secondly, how were all those people now with-out a roof over their heads, for whom they couldn't very well build new houses, going to be housed?

So, as the gentlemen were leaving, one of the mayors said to my father, "I wish all Jews were like you."

To which my father replied, "I'm happy all Christians are not like you," refus-ing to shake his hand.

That man was completely dumbfounded. After all, he'd come to The Jewish Invalid, so he honestly must have believed that "anti-Semitism" was a real obscenity. And yet, he still had this very ambivalent attitude.

◆ SALKO HERTZBERGER

Being a doctor, I have always been surprised at how little non-Jews know about Jewish life. The odd one knew that Jews didn't turn on lights on Friday evenings and that a non-Jewish neighbor had to go over to do that. They thought it was a little strange, but nobody was surprised about it in the least. That was just the way it was. They didn't have the vaguest notion about Jewish attitudes, Jewish ideas, or Jewish traditions. Sure, you could get really good matzo at De Haan's. You had to have matzo for Easter. Easter Sunday and Monday you were supposed to eat matzo. If you were a Jew and had a non-Jewish visitor, he would say, "Before I go, I *must* have some of your matzos to take with me." Not that they couldn't get any at the store, but you got matzos from your Jewish friends and acquaintances. There was a lot of contact between Jews and non-Jews, and yet the basis of Jewish life was completely unknown to non-Jews.

Whenever I got new patients, I would introduce myself and ask, "How did you find me?"

---

[4]Nico Heijmans and Henk van Nierop, the president and founder of the prestigious Amsterdam Bank, were both Jews, and therefore not admitted into the Big Club.

And they would way, "Oh, I just moved into the neighborhood, and we asked people if there was a Jewish doctor in the area, because at home they always said that if you wanted to have a good doctor or pharmacist, you went to Jews." It's a far cry for me to call that anti-Semitism, but it's clearly a form of discrimination.

Jewish *Selbsthass* (self-contempt) is a unique phenomenon. It's almost unheard of in a group for the people in it to feel contempt for and to distance themselves from each other based on the fact that you are both being discriminated against by somebody who has no sympathy for either of you. It's a kind of disdain for traditional Jewish life. You think things like, "It's not very smart of those Jews to be sitting in the very front of that café, do they really have to? And do all those women have to wear every diamond they own, and do they really have to try to climb up the ladder? Do Jews really have to sit on every board, and do there really have to be four Jewish city commissioners?" But those same people would have a non-Jewish maid, and if they were sitting at the table talking "among family" about Jewish matters, and the goy maid came in, they would immediately talk about "Mexicans." The word "Jews" was not mentioned in the presence of non-Jews. They didn't want to be labeled as Jews in public. They thought it was an ugly word. They would say "Israelite" instead.

The whole concept of "being Jewish" was loaded. Shul at that time was also referred to as an "Israelite church community." Now it's called a "Jewish con-gregation." Being Jewish meant having a religion, not being in a separate popu-lation group.

◆ AARON VAZ DIAS

There were businesses like C & A where a Jew could never work. Which reminds me of the joke about the Jewish salesman who *did* manage to get hired at one of those places. The priest found out and went to the manager. So, the manager advised the priest to go and talk with the man himself. Later, the exhausted priest, looking absolutely miserable, comes back to the manager.

"And, Father, what are your findings?" asks the manager.

"You should keep that man on. He just sold me a double bed!"

Integration and Assimilation

◆ JOHANNES JUDA GROEN
When I was three or four years old, I had to go to a nursery school of course, like any child, so my mother sent me to a Jewish nursery school. For some reason or other, it didn't work out. I thought it was dirty there. I can still smell the smell of vomit. I couldn't adjust. I didn't want to eat there, even though my mother gave me sandwiches to take along, so she withdrew me from the school.

This was a bit of a problem for my parents because they didn't think it was a good thing for an only child like myself to be at home alone like that—my brother was born later. Evidently they looked around some, wondering what they could afford, and finally sent me to a "kindergarten"—this must have been around 1907—on Plantage Muidergracht. It was run according to modern principles by a Miss Zeilmans. Slightly better-off middle-class Jews who lived in the Plantage area, as well as some non-Jews, sent their children there.

I had as much of a crush on that teacher as I did on my mother. She wasn't Jewish. She took me out to the garden and showed me flowers, birds, and goldfish. For the first time, I lived in two environments, two cultural worlds. At home, there was the poor but warm Jewish family atmosphere, where my father spouted forthright socialist theories: strikes and no alcohol—so the family had none of the cultural drawbacks of a poor family. My father wasn't interested in flowers and plants and birds or in other cultures or geography, and so on, though. His ideal was the labor movement, and that filled his life. So, at home it was still a small world.

But this teacher taught me to look at other things, and that made a deep impression on me. At a very early age, I would wander around the city from time to time. I'd be gone, and my parents wouldn't be able to find me. I was five or six then. I'd have gone to Zeeburgerdijk or across the IJ or something.[5] When I was in second or third grade, I learned about Floris V, Duke of Holland, and Muider Castle, so I hiked all the way to Muider Castle by myself, but to my great disappointment wasn't allowed in without a chaperone because I was too young.

Exploring other worlds, the fantasy that I might become an explorer later on,

---

[5]The IJ is the harbor area behind Central Station into which the Amstel flows. North Amsterdam is on the other side.

these ideas definitely came from the non-Jewish world that I first got to know about through that preschool teacher and later through my non-Jewish elementary school teachers.

◆ BEN SIJES

In the Jewish families I was acquainted with, the attitude I noticed was: "We're living in rotten circumstances, we work ourselves to the bone, but we're going to give our children a better future!" Jewish workers distinguished themselves in that respect from non-Jewish workers.

Maybe for the Jewish proletariat there was something more involved than simply "my children should be better off than I am." Part of it was: "If my child, being Jewish, can become a lawyer or whatever, then he'll be more independent, so he'll be safer, and they'll need him." A Jewish orange seller wasn't going to get any protection from relatives or anything. The war proved that. But many Jewish intellectuals did get protection from the non-Jewish people around them, although we shouldn't exaggerate.

The opinion that "if you're Jewish, you have to insure yourself with knowledge and indispensability," I think was very much part of it. When I got to high school, it was the first time I was in predominantly non-Jewish company. But it was very coincidental that I went around with non-Jewish friends a lot. They came to our house too. At first, my mother objected because the cups would have to be washed extra well. Of course we never ate dairy and meat products together from the same set of dishes. That wasn't kosher, right?

Most young Jewish men moved out of the Jewish Quarter to work at factories, so they no longer went out on the street with a pushcart, like the old guys. They looked for work in different places, the number of mixed marriages increased, and social change was underway. Around 1930, you could no longer talk about "the Jews." That concept had been shattered, among other things due to the advent of the socialist movement, which resulted from the expansion of the capital means of production in the city of Amsterdam. More and more Jews worked as metalworkers or in the garment industry. They were also to be found at the harbor.

Even at the beginning of the twentieth century, there were sharp contrasts between rich and poor Jews. The rich and the middle-class voted the conservative Liberal ticket. In 1936 or 1937, they voted for Prime Minister Colijn, against the NSB.[6] The Jewish workers didn't do that. They voted for the Communist Party or for the SDAP, but primarily for social democracy.

---

[6]Colijn was also the leader of the Antirevolutionary Party.

◆ ROSINE VAN PRAAG
My parents weren't orthodox, and even my grandparents weren't. My father was
a member of the SDAP. He was a diamond broker with a strong socialist bent.

It was not important to him that we were Jewish. He was a Social Democrat
and Dutch, and after that he happened to be Jewish. The fact that socialism
bound these people together was more important than any differences among
Catholics, Protestants, and Jews. The most important concerns were workers'
occupations, social conscience, and intellectual and cultural development.
They were terribly proud of the fact that Monne De Miranda became a city
commissioner.

◆ LIESBETH VAN WEEZEL
We were a totally assimilated family. The only thing was that there would be a
little JNF (Jewish National Fund) container or one for The Jewish Invalid on the
mantelpiece. We also got the little Keren Hayesod (United Israel Appeal) paper.
My father contributed, but it was almost like pulling teeth.

De Miranda was a diamond worker at one time. It wasn't long before he was
on the city council, and later he became a city commissioner, together with
Wibaut and Eedje (Eduard) Polak. But then he was also "a Jew with a head on
his shoulders" as they used to say. I recall that one of De Miranda's sons had a
birthday on Christmas, and there'd be a Christmas tree and all the children of
friends and acquaintances would be invited. We wouldn't have anything like that
at our house, a Christmas tree. I thought it was fabulous, though! All kinds of little gifts would be hanging on it, and the best thing, I thought, was that you were
allowed to "exchange" them. I didn't even know what the word meant. I had to
have somebody explain it to me. You were allowed, though, to swap one gift for
another if you weren't happy with yours, a bead necklace for a bar of soap or
something.

My parents were broad-minded enough that I was allowed to go over there,
but my father's response to the idea of having a Christmas tree at our house,
which I whined about, of course, was, "No, I won't have it!" He also didn't want
me to go to Sunday school, which was at the school complex across from where
we lived, when all my little girlfriends started going. I didn't understand why *I*
wasn't allowed to go. That was never explained very well, which wasn't very sat-
isfying, to my feeling.

Socialism wanted to drop the distinction between Jews and non-Jews. We also
followed that road, my brother very consistently even. He became communist
when the OSP split off from the SDAP in 1932. Down to the day of his death in
Dachau, he was a proponent of official Communism, of Stalinism.

All of this didn't take away from the fact that we were still interested in *Yiddishkayt*. There were some mixed marriages in our family, though, and we had almost completely grown away from being Jewish.

Still, there was one funny thing. When my father was in a really good mood on Sunday, he'd sit at the table with his shirtsleeves rolled up (which was the height of shamelessness!) and start singing psalms in Hebrew. That had such a profound effect on me as a child! It stirred something inside me that I didn't understand, so I'd walk out of the room. I couldn't bear to hear it!

◆ EDUARD VAN AMERONGEN
In the Plantage area, there were only public schools, no Jewish schools. On the Sabbath, there would be no school, though, because the students were mainly Jewish. That way you didn't feel at all like you were in *golah*. This kind of thing was typical of middle-class Jews in the Jewish districts of Amsterdam. This and the fact that they called Amsterdam the "Jerusalem of the West" showed that you could feel completely free there. And yet there were some disadvantages to that great freedom. There was a kind of assimilation, even among pious Jews.

Jews living in Eastern Europe, who belonged to a national minority, would steep themselves in Jewish history, Jewish literature, and Jewish values. Amsterdam Jews, though, went through a considerable equalizing process. The overwhelming majority of all those middle-class Jews who went along with the Liberal Union was against parochial schools on principle, and so against Jewish schools as well. Why should Jews have parochial schools? You were supposed to be equal.

◆ BERNARD VAN TIJN
In 1922, I was regularly in touch with Jo Spier, a young mathematician, who had just started college and was living in the Transvaal neighborhood. He was the son of a diamond worker who had always worked in the SDAP and the ANDB and had been on the union board for decades.

The Transvaal neighborhood was a "Red" neighborhood with "new-Jewish" leanings that the residents themselves were barely aware of. A large number of them believed in assimilation, and if they hadn't ended up in the same neighborhood actual assimilation would already at that time probably have been much greater. Considering that they lived all over that network of streets, though, it was natural for them to marry someone like themselves in the neighborhood. The residents didn't feel that the neighborhood was a ghetto, although it did have the characteristics of one. It was a voluntarily selected ghetto, but they weren't aware of its character as such.

There were a number of mixed marriages, among the Spiers as well. Their daughter married a non-Jew under the influence of the AJC. That was an elite outfit, because even though Jews outnumbered the others, it had no more than twelve thousand members all told.

Still, all the Transvaal residents, Zionist or not, felt they belonged together. For a while, for instance, there were eight or nine Jews on the city council from the Liberal factions, the Liberal Democratic League, and the Communist Party, but especially from the SDAP.

One of the members of this last party once told me despairingly, "Did you know we've got a *minyan* at city hall?"

However, the required number of men needed to "make a *minyan*" is ten, so I said, "I only come up with nine!" Some of them were a far cry from being Jewish. They were Jewish in name only.

So then he said, "Bonn's wife"—she was a non-Jew—"is assimilated, and we're counting women."

Bonn's wife had converted to Judaism, and later she even went to Israel with her husband.

◆ SIMON EMMERING
The father of my uncle Boekman, the city commissioner, was an antiquarian bookseller like myself. His son was a typical self-taught man, just like my father. He studied hard and, as far as I can remember, finished the better part of his studies before he got married. Years later, in 1939, my uncle Boekman got his Ph.D. with a dissertation entitled "Art and Government in the Netherlands." Originally, I think, he was a typesetter. Then he passed the postal service exam, and by way of that job he was able to continue his studies.

We thought it was quite an honor that there was an opportunity for Jews to move ahead, and that they were also proving that they were capable of doing so, taking on high positions like that, like my uncle Boekman and De Miranda did— particularly my uncle because he was a person who retained his Jewish sensibilities, I'm not sure about De Miranda.

My uncle was a Social Democrat. That's the dilemma Jews often live with, in my view. Getting "into" Dutch society, living the life of a Dutch person, but being able to stay Jewish at the same time! *This* man always did. His ties with his Jewishness were always there. In spite of his significant position as an Amsterdam commissioner, and in spite of his integration into the non-Jewish world, he always consciously remained a Jew. And in my view, that should be able to happen. Everywhere. Not just among Jews, but also among other people.

◆ LOE LAP
I recall when I was seventeen or eighteen, all kinds of friends came to our house. Sometimes there would be talk about Jews and non-Jews. My father used to say, "Everybody is welcome here, but anybody who wants to discuss that should do

me the favor of leaving, because I don't know any Jews and I don't know any non-Jews."

I thought this was incredibly amazing for that time. I never forgot it, either, because it was how he taught me that it was all utter nonsense and that it was time to finally get away from it.

On the other hand, the socialist movement had a lot of influence on the Jewish community. It was certainly a liberation for them. I can't imagine, either, where Jews came up with the "image" of "rich Jews," because on a percentage basis, Amsterdam Jews, certainly at that time, were the poorest group in Amsterdam. This wasn't because they were stupid or retarded or anything, but simply because they were behind in their overall social, cultural, and economic development.

I was in the Workers Sports Association. I swam at Sports Foundation Pool East. Our division was called "Friends of the Water." Those Sports Foundation guys rode around with election signs on their bikes with, say, Vote Slate 1 on them.[7]

To my father, Henri Polak was Jesus Christ. And the man knew it—many people felt that way. Henri Polak was the pride of Jewish people in Amsterdam.

◆ GERRIT BRUGMANS

My wife came from the Joden Houttuinen area. Her father worked at Kaas's in an old metals business on Zwanenburgwal. They worked hard, and they lived pretty well. They earned some three guilders a day. Myself, I worked at a little bakery on Muiderstraat, near Herengracht, De Groot's. I earned twelve guilders a week there plus a loaf of bread every day. I lived on Korte Koningstraat. That cost three guilders a week, so I still had nine guilders pocket money for the week. I was already married then.

My wife's parents weren't devout, but they were traditionally Jewish. Food was as kosher as possible. On *Shabbes,* my father-in-law sometimes went to shul. Well, on the corner of Jodenbreestraat and Marken Square there was a café, The Bishop. We'd have a couple of drinks there when they came out of shul, although they'd pay up the next day, not on *Shabbes.* The café owner would write a tab for them.

My wife worked on Achtergracht. And if you see a good-looking girl, you naturally try to talk with her. They always thought I was a *Yehudi*—guess I'm handsome, got a pretty good-looking ponum, right? And I used to go around with a lot of *Yids,* there. A Jewish guy worked at the bakery with me, and I was good friends with his sisters as well. So, the odds were I would meet a Jewish woman.

---

[7]In the Netherlands, the slates of candidates for each party are numbered, starting with the party that received the most votes in the previous election. In Amsterdam, Slate 1 was the slate of SDAP candidates.

Well, my wife worked on Achtergracht. That was very close, so that's how I ran into her.

Before that, I dated one of Gerritsen's daughters. He had a salted fish shop on Zeedijk and a stand at Nieuwmarkt in the old Fish Market. Well, I'd go out at night, right? Go down Zeedijk, together with some other boys—the street was a hotspot for nightlife, with dancehalls and all that. Gerritsen's would be open at one o'clock in the morning, so I'd go in and sit down, and that daughter of his was crazy about me. Her mother pretty much accepted me, on account of her daughter. I was eighteen or nineteen. But later, when she started asking around about me and heard I wasn't Jewish, the woman took me aside and told me, "Gerrit, you're a fine boy, and I don't have anything against you, but I just don't want my daughter marrying a man who's not Jewish. Before you two get too 'close,' I'd prefer to keep things from getting serious. Don't be angry with me, but we just don't want that kind of thing." So, that's how I was sidelined, see. But when you're eighteen, it doesn't hurt so much yet, it's all still a game.

I continued to work in that neighborhood, on Lepelstraat, and I got to know my wife. I wasn't allowed over to her house, of course, because her parents had heard from other people, "You're daughter's going out with a goy." At one point, her mother said, "You're meshugge! I've seen that boy and he's not a goy."

What can I say? I never had but Jewish friends, and my best buddy lived on Joden Houttuinen, near the bakery. I stayed friends with him my whole life until he died.

Anyhow, the relationship with my wife started getting serious. My mother pretty much accepted her, but her parents, it was awful when they found out we hadn't broken up. She had a life you wouldn't wish on anybody. She had almost nothing to eat, so I'd bring her to our house to eat with us. Her parents were people without much judgment or insight, but they'd still cling to *Yiddishkayt*. They wouldn't accept our relationship.

That wasn't an exception by any means. Particularly among ghetto Jews it was terrible if a daughter married a goy or a son a shiksa. In non-Jewish families also, they didn't want that kind of thing in those days. Jews were nice people, but you weren't supposed to be too tight with them.

◆ Jacob Soetendorp

How large the percentage was of Jewish men who married non-Jewish women completely escaped me when I was young because this was never talked about. In my more immediate family, there was nobody who was in a mixed marriage, and *if* that happened in traditional Jewish circles, it was always kept quiet.

My mother did object to the term "shiksa" that was used at the time. But the idea that I might bring a non-Jewish woman home was unthinkable. A cousin of mine showed up with a half-Jewish woman, and that's why his marriage couldn't be solemnized right away with the Orthodox Jewish congregation. There was this whole big fuss over that, they whispered about it endlessly.

So the fact that my immediate family wrapped the issue in a veil of secrecy already shows how it was regarded in traditional Jewish circles.

I don't know if all Jews in fact "sat shivah" if a son married a non-Jewish girl.[8] It's hardly possible considering the number of times that happened.

◆ WILHELMINA BIET-MEIJER

All the Christians you want were allowed to come to our house, boys and girls, and were allowed to stay overnight too, but the idea of a mixed marriage wouldn't have occurred to my parents because they were far too consciously Jewish, albeit not orthodox.

I recall that two cousins of mine were married to Christian girls. The family didn't like that. The girls were appreciated on their own because they were nice, but people preferred not to talk about it. It was still always something like, "Two faiths on a single pillow, the devil is sure to follow." That doesn't sound very Jewish, but it was very much like that.

◆ LOE LAP

I myself have a non-Jewish wife. My parents accepted the idea one hundred percent, but there were people around who thought it was a lousy idea. I wasn't allowed to go over to my in-laws' for two years. They wouldn't acknowledge me. That was hard on my wife. But when they got to know me, after those two years, they grew to love me like a son. They were born and raised Catholics. They came from Tiel. They really had no idea what a Jew was. They told stories down there, like: Watch out for Jews, I hear this and this, you know. Jews were alien to them. They didn't want their daughter marrying somebody like that. That's the way things were.

My parents had a positive opinion about the situation, though, accepting her as they would have accepted any girl. That wasn't the rule among Jewish families though. My father was already very progressive in his thinking for those days.

Even relatively "liberal" Jews didn't think a non-Jewish girl was the best thing for their son. The very best thing, of course, was to marry in the shul, have the *chuppah*, be dressed in white, just as it was the ideal for Catholics to have a church wedding with all the trimmings and to marry in white.

◆ NATHAN STODEL

I told my mother that I was dating a girl, and the first thing she asked me was, "Is she a Jewish girl?" I said, "Yes," and she said, "That surprises me," because

---

[8]To "sit *shivah*" is when one mourns the death of a close relative.

I went around with so many non-Jews in the communist, syndicalist, freethink-ing socialist circles, in short, with everybody that was in any way to the left of the SDAP. This is why on my wife's side of the family they said, "That boy's no good." But my mother was actually happy, because I think she wouldn't have liked it if it hadn't been a Jewish girl.

◆ ELISABETH VAN DE KAR-STODEL

My father would really have taken me to task if I had come home with a Christian boy. In spite of the fact that there were mixed marriages in my family and only a few people were orthodox in the extended family, we always thought a mixed marriage was dreadful. The ones who had married that way were the fifth wheels of the family.

◆ MARIUS GUSTAAF LEVENBACH

My mother did Jewish social work. She played a pretty major role in that area. She did a lot of things, including being chair of a Jewish association that dealt with child abuse called Misgab Layeled. Rabbi Sarlouis was on the board, and the board usually met at our house. But when I became engaged to a non-Jewish girl, Sarlouis didn't want to set foot in our house. So then they had to meet at one of the other board members' houses, and he hardly took notice of my mother anymore. That was Rabbi Sarlouis, *nebech*. He was deported too, of course, but he was a staunch one!

I had a cousin who thought it was a bad idea for me to marry some "little goy." One time, when we were engaged, we were visiting his parents, and all he could do was make nasty little comments and tease her by using all kinds of Jewish expressions. My wife didn't just put up with it though. She went straight to my mother and said, "Teach me some Jewish expressions, so I'll be able to talk to him." The next birthday over there, she had a whole series of those expres-sions, and she started saying them back at him with a real flair. He has adored her ever since.

◆ ALEXANDER VAN WEEZEL

When we were getting to know each other, I said to my wife, "I'm Jewish." And my wife replied, "That doesn't really make any difference to me. It doesn't mean anything to me." I wasn't specifically Jewish, because when I was younger I'd read *The Communist Manifesto* and Marx's *Das Kapital*. That's how I learned to see that the world doesn't just consist of Jews. For me, it's not the background that's important, it's how human a person is—human in the truest sense of the word.

My mother never made any noises. My father-in-law was working in the police force when we were engaged. One day, though, when I said, "We want to get married on such-and-such a date," he said, "I won't give my permission." So, I said, "I don't need your permission, I'll get permission from your boss."

◆ RUBEN GROEN

If you're in a mixed marriage, like I am, the Jewish faith as such usually gets watered down. My parents didn't like that idea at first, of course. It wasn't appreciated in 1935 and '36 in those totally Jewish families. Sometimes they'd say to me, "I don't understand you. Are all the Jewish girls on vacation or something?"

But my parents were very modern and liberal in their views, and they quickly reconciled themselves with it and accepted it completely. Still, other family members sometimes dropped a remark, because people were very close in those days—maybe less so nowadays because of the war, but at that time family ties were very strong.

We were sixteen when we started going together, and in the beginning, I did sense that something wasn't quite right. That's why we split up a few times. Later on, though, her family always received me with incredible kindness and warmth.

◆ JOHANNA LOUMAN-GROEN

You couldn't convert to Judaism in those days, or I'd have had to go to Germany, I think. If it had been possible, though, I would have done it.[9]

◆ RUBEN GROEN

My father was always socialist, and I was a member of the AJC at one time. At our house, it was SDAP this and SDAP that.

◆ SIMON GOSSELAAR

We had a group of friends, most of whom were AJC members. Jo Juda was among them. My wife was also a member of the AJC, and she worked as a sales clerk. There was a friend at work who asked her if she would like to come along for a weekend. That was in the town of Blaricum. Jo Juda was going play violin and Jaap Nunes Vaz, a reporter at the Vaz Dias press agency, later a member of the Resistance—he recited poems beautifully—-was going to be there. He was the only one who'd been to high school.

Anyway, that's where I got to know my wife. We would always bike there on Saturdays from Amsterdam, and be back Sunday evening. Gradually she became my girl. The fact that she wasn't Jewish was considered very normal because in those days there were lots and lots of mixed marriages.

---

[9]It was possible, but the Dutch Orthodox Congregation required lengthy study, which was not the case with the German Reform.

Our families were just about the same. They were all workers, see. Many of our friends were in mixed marriages. The funny thing is that the non-Jewish partners were more assimilated into Jewish culture than the other way around as far as the whole atmosphere goes, the humor, and so on.

◆ Toos La Grouw-Gosselaar

I was a salesgirl in a business where quite a few Jewish girls worked. When they heard that I was going out with a Jewish boy, I rose in their esteem, especially when they noticed that I understood Jewish jokes and expressions.

I also had to get used to the food. The first time I saw lentil soup, I thought: What kind of sludge is this? And those arguments, so good-natured, there'd always be a joke to smooth things over. And chicken soup every Friday. My family certainly couldn't afford to have chicken soup every Sunday.

VI

ENTERTAINMENT AND
RECREATION

Many producers and consumers of both light and serious art before the war were Jewish. It is no coincidence that around 1900 two of the major hot spots for Amsterdam nightlife, the Rembrandt Square-Amstelstraat area and the Plantage area, bordered directly on the Old Jewish Quarter. The Paleis voor Volksvlijt on Fredriksplein was also close to the Jewish neighborhoods. In Amsterdam, it was common knowledge that once diamond workers were earning reasonably well, many of them liked to spend their leisure time at the theater and the opera, at cabaret shows and concerts.

When movies began to supplant theater during the 1920s, a night out at Abraham Tuschinski's opulent movie house was a special attraction for many Jews.

There was no such thing as an especially Jewish art form in Amsterdam, however. Cabarets devoted to presenting Yiddish songs, or theaters specializing in plays with a Jewish orientation did not exist in prewar Amsterdam. Even the Tip Top Cinema on Jodenbreestraat hardly ever presented specifically Jewish shows.

How "un-Jewish" the taste of the Jewish public was is revealed by the great popularity among Jews of Beethoven's *Fifth Symphony*, Bach's *St. Mathew Passion*, Bizet's opera *Carmen*, not to mention the Vienna Boys' Choir.

Things were slightly different where it concerned sports. There were types of sports that were practiced particularly by Jews, such as boxing and gymnastics, through Jewish clubs and otherwise. Consequently many Amsterdam Jews numbered among the Dutch national boxing and gymnastics champions. Some of the gymnastics clubs were not officially Jewish, although the majority of their members were.

Theater and Music

◆ JO JUDA

My grandfather was a cobbler. He had one of those little places below street level in the Jewish Quarter. He just loved music, and he was very modern for his day because he'd go to Wagner operas. He was crazy about them. How he got into doing that, I don't understand, because there was never enough money. They were dirt poor. They all lived in one room somewhere in the Jewish Quarter just like all the other families. But he'd go to the opera. He'd go to hear Wagner, and he really knew all his operas, particularly *Tannhäuser* and *Lohengrin*.

At that time—certainly among plain everyday people, which my parents were—they believed that socialism would come because Marx had said it would. And sometimes they'd dream about the "socialist utopia" being a reality. One of my uncles, Uncle Jaap, used to say, "It'll be great! We'll always be able to go to the opera for free!" He was a real opera lover too.

◆ ARON DE PAAUW

Diamond polishers were an extremely lively bunch, so an opera was a real party! During intermission, people would of course be discussing the singers. They wouldn't talk in terms of this character or that one, no, it would be, "What did you think of the tenor?" or "What did you think of the soprano?" And then the performer would either be criticized or praised, the way you criticize soccer players. It was marvelous!

I never saw diamond polishers go to the opera with their hands still dirty from the factory. But they did go out a lot.

They also sang a lot at the polishing plant. If they'd been out of work for a couple of months or so, it wouldn't take more than an hour or two of being back at the factory before they'd be singing again. Some of them had really good voices, too. Of course people always criticized them as well, but still, people liked hearing them.

Then there was the Wagner Society here in Amsterdam. It celebrated its twenty-fifth anniversary in 1920 or 1923, and they invited a French opera company to perform *Carmen*. The entire diamond-polishing world was in an uproar with everybody crowding the box office to get tickets. They weren't cheap, but people were earning, and they spent money easily, certainly on this kind of thing.

One time I had a ticket for a seat all the way in the top balcony on the side. I couldn't see even half the stage, but I could hear the singing! The singers were accompanied by the Concertgebouw Orchestra, with Pierre Monteux conducting. It was a magnificent evening.

Now, you know there were always a lot of celebrities that visited Asscher's diamond factory, royalty and VIPs and so forth. The day after that performance, the opera singer who had sung the role of Carmen came to the factory, and when she crossed the hall to look at diamonds, they applauded her from all sides. So, Kleerekooper, the one who wrote the "Rebellious Scribbles" column in *Het Volk*, wrote in one of his "Scribbles" that she had said one of the highlights of her career had been when they had recognized her and applauded her at the diamond factory.

There were even people there who knew operas from beginning to end, and after a performance they'd go and sing it themselves.

◆ KAREL POLAK

My brother sang in the opera. He always had small parts. When he was on stage, he would look out into the audience to see where the empty seats were. If I were standing out in the corridor of Carré or the Paleis voor Volkvlijt during intermission, he'd come over to me and say, "Karel, there's still a seat in such-and-such a row." So, I would get to see half the opera. It had to be free because I couldn't afford it.

I saw the Paleis burn down to the ground. I was living on Utrechtsedwarsstraat. My brother came home around midnight and woke me up. "Get up! Get up! The Paleis is on fire!" Only small flames were to be seen at that point. We stayed up all night and watched as the Palace's huge cupola collapsed with a tremendous crash, and suddenly it was all just a piece of molten metal. I'll remember that all my life.

I saw an awful lot in that place, though, like the operetta *De koningin van Montmartre* (The Queen of Montmartre), which was something fantastic for that time.

◆ AARON VAZ DIAS

At Hanukkah, the Jewish Temple dedication ceremony, the Jewish teachers' association always organized big celebrations for the children. There would be performances of three-act plays that I always took part in. The festivities would be held at the Plantage Schouwburg on Franschelaan (now Henri Polaklaan). Usually at the end, *De Bruiloft van Kloris en Roosje* (The Wedding of Kloris and Rosie) would be performed.

It happened that on my mother's side of the family I had this uncle called Sam who married Aunt Rosie. Together with all the family members, we put on a performance of *The Wedding of Sam and Rosie,* complete with costumes and text about events from their lives.

◆ Sylvain Albert Poons

In the Plantage area, there were the Hollandsche Schouwburg, the Plantage Schouwburg, and many other theaters. It was a theater district. Amstelstraat was also a theater district, and had Flora, the Grand Theater, and the Central Theater (which used to be called Panopticum). Well, if Amstelstraat filled up, which it always did down there, people would go farther afield. They'd go to the Plantage area.

Operas and operettas were put on at the Rembrandt Theater, which is now the Caransa Hotel. They had a choir of beautiful voices, all *Yids:* Koster, Levison, Waterman, you name it. One evening, Meyerbeer's opera *Les Huguenots* was being performed, and a diamond polisher and his wife were sitting in the very back row.

His wife says, "Bram, what's it supposed to be about anyway?"

So, Bram says, "It's the struggle between the Catholics and the Protestants."

To which his wife replies, "Well, what do you know, I thought they were all *Yids.*"

Before I was with Heijermans, I performed in a lot of operettas at Flora. Then I received word that I was to go to Heijermans' office, and I was engaged on a trial basis.

I had a tremendous respect for that man. As a boy, I'd always read his books. I completely idolized him. For me, he was a man with a slouch hat, a cloak, and long hair and everything. When I arrived at his office, I saw a fat little man with short straight hair and bulging eyes. He really scared me.

We performed *Een kostbaar leven* (A Precious Life), arranged and adapted by Heijermans, and I happened to play a Jewish role in it. After fourteen days, I had to go down to his office. I'm thinking: "I'm out. It's all wrong." Heijermans was there waiting for me, and he said, "Mr. Poons, did you bring your contract with you?"

I say, "Yes, Mr. Heijermans."

"May I have it for a minute?" And he crossed out the seventy-five guilders trial pay for that month and made a year of it, then raised the salary to a hundred guilders per month. That was my first major artistic triumph.

He had two troupes at the time. The one with the biggest names, like Hubert La Roche, a famous Belgian actor who'd fled to the Netherlands, played at the Holland Theater. We played at the Grand Theater on Amstelstraat.

It wasn't a very rosy time because Heijermans was up to his ears in debt, although in terms of accomplishment, more was demanded of performers then than nowadays. Acting was done more from the gut, not technically.

The stage actors went on strike once. Heijermans was at The Golden Head, on the corner of Bakkersstraat and Rembrandt Square, eating chicken at a table by a window. The striking actors were standing in front of the restaurant in little groups, watching. When Heijermans came out after his meal, they said, "Mr. Heijermans, it's shameful. We're standing here on strike and you. . . ."

And he said, "I know, but I have to eat, don't I?"

◆ HERMINE HEIJERMANS
The famous Jewish actor Louis De Vries, who was the president of the Hollandsche Schouwburg, was a very good friend of my father's. What he had in common with Querido was that if they disagreed with him, they could both tell my father the truth without beating around the bush. He took that from them.

Louis De Vries also performed in *Schakels* (Cogs) and in *Ghetto*, which was quite an achievement.

There was a glorious public at the time. Everybody would hang over the railing at the very back. Those were the workers. They stood. They'd get so caught up in what was being performed. They had an instinct for the differences among the popular plays, like Adolphe d'Ennery's *Les Deux Orphelines* (The Two Orphans) and *Zwarte Griet* (Black Meg), which ran at Plantage Badlaan. Those were the so-called volks plays, the popular plays, like *Het kind van de buurvrouw* (The Neighbor Lady's Child). These were sentimental plays, the tear-jerkers of the time, and the workers didn't know any better either. But they started discovering that my father was a real person who didn't present sentimentality, just reality. That's why they were nuts about him.

It was the mixed proletariat that went to the theater, both Jews and non-Jews. The negative description of the Jewish ghetto my father wrote was meant to wake up the people in the ghetto, to lead the people who read it to socialist transformation of society. If he points out their dirtiness, he means to say that a life like that isn't human.

"This will ruin you all. *See* that, why don't you, and resist the conditions under which you live!" And it actually worked.

My father wrote his roles "for" the actors, the same way Molière did. In his mind, he'd see the actress Esther De Boer as Eva Bonheur or Kniertje, or Angel in *Het zevende gebod* (The Seventh Commandment). That was psychologically brilliant on his part because she was, in fact, a very multifaceted person, very charming on the one hand and a bitch on the other (The Razor was her nickname), but sentimental. She'd do anything for her family. She came from a very Jewish family. She was a great actress, the intuitive kind. She understood each of Father's intentions, the humble Knier, the shrill Eva Bonheur, and Angel, that landlady in *Het zevende gebod* who makes life hell for the student and his girlfriend.

My father's work most certainly had an influence. For instance, the government shipping inspection agency was "in the dog house" as far as the Lower House was concerned, but *The Good Hope* got things going. His fight against hypocrisy and middle-class conventionality generally gave him an enormous following among people who felt frustrated by society, people who thought that something was wrong.

At a certain point, people claimed there was going to be war—the First World War—so, my father said, "We'll go to Schiller's so we can flee the moment we're occupied." We stayed at that hotel for four years. Our furniture was in storage, and in fact we were constantly at the point of leaving.

Schiller was so completely nuts about real artists that he gave my father large amounts of credit. Then war broke out, and my mother started hoarding. At one point, she bought flour and started baking loaves of bread, up in those rooms, on the kerosene stove. I'll never forget it. Schiller would knock on the door, and she'd say, "Shhh!" because the dough would be rising and if he slammed the door, it would cave in. He'd come in with his hand, fingers spread, in front of his eyes.

We celebrated Christmas there with enormous trees. My mother would bake and fry. We had an enormous circle of acquaintances, so all kinds of people would stop by, including the writers who wrote the plays that my father directed, like Adama Van Scheltema, Kees Van Bruggen, and even J. C. Schröder, who was called Barbarossa. Actresses like Julia Cuypers, who was performing in his production of *l'Aiglon* (The Eaglet), came too.

The Grand Theater was halfway down Amstelstraat where there's a bank now. After an opening night, my father always took just about the entire company along, like Jan Musch and Mrs. Van der Horst. The famous pianist Frédéric Lamond also went there. He was interned during the war because he was a Scotsman.[1]

◆ HARTOG GOUBITZ

There was some progress. Incomes were a little better, and the labor unions thought that workers had to educate themselves. All that had an effect on a person, you know. It made you go out and do uplifting things that were outside of your everyday life.

I remember the first Beethoven cycle. Whenever I could, I'd go to the Concertgebouw. The public concerts cost next to nothing, right? They were subsidized, and for a quarter you could go to a public concert on a Sunday evening. The first concert I ever went to, I listened to from the gate outside the Concertgebouw. There used to be a garden out there, where they built houses later. It was the same at the Paleis voor Volksvlijt. If you didn't have money to go

---

[1]During World War I, citizens of the countries at war were interned in the then neutral Netherlands.

to a concert but you wanted to hear music, you could stand at the gate and still hear it. It cost nothing. You'd be what they called a "gate subscriber."

◆ Jo Juda
We lived on Graaf Florisstraat, and Max Tak was our upstairs neighbor. When I was two or three, my mother used to take me for walks, pushing me in the carriage. One time we ran across Max Tak and a couple of his friends on the corner of Graaf Florisstraat and Weesperzijde. They all had violin cases, except for one who had a really big case, a cellist, of course. They were on their way to Max Tak's, so my mother immediately turned around and we went back home. Those people were going to play a quartet, so my mother sat and listened to them. She just sat there. I thought they were playing for an awfully long time up there.

At a certain point, my father came home, and usually by that time my mother had the table set and dinner ready. But this time she hadn't done a thing. She had just sat there listening.

So my father comes home and says, "Leentje, isn't it time to eat?"

My mother just pointed upstairs.

Then he heard it too, and went and sat down to listen as well, still wearing his coat and hat, until they had finished playing. I still remember that very well.

My parents went to the public concerts if they had the money. It cost a quarter, so two quarters for two. These were Sunday evening performances, and the hall would be full of diamond polishers. Monday morning at the factory, they'd go on and on about what they had heard. Willem Mengelberg was hugely popular among the diamond polishers, and Mengelberg conducting Beethoven was absolutely tops. When I was a boy, I also identified Mengelberg with Beethoven.

I remember I wasn't allowed into a concert because the door attendant thought I was too young. "How old is he?" he asked my father.

My father said, "Hmmm, ten." I was eight and my father wasn't a very good liar.

So then the door attendant said, "Well, he has to be twelve years old, sir, so I'm not allowed to let him in."

My father said that we had come a long way and that I was so musical and also played violin, and that it would be such a big disappointment. So, we were allowed in anyway.

At one point, somebody, a violinist who often played for Mengelberg, was playing by himself, and my father whispered, "That's Louis Zimmermann." I'd already heard that name a lot at home, so then I looked at that Louis Zimmermann with even bigger eyes. I thought it was absolutely fantastic. When they were done, Louis Zimmermann stood up, and Mengelberg shook his hand, at which Zimmermann started bowing to the audience. The applause didn't stop.

He was beaming, as if he'd received the most beautiful gift. That's what I thought back then.

I also heard Hubermann. That must have been during the First World War or right after, at the Holland Theater. They had lots of concerts there. All during the intermission, we kept running into friends of my father's. They were all beside themselves with enthusiasm. Hubermann later also became one of my favorites.

◆ HUBERTUS PETRUS HAUSER

I'm a Catholic, and the Moses and Aaron Church was our parish. We had permanent seats there with our name plate on them, the way it used to be done.

One time the Vienna Boys' Choir sang there. It turned out that hardly a single Catholic could get into the church because it was full of Jews who had come to listen to the Vienna Boys' Choir. They had all taken one-guilder seats. This was very unusual and really the priest's fault. A certain seating section in the church was rented to regular parishioners like us for the year. The rest of the seats were rented separately. He had sold so many tickets that the regular parishioners couldn't get in anymore.

The Jews were crazy about the Vienna Boys' Choir. It *was* tremendous that the group came to sing right in the heart of the Jewish Quarter, for just a guilder at that. What more could you want? To go to the Concertgebouw, you had to pay three or four guilders.

◆ EDUARD VAN AMERONGEN

There was an annual performance of Bach's *St. Mathew Passion* conducted by Mengelberg. It was on Sunday afternoon and the public concert was on Saturday evening.

There happened to be lots of devout Jews who were very interested in music and they would go Saturday evening. The performance would start at seven-thirty, though. The Sabbath wouldn't be over yet then, and they were bound to the laws of the Sabbath. So they would go to the synagogue closest to the Concertgebouw, on Jacob Obrechtstraat. They would do *havdalah* there—celebrate the end of the Sabbath—after which they were allowed to do whatever they wanted to do. Usually, though, they'd be too late for the beginning with its opening chorus, so right after the opening chorus, the doors would open and they would be let in.

The vice-rector of the Jewish seminary, Dr. De Jongh, would be in the lead, followed by the seminarians, cantors, all very devout people with beards. There'd be some ten or twenty men. It was very interesting to see that procession of devout Jews at the *St. Mathew Passion* on Saturday night. That was something unique and unheard of anywhere in the world, and typical of the Jews in Amsterdam.

◆ MEIJER MOSSEL

I went to the *St. Mathew Passion* once, I think, because the whole seminary was going. I could see our vice-rector sitting there with the entire score in front of him. It did make for bad blood sometimes, because strictly orthodox boys thought you really couldn't go hear it if you were a Jew, since it was an anti-Semitic text.

I was still young, and I thought my vice-rector was really something because he could easily follow every note in the score of the *St. Mathew Passion*. I knew him as a rabbi who had a doctorate in classical literature.

◆ SALKO HERTZBERGER

I looked through the text of the *St. Mathew Passion,* and particularly in the beginning it contains veiled anti-Semitic allusions, typical in the sense of creating distance between Jewish and non-Jewish population groups. I also saw at the time how utterly dubious it was for a Jew living with positive Jewish feelings to perform this piece in public. I thought it was a terrible business, and lots of fellow students and others of my age did too.

This was while I was at grammar school, 1936–37. We started waging very radical Zionist politics. We thought going to the performance was a form of assimilation, of integration, particularly among devout Jews, although in fact they didn't bring that up very positively at all.

Theo Van Raalte made up a satirical "National Hymn for Jewish Dutchmen" for the Zionist student organization on the occasion of the Hanukkah celebration. It went like this:

> *We Jewish Dutchmen of every rank and station*
> *We want to give our best for fatherland and nation*
> *We Jewish Dutchmen, through Torah and tradition,*
> *Are to our very marrow united with Holland,*
> *United with Holland.*

There's a certain amount of humor in it. It's a rich little song. These were the kind of Jewish Dutchmen who went to hear the *St. Mathew Passion*, preferably wearing their little skullcaps, of course! They weren't ashamed of being Jewish, but for the rest they were diametrically opposed to what the radical young Zionists were bringing up.

Zionist students were very much against it.

◆ DAVID RICARDO

The fact that *I* went to the *St. Mathew Passion* is no big deal, but the fact that
the wife of the chief rabbi also went maybe throws another light on the issue. My
mother went, and I went with my wife. The year before we went to Israel, I heard
it again at Easter at a church in the town of Naarden.

It's the music. The rest doesn't interest me. I had a friend in Israel, a doctor,
very learned, and an extremely devout man, Premsela, Meyer Premsela. He lived
on Herengracht in Amsterdam. He went to it every year too. And Professor Leo
Seligmann from Jerusalem, who is still very devout, also went every year to the
St. Mathew Passion. Nobody ever said anything against it, which does underline
how extremely liberal the opinions of devout Amsterdam Jews were. My father
always said, "I'd like to go too, but it's forbidden for a devout Jew to hear
women sing."

It's really part of a good education, a bit of *St. Mathew Passion*.

The Lighter Muse

◆ Ruben Groen
My father and both my grandfathers were diamond workers. I was a very musical child, and when I was five, someone in the family brought me a violin. When I was seven, I took lessons, and I started playing pretty well on that thing. When I was nine, the milkman, who came to our door every day and knew that I played violin, said to my father, "Why not let the boy try out for our brass band?" So, off to the brass band I go. It practiced at the dry docks on Meeuwenlaan every Friday evening in the canteen. I went over there with the milkman, who played trombone. I think I was the only Jew playing in that band at the time.

Then I had to learn how to play clarinet. I started taking lessons from one of the band members who lived on the other side of the North Holland Canal. I went there faithfully with my clarinet, which belonged to the band, and then I had my violin lessons too. When I was fourteen, I was already first solo clarinetist.

Entertainment appealed to me the most, though, and that's what I finally went into. From the money I earned, I gave my mother money for room and board, naturally saving up the rest so I could get married. I also bought an alto saxophone. I was sixteen by that time, and we put together a band, with Jonas Van den Berg, who had a grocery store on Korte Houtstraat. He played violin. Then there was a drummer, that was Leendert Porcelein, and a trumpet player, Sal Bremer, who lived near me. He was going to the conservatory.

I was a diamond worker. It happened a lot at the polishing plants that people did other things besides. I worked at the Lamon firm, and above us was the Goudvis firm, where the well-known Lex Goudsmit worked, along with Meyer Hamel, who later wrote vaudeville shows.

Later on I performed at Marigny. That was on Rembrandt Square. Two orchestras played there. Later it was called The New Karseboom. That's when my father bought me my first pair of dress trousers and a smoking jacket, because I was hired to be in a gypsy band at Marigny. That happened when I hit the "music exchange" at The Crown on Rembrandt Square. All the musicians and performers went there to pick up *snabbels* (gigs on the side). You could often get a snabbel while playing billiards. Everybody knew everybody else. Lots of Jewish performers went there. Sixty percent of the music world at that time was made up of Jews.

◆ JOOP EMMERIK

In my time, 1926–28, there were entertainment societies where you'd go dancing. You had Handwerkers Vriendenkring (Craftmen's Fellowship), the upstairs place on Roetersstraat. Downstairs there was a large ballroom we often went to for formal dances on Saturday nights. You could have three or four drinks there for one guilder.

Concordia was where the Weesper Square Hospital is now. Concordia made way for a new building designed for The Jewish Invalid, which in turn became Weesper Square Hospital after the Second World War. Before all that, though, it was Concordia, across from the Diamond Exchange. They would rent the space out for parties and political events.

The orchestra there was always made up of Jews. Ab Witteboon, who also used to play with the AVRO radio dance orchestra, played piano there. They played contemporary dance music, Charleston and Black Bottom.

◆ GERRIT BRUGMANS

What good times we had at the Tip Top! People would sit there and eat a bag of *kesause mangelen* (peanuts) they'd picked up on Jodenbreestraat. They'd eat them while they watched a movie. A bag like that cost four cents, and I'd stand around on the corner of Jodenbreestraat, eating them with friends under a street lamp.

◆ BAREND KROONENBERG

The Tip Top Cinema opened in 1914. It got off to a good start right away. It was always sold out because there wasn't much entertainment going on in that part of town. After a few months, the First World War broke out. That was a big setback, but as the conflict wore on, business slowly picked up again.

A few years later, the Tuschinski Theater opened, which was tremendous, of course—the interior was particularly exceptional. The well-to-do started going to the Tuschinski, and afterward they always said they felt like they'd "really gone out." My father thought the interior of the Tuschinski was so beautiful that he had the Tip Top remodeled in the same style. After that it ran as it had before.

On the other side of the Blue Bridge, there was Flora and the Central Theater and other attractions, but on the Waterlooplein side there weren't any nightspots. There was a little movie house on Rapenburg, one on Weesperstraat, East Movie House, and then Rubens Movie House, but that had to go because of competition from the Tip Top, which ran two shows including variety shows.

If you had an afternoon off, you'd ask a couple of friends if they felt like going down to the Tip Top Cinema with you. In those days, it cost a quarter to get in, which people could just manage to pay, and the whole afternoon would be taken care of.

A lot of very well-known performers played at our place, including Lou Bandy, Willy Derby, Kees Pruys, Stella Fonteyn, Bigoni and Isalbert, and last but not least "Little Caruso," Bob Scholte, who's still an active performer. He was a tremendous success for us. He packed the house for months on end. Isalberti was a very famous tenor and one of the most famous opera singers in the world. They all performed at our place!

One day my father heard a singer in Italy, at the Scala in Milan, named Bigoni. My father thought he sang so beautifully that he went up to him and asked him to come perform in the Netherlands. He agreed and gave my father a contract for February 29, eighteen months later. My father had completely forgotten about that contract, and he hired the great singer Isalberti for February 29. To his great dismay, Bigoni honored his contract and reported two days ahead of time. "What now?" thought my father, because this was all going to cost him a lot of money. Then he got the idea to have the baritone Isalberti and the tenor Bigoni sing opera duets together. For months, he was sold out!

One week we ran a Jewish film entitled *Yidl mit'n Fidl,* which was filmed in Poland. That week there was a woman in the house who was going to the movies for the first time in her life. She was Polish. She heard them speaking Polish on the screen and during intermission she came up to me and asked, "Mr. Kroonenberg, would you do me a favor?"

I say, "Which is?"

"I'd like to shmooze a little with them!"

At which I say, "With who?"

She says, "With those people I saw on the screen!"

I couldn't talk her out of this notion she had. She thought that these people were standing on the stage. She just couldn't understand it at all!

Of course we also had a time when we played silent movies that were accompanied by an announcer who explained things. He would speak while the images played on the screen. One time in one of those movies, the countess pulls the count close, and the announcer says, "The countess whispered into the count's ear . . .," and at the same time we happened to hear a shout coming through the cinema doors, "I've got sweet prime pears!" Or somebody on the screen would give somebody a kiss, and you'd hear somebody shout, "They be tasty!"

Occasionally somebody would knock on the door and then shout, "Mamma, the potatoes are boiling!" Sometimes somebody would ask Mr. Hes, the doorman, "Mr. Hes, would you be so kind as to get my husband for me? I've got an urgent message for him."

So the doorman would go inside and walk down the aisles with a flashlight. He knew everybody, and if he saw the fellow sitting there, he'd say, "Sir, would you step outside for a moment?"

Then the wife might say (I actually heard this!), "David, there's a message from the factory that they have work. You have to start this afternoon!" The man was a diamond worker. So, they went straight to work from the cinema.

There were also times when there wasn't anything to be earned. During the Depression, the 1930s, many people were unemployed, so my father organized morning shows for them. They'd have to hand in a coupon from a packet of margarine, and then they could go in.

◆ LOE LAP

Sylvain Poons also performed at the Tip Top, just like Heintje Davids, and bigger performers, like Bouwmeester. Whenever they showed a movie, there'd also be a half an hour of cabaret. That was done all over the Netherlands. They all performed at the Royal Cinema, too, Kees Pruis, Willy Derby.

At the Tip Top, they'd toss plenty of Yiddish words around on the stage to please the audience because people loved to hear a little of their own language. Most of them did that, but then every performer spoke as much Yiddish as the Jews. It was the language of show people, used at Schiller's Cafe too.

◆ HIJMAN (BOB) SCHOLTE

The conductor of the Jewish choir I sang in was Mr. Koopman. He had a drug store on Nieuwe Kerkstraat.

One day he asked me if I'd sing some Jewish songs at some society party, because I only knew Jewish songs. That night a Jewish dance instructor also came, Jules Monas, who heard me sing, and the next day he went to Bram Godschalk, a well-known impresario in Amsterdam. He said, "Uncle Bram, yesterday evening I heard a boy with a beaut of a voice. There's money to be made with him. He sings at the shul on Rapenburgerstraat."

That man came to hear me at the shul, and then he went to my father to convince him to let me sing on stage. I thanked my lucky stars that this happened, because I didn't want to sing at shul anymore. I wanted to become an opera singer, hit the "big stage." At first, my father didn't want to hear about it because he'd have liked to see his son become *chazzan*. But I begged and pleaded, and finally he gave in.

I appeared at the age of fourteen in Franz Léhar's operetta *Der Rastelbinder* (The Tinker) at Carré. I received a fabulous review, which said, "The directors of the operetta company Nap De la Mar have provided an anonymous fourteen-year-old with flowers and success. He has a beautiful voice, and we think he will be tomorrow's Caruso."

Fien De la Mar, Nap's daughter, made her debut in that same operetta, along with me. She had to play my fiancée. She was sixteen and I was fourteen, and at rehearsal she suddenly turned to her father, to Nap, and said, "Dad, do I have to sing with that little boy?" And her father replied, "Yes, you have to sing with that little boy, and if you sing as nicely as that little boy, you'll make me very happy, Fien!" That was how I got to know Fien De la Mar.

After that, I was hired by Jozef Kroonenberg, the owner of the Tip Top Cinema. He profited from that "Caruso review," and on every poster he put, "Performance by the Little Caruso." Ever since that time, I've had the nickname "The Little Caruso."

I performed twice, fifteen minutes in the afternoon and fifteen minutes in the evening. I couldn't sing longer because this was during the break between two features. In those days, a lot of great performers could be seen there, a different one every week. The fact that I was a boy from their own neighborhood of course attracted big audiences. The house I was born in was only fifty yards away on Houtkopersburgwal. At least ninety of the hundred people sitting in the theater spoke Yiddish. I sang popular songs.

Nap De la Mar had a vaudeville company in addition to the operetta company I performed with. I also participated in the show *Had-je-me-maar* (If-You-Could-Only-Catch-Me) named after that well-known street character back then. They had a song and it went like this:

> *If-You-Could-Only-Catch-Me with a two-guilder bribe,*
> *If-You-Could-Only-Catch-Me with a little coaxing on the side . . .*

Louis Davids, he was at the peak of his career then, was in that too, as were Fien De la Mar and Emmy Arboes.

Later I sang all kinds of Max Tak songs. In 1914, I was already singing "Amsterdam, Nothin' Even Comes Close to You" for the radio and for a record. And "Under the Trees of Rembrandt Square" and "Girlfriend" which he wrote together with Alex De Haas.[2]

◆ SYLVAIN ALBERT POONS

I played a Chinese peanut vendor in a show at the Grand Theater that I was in together with Henriëtte Davids. Jaap Spijer was sitting in the audience, the one

---

[2]The original Dutch titles of the songs listed are, in order: "Amsterdam, er is toch niks wat ook maar effe an je tippen kan," "Onder de bomen van het plein," "Vriendinnetje."

who later directed *De Jantjes* (Sailor Boys), and he said, "I have to have those two for the movie."

Moviemaking as a profession was "brought" here by German emigrants. These directors were usually Jewish. It was in 1934 that they came, and they were usually hired right away by various entrepreneurs and cinema operators to direct films. Movies were being made before that time, but the boom really hit when they started fleeing from Germany. Some went to the U.S., and others ended up staying here.

Spijer was Dutch by birth, but he always worked as a director in Berlin. He started working here as well. The pioneer, though, was Alex Benno. He hit up all the cinema operators to collect money for *De Jantjes*. He must have gotten fifty thousand guilders together, which was a lot of money, but in the middle of shooting, it evidently wasn't enough. It was the first talking film. Nobody wanted it. Then Barnstein, the film producer who was going to produce the movie, gave all those operators their money back, and he started doing it himself. He made a quarter of a million on it.

◆ WILHELMINA BIET-MEIJER

The Nelson Cabaret came to the Netherlands very early on, because they did political cabaret in Germany. It wasn't until 1939, when they were putting on a new show ever two weeks, that I first saw them. The Nelson Cabaret also had some non-Jewish members, like Harold Horsten.

The Emigration Department people were occasionally invited to go to a show for free at Gaité, which was above the Tuschinski. Once they also organized an entire evening for the Refugee Committee. They were incredibly spiritual. Their songs were timeless.

Rudolf Nelson was the director. His son Herbert Nelson performed as well, along with Fritz Schadel, Dora Paulsen, and Harold Horsten, and they performed in German.

There was also another German cabaret, with Franz Engel and Ehrlich. It wasn't as sharp as the Nelsons. During the war, when Jews were prohibited from going to the theater, you could still go to a cabaret. They performed at the Holland Theater, with Heintje Davids joining them.

The Nelsons had a lot more "spirit." There was a song, for instance, by Harold Horsten in German about boots coming closer. That got you right down to the bone. They weren't as political as Erika Mann's Pfeffermühle (Pepper Mill) troupe, but they did expose things.[3]

---

[3]Erika Mann (1905–1969), daughter of Thomas Mann, left Germany in 1933. Her theatre troupe Pfeffermühle performed anti-Nazi political cabaret in Holland and the United States.

During the summer months, the Nelsons had no jobs, so they would get support from the Refugee Committee and have to go pick up their money every week. I'd think, "That must never happen to me," because I knew that I would never want to emigrate, would never dare or want to flee the country.

I recall that they had a song they sang, in German like most of their songs, where they'd sing with their shirtsleeves rolled up: *Lieber Teller waschen in Amerika, als Angst haben in Deutschland* (It's better washing dishes in America than being scared in Germany), and I thought, "No, never!" That was probably my pride.

Sports

◆ Joël Cosman

A specifically Jewish boxing association called The Young Boxer was set up in Amsterdam. It came out of the KDO wrestling and power sports association. I became a member of The Young Boxer, and we trained in a space behind a cafe on Rapenburg. After the First World War, a boxer by the name of "Battling Sikhy" came to the Netherlands. He boxed in a match at the Concertgebouw, I think, got to know a Dutch girl, and stayed. We managed to convince him to teach the boys in The Young Boxer.

The popularity of boxing as a sport was on the wane mostly because boxing was banned in Amsterdam. No public matches were allowed, but that's just propaganda, right? That's how you get more members. Mayor De Vlugt was strictly opposed. A rift developed in The Young Boxer, too, and that's when I left to set up my own club, Olympia, in 1928.

The first year I had two good students in Olympia and that same year they also became champions of the Netherlands, Appie De Vries and Ben Bril. When Ben Bril became Dutch champion, he wasn't even sixteen yet, but the Dutch Boxing Federation didn't know any better than to think he was. He was allowed to participate in the Olympics in Amsterdam as a flyweight.

During his first match, he won in the first round with a KO. That was on his sixteenth birthday too.

In those days, boxing was practiced mostly by poor boys. There wasn't any entertainment, television didn't exist yet, people often couldn't afford to go to the movies, and the contribution to our club was pretty low, ten cents a week. They thought it was great that they could train three times a week. That was their opportunity to broaden themselves. Obviously most of them came from real working-class families, people who had it bad, especially in the winter.

Before they fought a match, I'd often hunt up people who were a little more middle class who'd let the boys go and eat at their place for a couple of days before the match so they could gain some strength. Boxing became so popular among the Jews that storekeepers and people who had it pretty good supported us and also often gave the boys clothes.

The boys in my club weren't active in politics. For them, engaging in sports was their outlet, their way of getting out of the daily grind. If they could excel in sports, they had a chance to have their moment in the sun, which they wouldn't have had otherwise because they always lived in the shadows.

Boxing is not a rough sport where guys punch each other out like most people think. It's a sport of defense, where you have to make sure you receive as few punches as possible. You achieve this through technical control, going along with a punch that connects, footwork, reacting well. In boxing, technique is very important because you're standing at such a short distance from each other that a punch flashes toward you and you have to react in the same instant to avoid it or take it.

That quick reaction speed is something native to Jewish people, partly because of studying the Talmud, which teaches them to be resourceful and to dot their i's, and partly because of their fight for survival. Boxing also appealed to them because they felt that they weren't considered to be a hundred percent Dutch. Their nasal way of talking was sometimes overly exaggerated to let you know that they were still Jewish and still considered an exception.

One year we had all the champions of the Netherlands in all the weight classes. In the flyweight class, Folie Brander, in the bantam class, Nathan Cohen, in featherweight, Japie Casseres, lightweight Appie De Vries, welterweight Ben Bril, middleweight Sam Roeg, and in the heavyweight class, Barber.

One day the chairman of the Maccabi of Berlin, *Herr* Glaser, came to ask us if we didn't want to visit over there, because German Jews no longer had the opportunity to take part in matches publicly. So we went to Berlin. We boxed at the Gaststätte Friedrichsheim. The German Jews weren't allowed to sit on the bus, but we were. The German Jews were shoved off the sidewalks on purpose by the Hitler Youth, and we could just walk. You could already see it, right? That terror aimed at the Jews. We thought it was awful.

Then we got a visit from the chairman of the Dutch Maccabi Federation who asked us if we wanted to represent the Netherlands in the Jewish Olympic Games, the Maccabia in Tel Aviv. That was 1935, the second Maccabia. Appie De Vries and Ben Bril went, and both of them became Maccabia champions. That was an enormous achievement, because a lot of countries took part.

When we got back to the Netherlands, supporters were already greeting us on the train in Roosendaal right after the border. By the time we got to Rotterdam, half the train was full of supporters. Amsterdam gave us a real welcome. We had to go to the first-class waiting room, and I got a big wreath around my neck. Down on the street, there were two stagecoaches and two mounted police bands, and that's the way we went through the Jewish Quarter. Everybody had hung the Dutch red-white-and-blue out their windows. Later we went to Hotel Krasnapolski. It was an unforgettable evening.

◆ SAL WAAS

Many champion gymnasts were Jewish. In December, there would be the "Stone Competitions" at the Marnixstraat Gym.[4] I remember names like Biet, Fortuin, Israel Wijnschenk, Melkman, Zwaaf, Miss De Levie, and Polak.

My oldest brother was a gymnast, and for my bar mitzvah he gave me a membership to his gymnastics association. That was the Workers Gymnastics Association for Men and Women, made up mostly of Jewish members, although there were also non-Jewish members—that wasn't a problem at all. Later its name changed to Bato Gymnastics Association.

When I turned eighteen, I became a board member, and I stayed on the board for about forty years.

There was also a mainly Jewish association called Spartacus. Its members weren't organized into a union. We thought that wasn't right. If you're a worker, you have to be a member of a union, and for us that was the ANDB of course.

Then there was Power and Speed, the association Rosine Van Praag was a member of. Those were people who were better off. These associations were all set up between 1906 and 1910. Jewish people really liked sports. There was also an association of Jewish gymnastics teachers called Plato.

◆ ROSINE VAN PRAAG

Gymnastics was a specifically Jewish popular sport. The "better" Jews weren't very active in gymnastics. Most gymnasts were normal everyday people, diamond workers and so on. At the end of the year, the so-called "Stone Competitions" were held. The name of the winner was engraved on a plaque on the wall in the Marnixstraat gym. That "stone" bearing the names of many Jewish winners is still there.

Originally it was a competition just for men, although later there was also a Stone Competition for women. Gymnastics is something that suited Jews to a tee, and on an international level, they had a good deal of influence. I recall a women's gymnastics team that was sent to the Olympic Games in London, and it included quite a few Jewish girls.

Gymnastics has always been a sport for the little guy, requiring low dues so that the bulk of the population can participate. As a result, the gymnastics associations in the Netherlands have lots of active members. It's a "doing" sport, not an armchair sport, the way soccer can be, where there are more people watching than actually taking part in the sport. With gymnastics, it's the other way around.

There was also a Jewish sculling club called Poseidon, because there were no Jews in "The Hope" or "William III." They were usually excluded. It's a funny thing, but I think that in the "better" circles there was more anti-Semitism than among everyday people.

---

[4]Stone Competitions (Steen-wedstrijden) were held at the Marnixstraat Gym, which still exists (along with the stone on which winners' names were inscribed).

VII

IMMIGRATION

Between 1870 and 1940, a good number of Jews living out in the provinces moved to Amsterdam. The degree to which they integrated into Amsterdam Jewish life was significantly dependent on the degree to which they had assimilated into their non-Jewish environment prior to coming to Amsterdam. The more assimilated Jews often kept themselves at a slight remove from Amsterdam Jews on a personal level. They were partially or completely absorbed into the non-Jewish environment and so did not form a separate group.

Things were different for immigrants from Eastern Europe and the German-speaking countries. In czarist Russia, and in the state of Poland after 1918, the Jews formed a national minority with its own language, Yiddish. Among these Jews, there were orthodox religious Jews as well as revolutionary socialists and even anarchists with no belief in God at all. All these differing views were represented among the small groups of Eastern Jews who came to Amsterdam starting around 1900. The slightly haughty attitude of many Dutch Jews regarding these Eastern Jews and the latter's love for their own national culture pushed them into relative isolation. Until 1940, they remained a separate group, albeit one that was not completely cut off from Dutch Jews and Christians.

In general, the Eastern Jews who moved to Amsterdam came from extremely poor families, in contrast to the ten thousand German and Austrian Jews who fled to Amsterdam after 1933. The German emigrants were primarily upper middle class. This group included a strikingly large number of artists and intellectuals. Their culture was mainly German. In the comparatively provincial Netherlands, they felt themselves more like displaced Germans than like displaced Jews.

Most German emigrants moved to South Amsterdam. Conglomerations of German Jews were to be found on Merwede Square behind the so-called "Skyscraper" and on Beethovenstraat.[1] Consequently tram 24, which ran down this last street, was sometimes referred to as the Berlin Express.

---

[1] The German Jewish community on Merwede Square included Anne Frank and her family.

Jewish Immigrants from Eastern Europe

◆ ROSA COHEN-DE BRUIJN

There was a transitional home on Weesperstraat for Russian emigrants who had fled the pogroms.

It was very strange, but at our house, my parents didn't talk about it much when we were around. Our yard ran alongside the yard of the house where all those people lived—I can still see it—but we never saw any children or adults in that yard. Those people, coming in dirty after such a long trip, were taken care of there and prepared for their journey overseas.

◆ DAVID MINDLIN

My parents came from Russia, from the Ukraine. My father deserted the army in 1905 because of the Russo-Japanese War, and also because there were already a lot of pogroms taking place in the area then.

They talked about it a lot, in Yiddish, about there being lots of pogroms and about how lots of people were leaving, headed for England and America by way of Rotterdam and for the Netherlands too.

My father was a tailor like most of the other foreigners. There were also some cobblers among them. He came here in 1906. First, they were in the transitional home on the corner of Weesperstraat and Nieuwe Herengracht. All the foreigners who didn't have a place to sleep ended up there.

My parents looked for and found an apartment on Manegestraat, a street known as "the little Russian street."

Among the many refugees was a formerly well-known violinist, Alexander Schmuller.[2] He was the first violinist and concertmaster for the Concertgebouw Orchestra. He came to visit my father a lot when I was little because he came from the same town where my parents had lived, very close to Kiev.

At home, we always spoke Yiddish, although my parents tried to speak Dutch with us. They always kept that Russian, Eastern-Yiddish accent.

I was born on Manegestraat. My parents usually stayed home. They always had company. There were always plenty of foreigners coming by, all of them Russian and Polish Jews. Day and night, discussions went on about the revolution and that

---

[2]Schmuller did not come to Amsterdam as a refugee, but came to accept the position of chairman of the violin studies department at the Amsterdam Conservatory.

everything would get better. That was their dream world. And all of this in Yiddish.

My parents were absolutely not devout, and they also didn't go to shul. In fact, they had leftist leanings. Things were hard for them. They were very poor. I can still clearly remember that we always wore clogs, that the school fed us, and that everything had to be bought in installments. We were, understandably, kept down. My parents were fearful people. We were raised to be afraid, it was *inside* them. You weren't allowed to swim because you might drown. You really weren't allowed to play soccer. Soccer was dangerous, awful!

There were also a great many refugees who weren't afraid in the least, who were very gutsy in fact. I'm thinking of Broches, a well-known prewar cigarette manufacturer, and I'm thinking of the carton factory near me on Govert Flinckstraat, where I live now. That was a Russian family too. Those people were active. There were lots of people who built up a position for themselves here.

Manegestraat was a well-known street that was always crowded with Russian and Polish emigrants, which is very logical. When Turks or Moroccans come here, they always seek each other out as well. There wasn't much contact with other people in the neighborhood. There was a tremendous hatred on the street between the Dutch Jews and the foreigners. The Dutch kids were always breaking windows. They always jeered at us. Life was made impossible for us. They'd shout, "Filthy, stinking Russians, go back to your country." I remember I was about seven and we were playing on Nieuwe Prinsengracht where a lot of cargo boats were moored. I fell into the water, and there was this man who rescued me. When I was back up on the side and he saw that I was a so-called "Ruski," he said, "If I'd known you were a Ruski, I'd have let you go under." He was just somebody from the Jewish Quarter. So, there was absolutely no solidarity.

We hung around together when we were kids because the Dutch kids didn't want to play with us. Our clogs were always being smashed. They'd tear the clothes right off your back. Later on, though, when we got older, say eighteen or nineteen, we became friends with those guys.

Next to us lived a terribly poor family with eight or nine children. I still remember that they used to go to the Olympic Stadium with Kwatta bars to sell them to the fans. They asked me if I wanted to help. So, we'd sneak in and sell those chocolate bars. We were good friends by then, and that friendship lasted. These were Dutch Jews who had taunted us horrendously at first. They would also sometimes secretly put a stone on the landing in front of Russian people's doors and then pull on a rope from down below. Those poor people thought all that awful thumping meant their children were falling down the stairs! Those kinds pranks. A lot of people are into that. It still happens.

Of course, I have nice memories of it all as well. Friday afternoons after four o'clock, a harmonica player would wander through the Jewish Quarter to cheer the neighborhoods with music. A well-known street singer named Buiki (Pot Belly) because of his fat stomach accompanied him, and they'd do popular folk tunes and dramatic songs. And then, too, a lot of organ grinders came down our street with their barrel organs.

At home, we always sang Yiddish songs. There was also a Yiddish society here called Sha-Anski that organized parties that only Yiddish people went to. They always sang freedom songs there.

That Eastern Yiddish music had beautiful, haunting melodies. They were what you'd call tear-jerkers nowadays. I remember one song very well. It was about a family that was very poor. The mother, the father, and the children all had to help sew clothes. They had to work by the light of kerosene lanterns. It was all very sad, and that's always when melancholy songs are sung.

◆ BEN SIJES

We lived on Nieuwe Kerkstraat, between Weesperstraat and the Amstel River. It was the proletarian part of Nieuwe Kerkstraat, a poor neighborhood. My grand-parents lived on a different part of Nieuwe Kerkstraat, between Weesperstraat and Roetersstraat. That's generally where people who were better off lived.

One of the side streets was Manegestraat. That's where a number of Russian and Polish Jews lived. They were poor too. There were two little shuls there as well, a Russian shul and a Polish shul, I think. We weren't allowed to hang around with those boys, but I did. One of them was called Herschel.

It's true. You weren't allowed to spend time with them because those Polish Jews had other customs and ways. They danced in their shuls. Well, that was not something for those stiff, mostly Portuguese Jews on Nieuwe Kerkstraat between Weesperstraat and Roetersstraat. They looked down on the Manegestraat people.

◆ ABEL JACOB HERZBERG

The Amsterdam Jews had settled down. They were natives, and the Russian Jews were outsiders. They spoke Yiddish, and the Amsterdam Jews didn't. There was even a kind of revulsion for Russian Jews in certain circles.

The Russian Jews were *real* Jews, they were *different,* and they accentuated this. While the Dutch Jews assimilated, the Russian Jews came and accentuated their Jewishness and thereby the problem that unconsciously still lived on.

Although Amsterdam Jews hadn't let go of their Jewishness, they weren't overly attached to it either. The chief rabbi of Amsterdam was a confirmed anti-Zionist. In fact almost all of them were against Zionism! Jews would return to Israel, but only by means of the Messiah. In other words, "No, thank you! Let's please just go on living here quietly, we're fine here!" For Dutch Jews, there was no political problem. At most there was a social problem.

And then suddenly along come these Russian Jews, and *they* go and demonstrate the Jewish question.[3] Well, that just sends chills down your spine.

◆ SALKO HERTZBERGER

When a large number of emigrants from Eastern Europe went to America, a whole bunch of them came to Holland too. Dutch Jews were extremely apprehensive about increasing the number of Jews in the country through immigration. They had to get rid of the immigrants as quickly as possible. There is a "law" regarding minimums: a certain number of Jews will be accepted by a non-Jewish environment, but if that number gets too big, anti-Semitism crops up.

So, those people coming from Eastern Europe, victims of pogroms in places like Chernovitz, where dreadful things had happened, were taken in on Weesperstraat at a place called Hachnosas Orchim (Assistance to Guests). They could get food there, and there were sleeping wards where they could sleep. They'd get a little money, somebody'd find out about the next boat to America, and they'd be sent off on that boat as quickly as possible.

◆ BAREND DRUKARCH

I was born on Valkenburgerstraat. My parents came here in 1914 from Belgium. They were originally from Eastern Europe. When the war broke out in Belgium in 1914, they came to the Netherlands along with a whole flood of refugees and ended up staying.

There were a large number of people from Eastern Europe who ended up in Belgium with the purpose of traveling on to England or America. The war forced them to speed up that plan. When they came here, they saw that it was impossible to get away again, so they stayed.

My father was born in Kazanov, my mother in Sodkob, both in what was then Russia. They preferred not to talk about the persecution. It was enough that they had had to bear the suffering, so they wanted to spare us children. They didn't talk with nostalgia about Russia. Of course they had carried a part of it with them, because you can't avoid that.

In Antwerp, it hadn't been so difficult because the Eastern European element there was sizable by then. The Eastern Jew was no oddball. In Amsterdam, however, it was a strange business, and that's why two separate little Eastern

---

[3]The Russian Jews made it clear that there was a promblematic regarding Jews from czarist Russia, because Jews there were constantly confronted by serious discrimination that resulted in terrible pogroms. The situation for Jews in the Netherlands was incomparably much better. The term "Jewish question" or "Jewish problematic" has been used in Holocaust scholarship, referring the plight of Jews whenever anti-Semitism arises or whenever they have been persecuted.

European shuls were set up, on Nieuwe Kerkstraat and on Swammerdamstraat. They held their own services.

◈ Max Reisel
Because of the songs we sang around the table at home on Friday evenings, life at our house was oriented toward Eastern Europe. My parents spoke Russian or Yiddish to each other. The kids didn't adapt to this though. They very consciously spoke only Dutch. They wanted their parents to adapt to them. So, there was a distance with respect to the culture that the parents had brought along with them and that they wanted to maintain, but that the children didn't want to accept. Russian we didn't understand, and Yiddish we thought was an ugly dialect of German riddled with Hebrew words. Precisely because we were learning proper High German at school, we could tell the difference. We had adapted too much to be able to appreciate this deviation from what was taught at school.

◈ Joannes Juda Groen
I was changed by several influences. The first influence came from a fellow student, Kantorowicz, a Jewish boy who had been born in Poland and ended up here because the situation during the First World War had torn his family apart.

He said to me once, "You speak like a real Dutch Jew. You only think about freeing the working class because you've never experienced discrimination for being a Jew. You should have grown up in Poland like I did. Even today, if I go to Poland to visit my parents and I ask a policeman for directions, there's a chance that he won't answer me or that he'll say, 'I don't have time for Jews.' And when I see how my family has to live. . . . If my brother, who runs a business, thinks he is being overtaxed, he goes to the tax office. There he'll get to hear that the tax inspector won't speak to Jews. Then he has to send the secretary inside again with a bank note worth so many zloty, and only then will the man be prepared to listen to a Jew. I can't breathe anymore in that Poland because I'm a Jew, and only here in the Netherlands have I noticed that Jews are people. So, your idea that the liberation of the Jews will happen when socialism is a reality only applies to the Netherlands. The Jews here aren't in any hurry for liberation. They have it really good here.

"But over there, there are people who are waiting, who are being oppressed. For them, that's the most important thing. And did you know that if Jews in Poland want to become members of the Socialist Party, they can't? They have to set up their own socialist party!"

All of that turned out to be true. That was in 1921 or 1922. It made a deep impression on me.

◆ Sal Waas

Many Eastern Jews came to the Netherlands from Russia, Poland, and Romania. They had to keep fleeing the pogroms.

Those people had a very peculiar approach to life. When a boy was born there, the birth wouldn't be registered. That happened only after something like two years. Then, before he had to go into the service, they would send the boy abroad. That way he was two years younger and not yet eligible for military service.

They would bear their mother's name because they were married only in the Jewish religion, which means they only had a *chasseneh* and not a civil wedding. I *still* know people who use their mother's name!

◆ Mozes Heiman Gans

I remember that when I was young a ship arrived in the Netherlands with illegal refugees, and they all disembarked. The police were looking for these people, some of whom were children. A bunch of them slept at our place in our beds, and we slept over at The Jewish Invalid as supposed invalids. When the police came, they thought, "Aha! There's a couple of those refugees." When they spoke to us, we naturally just answered in Dutch, and everything was all right. Those refugees were sleeping at our place though.

We did have a lot of trouble with the police back then. They weren't giving anybody an easy time at that point. There was this family, for instance, originally from Poland. They would say their name was Neumann, but they'd have Muller in their passports. So they were deceitful liars! In Poland, the couple wouldn't have been married in the eyes of the registry office, so the husband's name would be Neumann and the wife's Muller. Officially she was still Muller, but she called herself Neumann. It was a terrible problem. We were busy all night trying to convince the police that those people were trustworthy.

German Jews after 1933

◆ WERNER CAHN

I was a student in Munich. Politically I leaned to the left without being a member of any party. In 1933 I lived in Berlin. I was friendly with Lion Feuchtwanger, also worked for him, helping him collect material for his book *Der jüdische Krieg* (The Jewish War). When Hitler came to power, I thought, "I'll go away for a month or two. The south of France is very pretty. There's sun down there, and after a couple of months this con game will be over and done with!" The perpetual mistake of all emigrants! April 1, 1933 was proclaimed the day of the "Jewish Boycott." I disappeared to the south of France on March 31. Feuchtwanger was already there, so were Thomas Mann, Heinrich Mann, and Wilhelm Herzog, who wrote *the* German book on the Dreyfus affair. I stayed there until 1934. Then one day, Landshoff arrives.[4] He had gotten in touch with Querido in Amsterdam through Nico Rost to set up an imprint for emigré writers.

Books by many writers had already been seized in Germany by then.[5] They weren't allowed to be sold any longer, and the publishers were stuck with stock they couldn't get rid of. The Nazis sold part of this stock abroad in order to get foreign currency. I remember one book that had been printed in Germany, sold to Querido in plano sheets, and bound here. That sure brought foreign currency into the German till!

When the con game wasn't over and done with in a couple of months, I played waiter in a hotel in the south of France and was a sports instructor for a while. I worried how I was to make ends meet. Then along comes Landshoff, who says to me, "You, I can use!"

In June 1934, I came to Amsterdam. At that time, the entire staff of the German imprint consisted of Landshoff, his secretary, and myself. The secretary was also an emigré who had left the same day I had. She had a Christian

---

[4]Fritz Landshoff (1901–1988), who until 1933 was an important editor with the German publisher, Gustav Kiepenhauer. After emigrating to Holland, with the support of the Dutch Jewish publisher, Emanuel Querido, he established the imprint Querido Verlag to publish German writers in exile. After the occupation, Landshoff traveled to Britain and the U.S., setting up G. B. Fischer Publishers with Gottfried Berman Fischer there.

[5]For the Nazis, undesirable writers included socialists, communists, supporters of the Weimar Republic, and Jews, among others—in short, anyone who did not support Nationalist Socialism and who was not Aryan.

boyfriend, which was dangerous even at that time. That was "racial defilement."[6] She later became my wife.

I spent my first night in Amsterdam in a small hotel on Warmoesstraat. It cost two-fifty, including a breakfast I could go on the whole day. I thought that was sensational. The whole setting—that narrow little street, the hotel with those curious Dutch stairs—was something new for me. How can anybody build stairs like that, right? The view onto that nice little building where Commercial Affairs is now. The hotel was called the Eden Hotel. It's gone.

Joseph Roth also lived there for a while. I spoke with him a couple of times. I had to pick up sections of a manuscript from him every now and then. He was a very charming talker. It was a real delight listening to the man, except for the fact that he always started drinking the hard stuff early in the morning. I'd sometimes go there on Saturday mornings, and when I returned to the publishing office in the afternoon, I'd feel like I was tanked. He began breakfast with a bottle, and I had to join in.

At the publishing office, I was a jack of all trades: copy editor, correspondent, and acquisitions reader—although there wasn't much to read. Querido Verlag's list consisted primarily of books by well-known writers like Feuchtwanger, Heinrich Mann, and so on.

Of course there were others who had fled Germany and who were literarily active here, like my old friend Fritz Heymann who wrote an extremely curious book about Jewish adventurers called *Der Chevalier von Geldern* (The Chevalier of Geldern). That book recently appeared in Germany again in photo-offset. Then there was Erich Kuttner who wrote a book about what's known as the 1566 "year of hunger" in the Netherlands. It was published by the intercession of the prominent Dutch historian Jan Romein, who had been very impressed by it. Konrad Merz, a physiotherapist who still lives in the Netherlands. Later on came Klaus Mann, one of Landshoff's friends, editor of *Die Sammlung* (The Collection), a literary magazine put out by Querido, which had a two-year run here.

The Netherlands was a relatively favorable country for German emigrants. The tolerance in the Netherlands with respect to the Jews is something that you could say every Jew in the world knows about. Also, the fact that Jews here played a role, particularly in Amsterdam, in the culture of the Portuguese congregation and so on. So, this was the country where a Jew could live, the Netherlands, especially Amsterdam. It was so close. There was no visa requirement like there was for France and many of the Scandinavian countries. And also the notion, albeit unfounded, that the language is supposed to be easy to learn was very appealing for emigrants.

---

[6]"Racial defilement" is a literal translation of *Rassenschande*, the Nazi term for sexual relations with a non-Aryan.

The emigrés formed a relatively closed circle. There was generally little contact with the Dutch. Of course we were pretty odd characters. I mean, we didn't have a cup of coffee at eleven o'clock in the morning! I never forced myself to adjust to these things. As soon as you cross the border, wherever that may be, there will be other norms and customs. We also had the feeling a little bit that in coming to the Netherlands we had come to a country where people were still living back in 1912. It was more staid, more bourgeois. People here hadn't gone through anything yet, no inflation, no revolution, no war. It had all passed the place by! Of course the emigrés felt like they were in exile here. They got the impression that the pattern of Dutch people's lives was so old-fashioned. The idea of "It seems like 1912 here" completely disappeared after the Second World War. But at that time, before the war, there was a very prevalent patriarchal "regent" mentality here—think of the way a man like Querido was the "pasha" of his business! On the one hand, everything was much more democratic than in Germany, but on the other you also had, "Us old boys will take care of it."

When I first came to the Netherlands, I tried to find a place in the same neighborhood as the other emigrés. That was the Beethovenstraat neighborhood. Most of the emigrés there rented a room or found an apartment. Beethovenstraat was jokingly referred to as the Brede Jodenstraat or "Broadly Jewish Street" and tramline 24 was called "the Berlin Express."[7] That neighborhood could muster the style in which those people had lived in Germany. It was pretty new, just a tad elegant. It wasn't such a big step from Kurfürstendam in Berlin to Beethovenstraat in Amsterdam. It was also a question of "standing." South Amsterdam, Merwede Square, was relatively Jewish before the war, and proportionately many emigrés still live here.

I can't say we had the feeling we had ended up in a lesser culture, absolutely not! I also knew too much about Dutch history to have that feeling. But you did have those "at-home-in Germany" people who took every opportunity to tell you, for instance if the plumber came in with a lit cigarette, *Bei uns* in Germany, that would never happen."

There were occupations that were economically very interesting for the Netherlands. Those few books that Querido sold to other countries weren't all that interesting, but the entire Berlin garment industry came here. Just before the war, you could say the Netherlands had a garment export business of great economic significance for the first time in its economic history. It was all Germans. Particularly women's clothing was an almost purely German emigré business in the Netherlands.

---

[7]Jodenbreestraat or Jewish Broad Street was an actual street, so the joke lies in the inversion of the words.

Then of course there were those rich kinds of people here that annoyed us no end, like that banker Mannheim, who naturally had no problem becoming a Dutchman. That was impossible for us before the war, having small-time jobs that paid little.

I was born in 1903. I remember the First World War very well, not only because my father, a good Jewish soldier, was killed, but I was also very interested in politics. I was familiar with antifascist groups here, but I was much too scared to get involved in them. Emigrés were forbidden to take part in political activities here. Doing so entailed the risk that you could be immediately deported across the border. We weren't Dutch. I was naturalized only after the war. It was already a little suspicious working for an antifascist publisher. We were made aware of this occasionally by the immigration police.

There were various reasons why the emigrés couldn't play a very major role here. First, there was the fear of doing something political, which was strictly forbidden. Second, the fight for survival was extremely hard for many emigrés. Most of them were middle-class, business people. Of course there were also some academics who had a particularly hard time of it. What was an attorney supposed to do in this country? What was I supposed to do here? Of all the emigrés, I probably had the only job for a German language specialist! Until I had to become a grocer, that is.

In 1938, when Kristallnacht happened in Germany,[8] even a conservative leader like Prime Minister Colijn went out on the street with a collection cup to support the persecuted German Jews. Things like that happened here with great enthusiasm and with a certain amount of courage in view of the German regime. On the other hand, it was extremely dangerous to say something *against* Hitler if you were an emigré. That journalist, Lippmann, had terrible problems here.

When I first came here, I didn't need a work permit. Only people in certain professions needed work permits. To work for a German publisher as a German reader, that was an occupation that could really only be done by a German who was literarily up to date. In 1935, work permits were introduced for all emigrants in general, regardless of occupation. They had to reapply for a permit every six months. The publishing house did that for me until the permit wasn't renewed in 1936. As I was told by the immigration police, this was a kind of revenge the

---

[8]When seventeen-year-old Herschel Grynszpan, living in Paris, heard of his family's expulsion from Germany, he went to the German Embassy in Paris and assassinated a German official, who died on November 9, 1938. Hitler's propaganda minister Herman Goebbels used this attack to incite German youth, who on the nights of November 9 and 10 roamed through Jewish neighborhoods breaking the windows of Jewish businesses and homes, burning synagogues, and looting. In all, 101 synagogues were destroyed along with 7,500 Jewish businesses, and 26,000 Jews were arrested and sent to concentration camps. This pogrom has come to be called *Kristallnacht* (Night of Broken Glass).

Dutch government was taking on the Germans. Evidently the Germans had started looking closely at lots of Dutch people working in Germany—there were a lot of Dutch miners, particularly in the Ruhr valley—to check whether they were politically "reliable" or not. Then the Germans cancelled about four thousand work permits for Dutch people, who had to go back. So, people here said, "Whatever those Germans can do, we can do too. After all we have so many Germans here!" Consequently four thousand work permits were cancelled for people with German passports, and my name's at the beginning of the alphabet. Whether this story is true, I don't know, but I was told this at the Immigration Service. It's possible. Stranger things have happened.

I had to be able to show the Immigration Service proof of income. I did have a residence permit, but that's not the same as a work permit. Later, we got alien passports because we'd lost our nationality, but in the beginning I only had a German passport. So, in order to be able to tell the immigration police that I had an income, I took over a grocery shop, including the clientele, from another emigré who was going to the U.S. I paid a hundred and fifty guilders for it at the time. That was a large sum, one-and-a-half months' wages. I earned a hundred guilders a month at Querido.

Once I had become a grocer, finding my customers particularly in emigré circles, I also went to Merwede Square to make deliveries. There I met *"Herr* attorney so-*und*-so." He was selling sausage! And one day I'm going up the steps, typical stone stoop steps, and a man walks toward me. He clicks his heels and introduces himself as, "So-*und*-So, cand. phil." That means candidate in philology. That had been my study specialty, and the man knew me. He was going around peddling bread.

Lots and lots of people crossed the border illegally and lived here illegally. They often didn't have the right papers or had none at all. There were Jewish emigrants from, say, Hungary, who had lived in Germany without the proper papers and who simply crossed the border like that. I know the story of a certain Braun who was going to Czechoslovakia. The police caught him there because he had no papers. They had to get rid of him, and so, at some ungodly hour, they dropped him off across the border in Austria, which was still free at the time. The Austrians dropped him off across the border of Switzerland. He came to the Netherlands by way of France in the same way. The man didn't know what to do. The danger was that they would bring him to the border again. Which they did, but they were humane enough to bring him to the Belgian border. There he was caught again and sent here. The man found a circle of people to which I also belonged. We had a kind of illegal "Jewish Council." We went into action to pull thirty-five guilders together for him, which was a fortune for us back then, because then he'd be able to go to England. There was a boat that sailed between

Antwerp and England, and the captain took people along illegally for thirty-five guilders. You were safe in England. You wouldn't be deported. Instead, you'd spend a month or two in jail, and then you could stay.

In those days, I'd rented a cellar on Jan Steenstraat for my produce, across from the dairy. A few people would get together there, including Fritz Heymann. Somebody or other would know that we knew ways to help people. My occupation as a grocer put me in touch with numerous emigrés. Naturally my customers were mainly Jewish emigrants. I had a kind of home-delivery business. I'd go out and take orders and then make deliveries from my storeroom on Jan Steenstraat. We were able to help people because I had the opportunity here and there to tell clients, "Listen, I need money!" On what was then Euterpestraat (now Gerrit Van der Veenstraat), for instance, behind the National Insurance Bank, there was a boarding house where I ate many a time. Emigrés with money, bankers and the like, lived there. So, I'd go there and say, "Let's see some money on the table. We have to help somebody!" And that's how that Braun fellow finally reached England by way of Antwerp.

Braun's wasn't an exceptional case. People wanted to get rid of those people. Too much trouble. We were administratively "expensive"! How many officials at City Hall weren't on the immigration police force? We had to show up every six months or every three months. So anybody who wasn't really very welcome here, away with them, please! The immigration police here in Amsterdam were generally very flexible and sympathetic with emigrants. They just couldn't get around certain things, although of course there was somebody there who was on the "wrong" side, as it turned out later. In Braun's case, he was also in danger because the immigration police knew where he was illegally living, and they'd warn us, "Make sure that man isn't home tomorrow morning!"

My mother came here in 1938. After my father died, she had remarried a so-called "Aryan." When the Nazis came to power, the "Aryan" thought it best to divorce her. So my wife and I had to care for three people: my mother and my in-laws. We had given guarantees for them at the Immigration Service. This was also a reason to always be able to say to the immigration police that my wife and I earned enough to take care of those people. Before the war, we often declared our income to be higher than it really was in order to be able to prove that we could support our parents.

Of course it was also true that we were able to spend more than we officially earned by selling things that our parents had brought with them. There were people who made it their profession to bring emigrants' money across the border. I know the case of one man who was an invalid from the First World War. He had a wooden leg and lived well from it. He brought emigrants' money across the border. He had a well-camouflaged compartment in his wooden leg!

◆ MARIUS GUSTAAF LEVENBACH

Before the First World War and during the days of the Weimar Republic, Professor Sinzheimer was the big man in Germany in the field of labor rights. He was at the assembly to write the Weimar Constitution and wrote the paragraphs about human rights together with his friend Radbruch. He was also a professor in Frankfurt and chief of police in Frankfurt in 1933.

Professor George Van den Bergh knew him well from SDAP meetings. He's the one who brought him here in 1933 so he could visit for a couple of weeks and recuperate after he'd been fired from his professor's job and discharged as chief of police.

I went along to pick him up. I still recall that we went to George Van den Bergh's house in a cab, Sinzheimer and his wife and Van den Bergh and I. We asked him, "How are you?" And he said, "Shhh . . . ," pointing at the cabdriver, because he didn't trust him. That didn't occur to us in 1933 that you couldn't talk freely about politics and about Hitler in a taxicab because the driver might turn you in.

Six months later we brought Sinzheimer here for good.

◆ WILHELMINA BIET-MEIJER

The Dutch Jews generally didn't like the German Jews very much, because they were able to recognize too much of the German element, we thought. The German Jews always fostered a certain pride in Germany and a certain disdain for the Netherlands. We'd tell the joke, for instance, in German, *"Bei uns* in Berlin the sun shines much brighter." People talked of the "if-we-hadn't" Jews and the "sideboard" Jews, as more refugees were coming here. The "if-we-hadn't" Jews were German Jews who didn't take the trouble of learning to speak Dutch. We resented that. They would live somewhere in a little room or a small flat in a so-so neighborhood and always say, in German of course, "If we hadn't been forced to flee Berlin when we did, we'd still have our furniture."[9] The "sideboard" Jews were German Jews who also lived in little rooms, but with nothing but paltry things around them, and they would say, "At home we had a big sideboard, but we couldn't take it with us."[10]

I saw those people slide, the ones I met at the Refugee Committee, who were cultural icons for me. They kept holding onto something that still gave them the

---

[9] Biet-Meijer refers to *"Wenn man nicht"*-Jews, saying (in German) by way of illustration: Wenn man nicht damals aus Berlin hätte fliehen müssen, dan hätten wir unsere Möbel noch.

[10] Here Biet-Meijer refers to *"Bufet"*-Jews, saying (in German): Zu Hause hatten wir ein grosser Bufet, aber das konnten wir nicht mitnehmen.

idea of some kind of luxury. They ate very little, for instance, because they didn't have enough money. If you worked for the Refugee Committee, though, you'd come out with more than those seven guilders support money. You'd get paid a certain amount for your work as well, and that would increase if you also had family members to support. Those people would eat, say, bread with nothing on it except a thick layer of butter, because a thick layer of butter was a symbol of luxury to them.

A girlfriend of mine who did illegal resistance work during the war belonged to the first group of German refugees who were granted Dutch citizenship after the war on the basis of her work in the Dutch resistance. She came here in 1937 or '38. I knew how hard it was for them to make ends meet, but my girlfriend ate less meat so she could ride in a taxi because a taxi was a luxury. My thrifty nature wouldn't let me do little things like that. I preferred to wear down the heels of my shoes, which was uneconomical, to riding the tram. But because of the fact that they had to cling to things that way, I actually got the idea that they were bereft of everything.

I remember Minister Goseling said that everybody who crossed the border illegally would be sent back, unless their life would truly be in danger if they were sent back. The flood of refugees from Germany started to take on such enormous proportions that the Netherlands actually couldn't absorb it anymore. These refugees weren't only Jews, because there was also the Catholic Committee and the Protestant Committee. People who had escaped from the concentration camps were also sent back, because according to the minister, a concentration camp was not life threatening. That caused a big stir.

◆ EDUARD CHARLES KEIZER

Most Germans weren't allowed into the country. They went to Westerbork. Originally Westerbork was a center to house German Jews in the Netherlands, which goes to show that there wasn't such a pro-Jewish attitude in the Netherlands after all.[11] The people were scared that if the German Jews came here, it would mean competition, and the government didn't want to let them into the Netherlands at all. So, finally Professor David Cohen, who was president of the Refugee Committee, took care among other things to set up a center in Westerbork.

Later I got to know various German Jewish families who settled in Amsterdam. Some of them were devout Jews. Our butcher's shop had pretty much all the German Jews with capital, bankers and the like, as customers. Those people *were* allowed into the Netherlands because they brought in enormous

---

[11]In July 1942, Westerbork became a transit camp for Jews en route to the Nazi death camps.

sums of money and had very important contacts. These people really never told us anything. Maybe they thought it was wiser not to talk.

◆ ARTHUR FRANKFURTHER

Shortly before the war there was a nondenominational committee here of which Abraham Asscher was president. An agricultural colony was set up in Wieringermeer. Young Germans received agricultural training there as well as training in various other occupations so they could emigrate to Palestine. These people were obviously looking for money. To allow emigrants in, the Dutch government made only one stipulation, which was that an organization had to guarantee that these people wouldn't become burdens to the Dutch state, which wasn't too surprising since there was a lot of unemployment here at the time.

I had good friends in the AMVJ (Nondenominational Society for Young Men) on Leidsebosje. I also gave talks to the members, and once I talked about the German Jewish emigrants. Their response was, "You may say that we should help them, and we think so too, but my brother has a barbershop in Amsterdam in the Jordaan district and if a German barbershop that was much nicer looking moved to the same street, his clients would walk away!"

So, I said, "Sure, but you should look at it this way. First, you'll get a kind of elite here. They aren't day laborers. And if a man like that starts a barbershop, right away he'll become the grocer's customer and the tailor's customer and so on. We Dutch people know very well from our own history that letting in good, intelligent foreigners enriches our society, even though in the beginning it seems like competition. The Portuguese and Spanish Jews, for instance, had a tremendous influence in the Netherlands. Just look at the Royal Library in The Hague and Suasso's house on Korte Voorhout, the house the Queen is using now, and all the family portraits in the Stedelijk Museum, which they also donated to the city. When I was a boy, that museum was even referred to as the Suasso Museum."

After the talk I'd given, these guys, office clerks and the like, were so enthusiastic that they came over to my place that evening to ask me to talk about it some more so they could explain it to their friends.

Somebody who also contributed a lot to helping Jewish refugees was Mr. Königs of the Rhodius Königs Handelmaatschappij banking firm. That was a German company in Amsterdam that was affiliated with Delbrück Schickler in Berlin and Delbrück Van der Heydt in Cologne. These were non-Jewish aristocratic German banking firms. That Königs, the big man behind the Rembrandt collection, he didn't let anything bother him. He supported the Jewish refugees here and still went to Germany to do business.

He also rented a house near the center of town that he had decorated as a club for these people. I went to the opening, and Königs himself was there.

◆ MOZES HEIMAN GANS

The Jewish Invalid was the first building where tables were set to feed refugees in 1933. Over the years, quite a few refugees were housed there too. They were put to work as staff members, but people who had to learn a trade because they wanted to go to what is currently the state of Israel could also learn it at The Jewish Invalid. That was what was called the *hachshara*.

I was sent to the train station by my parents in 1933 to receive refugees, wearing a strip of cloth around my arm with a large *magen David* on it. That was at the Weesperpoort Station, under the leadership of somebody we called the reception supervisor. We had to get these people into houses because there was no Refugee Committee back then, even though we knew that things were going wrong in Germany and figured that people would flee.

We really looked up to the refugees. They were much more than we were, culturally speaking, growing up as they had with Goethe, Schiller, and Heine. They recited these kinds of things by heart. We were complete hicks in comparison.

We didn't realize that something like that could ever happen in the Netherlands. That was out of the question, wasn't it? Where would the Dutch Jews go? The few Jews who happened to be rich would be able to get away, but most were appallingly poor, so they couldn't go to the U.S.

My father was working very closely on the refugee problem at a certain point with Mr. Visser, later the president of the Supreme Court.[12] Mr. Visser in turn introduced him to the minister to receive personal permission to allow certain people in. The day that my father suddenly passed away, he had just been to see the minister. I still had a chance to speak with him over the phone. That was right after Kristallnacht in Germany, and he had received permission for a large group to enter the Netherlands.

---

[12]Lodewijk Visser was a Dutch Jew who dared to confront the German authorities in 1941 to protest the deportation of Jews to the Mauthausen concentration camp. He had meanwhile been discharged as president of the Supreme Court, but still signed his correspondence "His Honor Lodewijk Visser, President of the Supreme Court of the Netherlands r.i." The abbreviation means "rendered inactive," to show that his dismissal had been illegal. He died shortly after.

VIII

ZIONISM

Zionism never gained a massive following among Dutch Jews before the war. Particularly the Jewish proletariat in Amsterdam remained generally unreceptive to the message of Zionism.

The Zionists were of the opinion that the Jews could become a free people not subject to discrimination and persecution only in their own national state. For the liberation or emancipation of the Jews, the realization of their own state, where Jews would not form a minority, was an indispensable requirement.

The Amsterdam socialist Jews generally attached little faith to this position. They had seen tangible improvement in the social, economic, and political situation of the Jewish proletariat with their own eyes. As far as they were concerned, Jews did not need to be emancipated by means of a Jewish state. Hadn't their Henri Polak and their Monne De Miranda considerably improved the standard of living of Amsterdam's Jewish proletariat through the Dutch SDAP and the Dutch union movement?

Until 1933, Zionism in the Netherlands and in Amsterdam continued to attract only Jews belonging to the middle class. After that time, a socialist Zionist organization was set up—Poalei Zion (Workers of Zion). Poalei Zion followers started playing an increasingly prominent role in the Dutch Zionist Alliance (NZB) so that the NZB lost its largely bourgeois character.

Nevertheless, most Jewish workers in Amsterdam remained indifferent to Zionist ideology.

In General

◆ ISAAC KISCH

I was very actively Zionist and was raised that way as well. My father and I had a very strong awareness of the international Jewish question. I was born with it, although I also thought that way on my own. The Jews were kept back everywhere, persecuted through the ages, driven out, and massacred, as they were during the pogroms in Russia, for instance. Some Jews didn't give it any thought. Others believed that as democracy progressed, the question would resolve itself if Jews assimilated into their environment through baptism and mixed marriage.

There were events that also determined my Zionism, for instance that my father traveled in France a lot during the Dreyfus affair and told me a lot about it. That underlined the thought that anti-Semitism can also break out in a community that has applied democratic principles.

When I was a student, I was the president of the Zionist Student Association. I was also a speaker there. I gave talks at meetings, spread the word, and supported the cause in various ways.

I was aware that Jews as a minority were always in a bad position because they had no country of their own. This had already been the case for twenty centuries almost everywhere in the world, except in a very few enlightened countries like the Netherlands. But these were the exception. There was strong anti-Semitism in Germany, France, and Austria that could very well intensify into more violent forms, as it did in Russia. The solution was having our own country and, in brief, you had to "sweat it out" for that.

◆ MIRJAM GERZON-DE LEEUW

When speeches were made in 1917 at the Concertgebouw in response to the Balfour Declaration, it was a great moment in the life of Jews.[1] When it was over, we said, together with Abel Herzberg, "Let's go to the Jewish Quarter and speak out. Maybe *now* they'll understand that in the long run it makes sense to leave

---

[1] During WW I, British policy became gradually committed to the idea of establishing a Jewish national home in Palestine (Eretz Yisrael). The British Cabinet's decision, taken in consultation with Zionist leaders, was made known in a letter from Arthur James Lord Balfour to Lord Rothschild on November 2, 1917. Known as the Balfour Declaration, it represents the first political recognition of Zionist aims by a major power.

the country!" That's what we did, with Abel Herzberg in the lead. Not a single response, although he spoke very well. We were standing out in the street on a cart, me too. The fact that there was no response was really to be expected. They couldn't grasp it all at once like that. But then they never did understand.

The situation of Dutch Jews was unusual, since they were in a country where they had been living quietly for a couple of centuries and were totally assimilated. They had no sense of the Jewish tragedy anymore.

During the 1920s, the Zionist Alliance was small. There were only a few Zionist students. Most of the Jews who were part of the proletariat, and that was the great majority of Amsterdam Jews, knew nothing about it. They were social-ist, also through the AJC youth organization, and it was hard enough just earn-ing a living. The Zionist Alliance was largely a group of intellectuals. They were Zionist in their minds, not in their hearts, like the Eastern European Zionists. The Dutch Zionists often hated the idea of their children going to Palestine, kids between the ages of sixteen and nineteen. The Zionist Alliance in Holland was focused on Palestine, which was fine, but they *themselves* intended to live in Holland. I'd ask them, "So, when are you going to Palestine?" And their response would be, "To Palestine? That's for the Russian Jews and the Polish Jews who couldn't take it where they were, but we're not going to Palestine, why should we?"

◆ Max Reisel

My father was a Mizrachist.[2] Mizrachi is a synthesis of Zionism and traditional Judaism. Such a synthesis was necessary because Zionism had taken up a neutral position with regard to being religiously Jewish. Its motto was, "Religion is a pri-vate matter." Reaction to this came from an internal Zionist group, the Mizrachi, who said, "That which is religious is not a private matter. It characterizes the Jewish community that as such has a task in the world."

Awareness of this Mizrachist mission contributed to the specific nature of my late father's *chazzanut*.

◆ Meijer Mossel

Whenever Meyer De Hond proclaimed his anti-Zionism from the pulpit, there were sometimes people in the shul who would slap the benches with their hands to let their displeasure be known. He'd say something like, "Jacob lived in Egypt. He *lived* in Egypt. Palestine is good for after you're dead."

He was probably anti-Zionist because he saw that the Zionists weren't ortho-dox, which he would have wanted them to be. Most orthodox families were

---

[2]"Mizrach" is Hebrew for "east," the direction Jews in the West pray in, facing Jerusalem and the Temple Mount.

against Zionism because they assumed that deliverance would come only when God determined that it was time and sent the *Mashiah*.

◆ DAVID RICARDO

We lived on Nieuwe Prinsengracht, and we had two enormous windows with wide windowsills facing the street along the canal. When I was three or four years old, I was always kneeling on those windowsills and looking outside at the long, flat barges with sand from the Amsterdam Ballast Company being pulled along down the canal by a little steam tug. My parents had probably told me, "When you're grown up, the *Mashiah* will come. Then all the Jews will go to Palestine, and you'll be a farmer."

Those poor people never realized what they triggered in that little boy, because when they were gone, I'd hear only, "When you're grown up, the *Mashiah* will come. When you're grown up you'll go to Palestine," and I'd think, "Then I'll wait until King David's barge comes by, and I'll go on that because my name is also David."

So, when it's time to leave grade school and go to high school, sonny boy says, "No, I'm going to be a construction worker because I'm going to Palestine." All those old people must have had the scare of their lives, because they used all their powers of persuasion to turn sonny boy's thoughts, even though it didn't help much. I did one year of high school, but it went nowhere.

My father was a rabbi. My uncle was a math teacher. There were no workmen in our entire family.

When I arrived in Palestine in 1931 for an orientation visit, I saw that becoming a workman was, in fact, the only way. So, I went back to Amsterdam and started looking for work. But it was 1932. There was a huge depression, and there wasn't any work to be found anywhere.

Then I remembered from the school of Maatschappij voor de Werkende Stand that there was a company called Jonker where friends of mine had worked. I went to Jonker's and said that I wanted to work there as a volunteer. "No work!" said the guy I talked to. I had been a sales rep for a couple of years, though, sold machines, so I made use of my sales tricks. I let that little reception window snap open and shut as many times as it took until , suddenly, with a very juicy curse, a door swung open and a guy came up to me and said, "God damn it, what's going on here?!"

To which I said, "Pardon me, but I'm a Jew, and I want to go to Palestine. I would like to work here as a volunteer because I have to learn before I go to Palestine." After that they were glad to help me. I was there until June 1933, until my marriage.

Before the Balfour Declaration, my father was a member of the JTO (Jewish Territorial Organization). After the Balfour Declaration, the JTO was dissolved, and my father stepped over to Mizrachi. They made him president right away. He remained president until his death.

On his hundredth birthday (in July 1972), I took the initiative to plant trees and greenery in a park in his name. At the planting I said a few words. I said that the reason for my presence in Israel had been my father, because he pushed me out, as it were, to be able to save the family. Because I went to Israel, I saved my immediate family—the rest of it had been completely wiped out.

My father suffered quite a lot from the fact that he was a Zionist. They detested him! There were even chief rabbis in Amsterdam who fired teachers from the Jewish schools because they had the courage to teach for free for the Mizrachist Youth Association.

◆ ABEL JACOB HERZBERG

The first night I was admitted to the NZSO, I met Jacob Israël De Haan. It was in a small meeting hall on Rembrandtplein. De Haan had just been to Russia where he had visited prisons. Because I had also just come back from there, although I had seen different things than he had, we immediately started talking with each other. I had gone there to see the ghetto.

I didn't know him. He had just left the SDAP because editor-in-chief P. L. Tak had attacked him in *Het Volk* about his homosexual novel *Pijpelijntjes* (Headlines). He went to the Zionists for comfort. He was a great poet, but a man without a home. In the first place, he was homosexual, which was totally unacceptable in those days, and in the second place he was a pathological character. He once said to me, "I have to destroy everything I love." I went over to his place a lot to visit him and his wife, and at one time they had this heavy ceramic dishware that was in fashion back then. The rims of the cups were slightly chipped, so he said to his wife, "Look, Johanna, the cups are falling apart, just like I am."

He also took me once to see the writer Frederik Van Eeden with whom he was good friends. Of course I thought that was marvelous because Van Eeden was a big name at that time.

He was never able to settle down here, never found recognition. He wrote a very fine dissertation about signification in law. His point of departure was: better law through better language. Thanks to him, we talk now, say, about being "able to bear responsibility" instead of being "accountable" as people used to say. He was in a circle of people at that time who busied themselves with signification, along with Brouwer, the mathematician, Van Eeden, and Professor Mannoury.

On a sociopolitical level, he couldn't find his niche either. So, first he was a socialist, then he became a Zionist, but that wasn't right either. Then he joined the devout Zionists, the Mizrachi, but they didn't want him either. Then he went to Israel, not so much out of Zionist convictions, in my view, but simply because he couldn't stand it here anymore. In Israel, he ended up with the very devout Jews, with the anti-Zionists, and also became chummy with Arabs. Then he was shot and killed. Nobody knows by whom, but they suspect that it was somebody Jewish and that he was considered to be a traitor there. And if it wasn't the Jews who shot him, he would have been shot a year later by the Arabs.

◆ JACOB SOETENDORP
During the time I was at the seminary, when I was freeing myself of Rabbi De Hond, I already experienced a certain form of Zionist organization. My first contact with this had been at home. My mother, who had read a lot, told many stories about the land of the Jews. My father, who died young, had leaves from trees in the Holy Land in his prayer book, and he always told us kids, "One day, you will all go there."

Over time, more and more boys at the seminary came into contact with the Zionist Youth Association. Initially the Zionist movement in the Netherlands had a conventional middle-class nature, and they barely managed to create a youth association. Later on, though, an orthodox group that did manage to set up a youth association came along called Zichron Jakov, which was named after Jacob Reines, an orthodox Zionist leader.

At a certain point, a religious revolution started within that group. They wanted to turn away from the "Ashkenazic" pronunciation of Hebrew, which they considered a "pronunciation of exile" and which was used in the official Ashkenazic synagogue. Instead, they started using the "Sephardic" pronunciation of Hebrew, which was used by the Zionists in Palestine and in the Portuguese synagogues. Those who wanted to do that in an official Ashkenazic synagogue were considered to be heretics of the worst kind. So, slowly we had our own shul service in what was later the chess league building on Plantage Franschelaan, now Henri Polaklaan.

Within orthodoxy, the Zichron Jakov group formed a very aware elite led by excellent people, like the Pinkhofs and the rabbinical Tal family. You really got the feeling you were involved in something meaningful. Slowly I also saw that there were other Zionist groups you could be in touch with, although initially this was limited to your own group.

◆ BEN SAJET
In 1906, at Casino, the building for the diamond dealers near the Blue Bridge, there was a debate between Mendels and A.B. Kleerekoper, who called himself "ABK."

Mendels was Jewish, a member of parliament, a prominent SDAP man, an inspiring orator, and a first-rate spokesman. So he was a socialist. Kleerekoper was a passionate Zionist at that time, wrote many poems, and was definitely not a socialist.

Mendels defended cosmopolitanism from the socialist perspective. Kleerekoper thought that Jews had to be Zionist first and that socialism had to take a back seat.

The curious thing about this story is that shortly after that, Kleerekoper became a member of the SDAP, a member of the House, a city commissioner, a member of the Provincial Council, and one of the best speakers the SDAP ever had. He expressly freed himself from the NZB (Dutch Zionist Alliance). And Mendels, like so many of us, went very far, thinking along Zionist lines!

◆ JOANNES JUDA GROEN

In 1923 or '24, at the time of my pre-med finals, I became a member of the NZSO, the Dutch Zionist Student Organization, and yet I was always "the red left-winger" there. I remember they almost threw me out once. That was in 1925, a long time before there was such a thing as a Jewish state, although we saw it as a future reality. I brought up the point that the Jewish state should really be open to all kinds of cultures, and that obviously something like the *St. Mathew Passion,* which I went to hear regularly, should be able to be performed there.

◆ LIESBETH VAN WEEZEL

The fact that the Zionist movement was led so exclusively by intellectuals possibly explains why it wasn't very popular among Jewish workers. The leadership and the bulk of its members were well-to-do middle-class people and intellectuals, particularly professors and lawyers. Those people all spoke a language that Jewish workers didn't understand. Henri Polak spoke a language that *did* connect.

◆ BERNARD VAN TIJN

I got to know Sam De Wolff in 1921 or '22. He had been a member of the SDAP since 1897–98, and a Zionist since 1903, I believe. In 1907 or '8, he left the Zionist Alliance because a motion was accepted that Jews who were married to non-Jewish women were not allowed to hold positions. That was of course a form of chauvinism that we always rejected. At that time, he said, "Although I'm married kosher, I still left the Zionist Alliance."

Many socialists even argued that there really were no nationalist issues. Others said, "Even if there are nationalist issues, you can't consider a group that has lived among others to such an extent and integrated to such a high degree as a 'nation' anymore. You shouldn't work against the process of assimilation and equal treatment!" And we have no special destiny, no special culture, no special ties. You could see that in the various families, for instance the Spier family. One of the Spiers was anti-Zionist while his brother was vehemently Zionist, particularly later in the 1930s.

The "We are Dutch" argument against Zionism often wasn't heard where you'd expect it. If you think of Henri Polak's position on this throughout his life, you can see in him something of a Zionist, sometimes outspokenly, sometimes not. In the 1920s, he was immediately won over for a membership to the trustees of Keren Hayesod, the United Israel Appeal. Although he never joined the Zionist Alliance, he sometimes talked like a Zionist—always as a Jew in any case.

◆ JAN DE RONDE

Wijnkoop was well read and had a solid philosophical background in Marxist ideology. That was the most important thing for him; being Jewish was not.

One time I was at a meeting with David Wijnkoop and Abel Herzberg, the Zionist, at Handwerkers Vriendenkring. We were "proletarian freethinkers" at the time. We saw the struggle against organized religions not as a goal in itself, but as a means against capitalism. We acted like we were a kind of "subsidiary branch" of the "godless" in Russia. With Abel Herzberg, the Zionists came out a lot more actively. Wijnkoop for his part insisted on the perspective that the only possibility of solving the Jewish question was assimilation. "We are Dutch first and foremost and after that Jewish, Christian, or Catholic. Assimilation is a requirement for improving conditions for the entire proletariat." That was Wijnkoop's and the Marxists' position.

Doorenbos was chairing that meeting. The man was so nervous he bit off a piece of his drinking glass. Wijnkoop was extremely to the point and thorough, and he was very well informed on the subject. The meeting was highly emotional, though, and when it was over there were thousands of people on Roetersstraat so the tram couldn't get through. So then the Communist Party decided not to convene meetings like that for the freethinkers anymore. People thought that it only magnified the differences between Jews and Christians, whereas we wanted to get away from all that!

Socialist Zionism

◆ ROSA COHEN-DE BRUIJN

I arrived at becoming consciously Jewish and also Zionist completely on my own when I read a Poalei Zion (Workers for Zion) paper one time. That was a Jewish socialist group and they published a paper, *Koemi Ori*. I was about twenty at the time.

In the paper, it said that there was also a division for young people and the name of S. Kleerekoper, M.A. was mentioned. I called him and said that I was interested, and where did they hold their meetings? They happened to be held every Saturday evening at eight in a building on Retiefstraat that they had remodeled as a center. I went, and there were no more than maybe fifteen young people. What appealed to me right away was that there were two things that were of concern to the group: both being Jewish *and* socialism.

In this club, we talked a lot about people who were working very actively for what was then Palestine, like Alozorov and Gordon, and we read Leo Pinsker's *Auto-Emancipation.*[3] It was very important that we freed ourselves.

Emil Premsela was the man handling the practicalities if you wanted to go to Palestine. I went to see him because I wanted to go, too, although it was unimaginable to my parents. So he freed up an evening to talk with my parents, who didn't appreciate it at all. I was twenty-one. Premsela managed to get them so far as to allow me to go for the required physical. And to my parents' great relief, I didn't pass. The physical demands were too high. Also, at that moment, the German refugees had greater urgency and therefore deserved to get one of those certificates before a citizen of the free Netherlands like myself did. It wasn't a big thing for me. Why would I have to leave the Netherlands? There was a general sense here that Jews in the Netherlands were not under any kind of threat.

◆ SALKO HERTZBERGER

In those days, I had no specifically Jewish orientation at all. I come from a very assimilated family, a rich Jewish family that was involved in Jewish organizations,

---

[3]Russian Zionist Leo Pinsker (1821–1891) wrote *Auto-Emancipation* in German *(Auto-Emanzipation* is the original title), calling for a return to Palestine as the sole possible solution to the Jewish question

as was customary back then, but that didn't get worked up about nationality or religion. *That* I learned from Sam De Wolff.

I got to know him through his son Leo, who unfortunately died in Bergen-Belsen. At the age of fourteen or fifteen, when kids usually want to get into sports or have fun, we were hotheaded socialists, and we studied—*nebech*—*Das Kapital* and works by Ferdinand Lasalle and Rosa Luxemburg.[4] We continued with this through the higher grades. Then events in Germany entered the picture more, and Sam De Wolff, who was a Marxist but with serious Zionist ambitions, came to give a talk.

On Friday evenings, we Jewish grammar school students, kids from assimilated families, met with Sam De Wolff. First, we would discuss a piece from the Talmud or the Mishnah or a section of the Torah, and after that we would talk about socialism. He was not religiously oriented at all, as he was more interested in the Jewish culture of antiquity. He knew volumes about that.

When the situation for Jews became more serious, we turned to a group of the JSS (Youth League for Socialist Studies), another one of Sam De Wolff's darlings, in which Taco Kuyper was also involved. We got together with them. However, when it turned out that those in the group felt they were more of a Sam De Wolff club, we set up our own Poalei Zion party. Poalei Zion was a party that already had an international presence. This was in 1934, '35, and our president was Jacob Van Blitz, the husband of the socialist city councilor Mrs. Bonn-Van Blitz.

The founding of the group took place in the ANDB Building on Plantage Franschelaan. We had a full house at first, but the meeting was made up solely of debaters, voices of the opposition. They were afraid that if Jewish socialists formed a separate group as Jews, it would arouse anti-Semitism. They wanted assimilation at all costs because they were afraid of jeopardizing their Dutch citizenship. In response, we said that it was not what Jews did or didn't do. Anti-Semites have never had a particular ideology, have they? They are convinced that Jews are bloodsuckers and capitalists, that they have fleas and dirty bodies, that they sit in the very front of cafes while being secretly behind everything, and that they invented communism. They maintain that Jews are so reactionary. It'll turn up in any corner they want to find it.

◆ BAREND LUZA

Sam De Wolff was one of the members of a family I knew. Once I became a physician, a good many members of that family were my patients. I talked with him a

---

[4]Ferdinand Lasalle (1825–1864), also known for his work *Science and the Working Man*, participated in the French Revolution of 1848 and created the Democratic Socialist Party in Germany. Rosa Luxemburg (1870–1919), born in Poland, was cofounder with Karl Liebknecht of the Spartacus League, Germany's first communist party.

lot, and I have to say that everything I know about the theory of Marxism, I know thanks to him. We also talked a lot about Zionism, although mainly about the tie that Jews did or did not have with Marxism. He knew a lot about that.

In his room he had a small bookcase that contained mostly books on Marx. He had a little green curtain in front of it. If he wanted to pull out a book—which I saw him do one time—he would stand in front of that little bookcase, put his skullcap on his head, say a *bracha,* put his skullcap back in his pocket, take the book out of the case, and let me see it. He went through the same procedure to return the book to its place in the bookcase.

◆ Ben Polak

I came from a non-Zionist family. My father was a rabbi in Nijmegen. I'm pretty sure that he was a Social Democrat and voted SDAP, even in the 1920s. All the rest of my family is Zionist.

I spent my early youth in the Zionist Youth Association and my later youth in the NZSO, the Dutch Zionist Student Organization. When I became a member, there was already a whole left-wing opposition that based itself ideologically on Otto Heller's book *Der Untergang des Judentums* (The Downfall of the Jews).[5] It was precisely among the Zionists that the socialists played a major role, and their criticism of the Zionists was precisely that the latter saw things in a fundamentally faulty way.

Now, once you'd been a candidate to become a full-fledged member of the NZSO for a year, you had to give an inaugural speech. The theme and conclusion of my speech was that the goal of the international Zionist Organization would never be achieved in cooperation with British imperialism. This was in 1933, and that's why I was not accepted as a member. The conclusion of my argument was confirmed in 1948, though!

Because I didn't get accepted, I was automatically placed not only outside the Zionist world, but also outside the Social Democratic world.

◆ Liesbeth Van Weezel

When Hitler came to power in 1933, Sam De Wolff together with his friend Jakob Van Blitz took it upon themselves to set up Poalei Zion, an association of Zionist workers. It always remained a very small movement. They wanted to be the shock troops of the Zionist movement, which was very active, particularly in supporting antifascism.

Sam De Wolff always used to say, it was his adage, "To really be able to think internationally, each of us will have to have found his own nationality first." In

---

[5]This work by Otto Heller was published in Vienna in 1931 and was about Austrian communists and the theme of anti-Semitism.

socialist circles, they had a very different way of thinking about this, but I know that city commissioner Boekman was of exactly the same opinion.

◆ BERNARD VAN TIJN

I slowly became estranged from the Dutch Zionist Alliance. I joined in 1918, became a member of the Alliance council in 1919, and then slowly lost interest. I was involved in lots of other things when I was a student, especially the SDAP, and later the Socialist Student Association when it started up. I sat in on a couple of Zionist Student Organization meetings, but stopped going because it was too bourgeois for me. The way they tackled the Jewish question, the things they talked about. . . . It was a world I didn't belong to. I became active again only after I had found a *real* Poalei Zion group in Berlin. For me, my earlier experience with Dutch Zionism was also the key to explaining what happened here after 1940.

During the 1920s, there were those Dutch Jewish socialist associations that couldn't arrive at a real Zionist organizational structure. That was because they weren't always appreciated in the socialist movement and because they felt there was something unpleasant about the Zionist movement, the way it was here, so conventional. That lasted until 1933.

In 1929, I was on the Poalei Zion board in Berlin, and I heard about what went on in 1933 only from a distance because by then I was in Indonesia. At that point, the Dutch socialists turned to Zionism by the hundreds. A socialist group arose within the Dutch Zionist Alliance, and between 1933 and 1940, that group was well on its way to being a majority.

Once there was a group like that, others felt comfortable with it right away. Here, again, Sam De Wolff did a lot of important work. When I was at those meetings and Jewish holiday celebrations here in 1936, '37, Sam De Wolff was one of the people who set the tone. Here he was the rebbe. The Jewish holidays turned into parties. The accent was placed elsewhere. Take the Hanukkah celebration, a celebration of national liberation, *that* was important! And Seder, the exodus from Egypt. Then there was Tu Bishwat (the 15th of the month of Bishwat) as well. It was also a celebration, although it hadn't been observed anywhere for hundreds and hundreds of years. It received some attention from Zionism, and for Poalei Zion it became a real celebration. I can still picture it in 1937. Tu Bishwat celebrates the budding of the trees. In the Netherlands, the date falls in January or February, but in what used to be Palestine, the natural world begins to stir again at that time of year. Ties to the land return! In the Dutch Zionist movement, though, Seder and Hanukkah received much more emphasis.

I sometimes used to say, "The Amsterdam socialist Jewish unbelievers had two rabbonim, Henri Polak and Sam De Wolff; one to organize the 'congregation' and the other to teach doctrine." They would go listen to Sam the way you went to a *chevra* school. Lacking a religious rebbe, they had this man as their *"rebbe."* Sam has often been underestimated by the socialist movement, but some of the Jews in this movement overestimated him in all kinds of things. He talked of this and that. *He* spoke. The *rebbe* spoke! The first speech of his I heard, this was in 1922, he talked about Heine and brought up the Torah. He couldn't ever resist doing that.

I would say that between 1933 and 1940, a real socialist Zionist movement with strong proletarian leanings developed here, which wasn't the case anywhere else except in Eastern Europe, of course, because lots of Jewish proletarians lived there, some of whom were very poor. The socialist Zionist movement provided the leaders of the Zionist movement even *after* the war, insofar as there were any Poalei Zion members left. Kleerekoper and Jaap Van Amerongen, who's been living in Israel for dozens of years now, going by the name of Jaäkov Arnon, were both chairmen of the Dutch Zionist Alliance, right after each other. The Poalei Zion party always had a pretty strong position within the Alliance. Melkman, who joined that movement later, was on the Alliance board for years.

IX

WAR

These testimonies once again clearly show that the Dutch, both Jews and non-Jews, having lived for generations in peace, could not believe the extent of Nazi crimes perpetrated on the Jews.

This understandable inability to imagine may partially explain the extent of the catastrophe that overcame the Dutch Jews during the World War II. The percentage of Jews killed by the Germans was higher in the Netherlands than in any other Western European country.

The Years Prior to 1940

◆ **LEEN RIMINI**

You didn't take the NSB people (Dutch Nazis) very seriously before the war. At the first NSB parade, I laughed myself silly. I was in the store and watched that formation march by. Sometimes you'll see children with paper hats on, held in place by bobby pins because they're too big. Well that's what that bunch looked like.

So in my shop, there was this photographer, Zegers, very well known, and he says to me, "What a sorry bunch they are, look at that lot of scum marching around!"

And I say, "Nicely put, sir."

During the war, though, he was collaborationist as hell! And after the war, I see him walking down the street. He couldn't take off fast enough. I hadn't done anything to him, had I?

◆ **MOZES HEIMAN GANS**

Our youth association paid the royal family a tribute in song. That was in 1937, when Queen Juliana and Prince Bernhard visited Amsterdam after they were married. It turned into an incredibly grandiose tribute because it was a moment when the Amsterdam Jews were actually able to express their feelings about what was happening across the border. That's why it became such a grandiose tribute, much more so even than it would have been under normal circumstances.

People resented those who were leaving. At best, it was said, "If we understand, that's one thing, but they better never come back!"

Prime Minister Colijn even asked the chief rabbi in The Hague if he couldn't do something about people leaving, because there was a flight of capital. It was the rich people who were leaving.

◆ **ARON DE PAAUW**

After 1933, there was Meyer Sluyser's paper *Vrijheid, Arbeid, Brood* (Freedom, Work, Bread), pointing out the dangers of fascism every week. And every Saturday evening, Henri Polak had a long article against fascism in *Het Volk*. Henri Polak was one of the first people they picked up at the beginning of the war. But he warned us enough about it, as they did in the courses offered by the

ANDB's Commission for Social Work, which provided the diamond workers with cultural education. Professor Bonger or Dr. Klinkenberg would explain in those courses how unsound the *"Blut und Boden"* theory was.[1]

◆ ABEL HERZBERG

I gave a speech in 1933 when Hitler came to power, and I told the people, "You can see by what is happening what it means when a people has no homeland."

So, Henri Polak jumped on me in *Het Volk,* where he wrote, "You're playing the NSB card, because they also say that the Jews have no homeland!" But that wasn't what I'd said! I'd said that the Jews as a *people* had no homeland.

◆ MARIUS GUSTAAF LEVENBACH

Mr. Gans, a lawyer here who was a year older than I, at his leisure one day in 1938 packed up his things, gathered his assets, and emigrated to the U.S. Why? Fear! Crazy and cowardly we thought it was. *That's* how we talked about it. "We're Dutch, and we're staying in the Netherlands."

We didn't apply the situation to the Dutch Jews right away. Someone who did do that in 1933 was Abel Herzberg, whose parents had come from Russia after a pogrom in 1903, I believe. His brother-in-law was one of the first to be shot point-blank by the Nazis. They went into his house and shot him dead, just like that.

So, the whole family said, *"Das ist pogrom!* I smell the pogroms again." Herzberg felt it coming.

◆ SALOMON DIAMANT

I once heard a talk by Henri Polak about fascism. He recounted that Hitler, when he was in prison along with Severing, Noske, and Scheidemann, was able to quietly write *Mein Kampf* there undisturbed.

Polak told another story. At a certain point, the Nazis stormed one of the German Social Democratic Party administration buildings. One of the German Social Democrats then suggested chasing the Nazis out of the building by force. Severing said, "No, we live in a democracy, and in a democracy we have to fight with democratic means." Polak's comment on this was, "Yes, that's true, except when the very existence of democracy is under attack." He wouldn't have objected had the SDP used dictatorial means. As far as that's concerned, his line of reasoning was ahead of the revisionist Social Democrats. He saw "Dictatorship Is Dictatorship" as a simplistic slogan. There is bourgeois dictatorship and then there is proletarian dictatorship.

---

[1]The Nazi theory of *"Blut und Boden"* (blood and soil) encapsulated the idea that political stability and power depend on unification of race and territory.

◆ **BEN POLAK**

In 1932, '33, a big group of us stepped over as a block to the Communist Party
of the Netherlands. We had an antifascist group of students and intellectuals that
was very active nationally as well as internationally at that time. We lived in The
Hague.

We saw the danger of Hitler's fascism for all of civilization and for the labor
movement. To us, the danger it posed to Jews was a component of that. The
thought of annihilating the Jews, the way it happened, was not on the horizon.
Not a soul knew that it was going to happen like that. But even if we had realized, it would not have changed our political position. We thought fighting
antifascism was the answer, not Jewish nationalism.

◆ **NATHAN STODEL**

In 1934, there was an illegal meeting here in February, in which Willy Brandt, the
later chancellor of West Germany, took part. It was a meeting of the German
Social Democratic Party. The meeting was in the province of North Holland, in
Laren. The immigration police were tipped off, and the mayor was able to pick
up a couple of people—Willy Brandt managed to get away—and chase them back
across the border to Nazi Germany. They were leftwing socialists: communists
and social democrats.

As soon as Hitler came to power in 1933, I was obsessed with the thought:
what am I supposed to do about it? So, you just took part in all possible antifascist actions. An awful lot of discussion, or, in vulgar Amsterdamese, *gelul,* went
on. Resolutions were accepted by the ton. Demonstrations, political weekends,
meetings, and discussion evenings were held. When the fascists were on the rise,
they organized their own demonstrations, which we went to disrupt. There was
a May first gathering at Huize Boer, that was a kind of festival hall, and all the
Deutsche Mädel, the young German women who worked here, came together on
the orders of the National Socialists.[2]

I remember as if it were yesterday one May first evening when I went to a
demonstration by Henk Sneevliet's party.[3] After it was over, we said "Boys, it's
time for a fight!" So, we smashed up all the chairs in the place. There *were* gangs
of Jewish toughs, but they shouldn't be overrated. If you hear about guerillas and

---

[2] The *Deutsche Mädel* (League of German Girls) was the female counterpart of the German
boys' *Hitler Jugend* (Hitler Youth).

[3] This was the RSAP, the Revolutionary Socialist Workers Party, a Dutch left-wing socialist
revolutionary party that was fiercely opposed to the Stalinist dictatorship in the Soviet
Union.

so on nowadays, it was just playing with wooden blocks in comparison, if you know what I mean.

I helped out with antifascist demonstrations. I painted and plastered "fascism is murder" on the streets, but in spite of that, it was never more than a slogan, because I just quietly stayed at home in 1939. The evening before the war broke out I was at the Municipal Theater. I'd gone to see the Fritz Hirsch operetta!

After Hitler seized power in 1933, the first movie from Germany appeared. It was called *Refugees* and it was shown at the UFA cinema on Rembrandtplein.[4] On Friday evening, I went there with a group of left-wing socialists, and I let a bunch of white mice loose in the cinema. There was a big panic. In the front row, there were a couple of guys with bottles of ink that they were throwing at the screen. The auditorium was cleared by the police.

In 1938, there was a play put on here called *The Hangman*, based on the 1933 book by Swedish writer Pär Lagerkvist.[5] Albert Van Dalsum was in the Dutch version. Disruptions by the fascists made performance impossible, because the play exposed fascism.[6]

Some people, Dutch Jews, were afraid and left in 1938 and 1939, like Flippie Truder, the tie man. They were people with money. They bought themselves tickets to America and left. The people who stayed here, though, felt pretty much betrayed, even though in reality it was a wise decision, a decision that the other Jews—and I was one of them—couldn't bring themselves to make.

◆ Jacob Soetendorp

Before the war, I really just didn't realize how much the founding of *Eretz Israel,* Palestine, was an answer to the Jewish crisis. We were always talking about "the Jewish question," but when we thought about setting up a Jewish homeland, we only thought about the idealistic aspect, not about the rescuing aspect.

We thought people who only went there *after* Hitler seized power were cowards! There was a cruel joke about that. We'd say in German, "What do you mean? Did you come to Israel out of love or are you coming from Germany?" Because that *wasn't* really how it was!

---

[4]UFA stands for Universal-Film-Aktiengesellschaft, a German film company.

[5]Pär Lagerkvist, playwright, novelist, and poet, received the Nobel Prize for Literature in 1951.

[6]Advance publicity in both right- and left-wing papers ensured a lively audience and the presence of 50 police in the theater. Fighting between the NSB members and the antifacists broke out, and 150 people were removed. The performance continued nevertheless. The mayor of Amsterdam refused to give in to pressure to discontinue the run of the play, and it was director Defresne and Van Dalsum who decided this.

In those days, I simply shut out the urgent nature of founding Israel because the reason for the urgency was about two hundred miles away, where a number of gentlemen were waiting to eliminate me. But at the time, we really didn't see this coming. German refugees told us what was happening, and even though you believed them, you said to yourself, "Boy am I happy I can live here!" You just didn't realize that the situation could change at any moment.

Only after Kristallnacht in 1938-which was a shocking experience-you thought, "Oh, my God, I'll have to talk about this day and night." So then you were busy taking every possible action, not just on behalf of refugees, but also on behalf of democracy. You were also thinking, "I have to shake other Dutch people and wake them up!"

We then went door-to-door with the Freedom, Work, Bread paper, *Vrijheid Arbeid Brood* It was also at this time that we clearly knew that the struggle in Spain was all about democracy and that we started consciously thinking much, much more politically. You began to realize that your fate and that of other Dutch people were two separate things, that you didn't share entirely the same fate anymore. I believe it was Reverend Buskes who asked me once on a radio broadcast, "What was your reaction on May 10, 1940?[7]

Oddly enough, it was relief. "Now we have the same enemy."

This shows that during those last years before the war, there really was the feeling you were in a different position precisely because the rest of the Dutch didn't feel as threatened as we Jews did.

◈ ABRAHAM DE LEEUW

Mirjam went to Palestine in 1920. I went in 1924. In 1925, we were married, and in 1927, Mirjam became seriously ill and we had to go back to Holland. We thought it would be for two or three years, but after a year I also went to Holland, and we only returned to Palestine in 1936.

During those years in Holland, I worked as an engineer for the Department of Waterways and Public Works at one of their biggest contractors, and we also worked a lot to help the young refugees and *chalutsim* (pioneers for Palestine) from Eastern Europe and Germany. Almost every week girls and boys would enter Holland, and they'd have to be taken in. The organization in Holland that did this was called the Deventer Association because right after the First World War, it started up with an agricultural program run by David Cohen's brother Ru Cohen and he lived in Deventer.

---

[7]Despite an official declaration of neutrality by the Netherlands and Belgium, Germany invaded the Netherlands, Belgium, and Luxembourg on May 10, 1940, without a declaration of war. Four days later, the Dutch army capitulated to Germany and the country was under occupation for the duration of World War II.

At the end of the 1920s, we started with a division of education for girls. Mirjam did that, and I handled technical subjects for the boys. You did this in your free time. It was all volunteer work, of course. We had about a hundred boys and girls, and in 1934 and '35 we got some certificates and were able to send kids to Palestine after a year or two of training.

Later on there was also the Wieringen work camp that took in boys who wanted to go to Chili, Argentina, Australia, or the U.S., although we didn't have much to do with them. In Deventer, we were completely focused on Palestine.

The Dutch government was very cooperative as far as my own experience goes. Now and then we had problems, but if we submitted a statement that these kids weren't going to stay in Holland, they got temporary residence permits and work permits. We never had enough certificates, though, so we tried other ways. For the British government, anybody who had a "capitalist certificate" (which was a check for a thousand pounds Sterling) was allowed to enter Palestine because that person was a capitalist. So, what did we do? We found a couple of rich Jews who deposited a few thousand pounds into a bank account in Strasbourg. A boy from our program would receive a check for a thousand pounds to take with him. Then, when he was in Palestine, that check would be sent back to Strasbourg, and in this way three or four boys per year went to Palestine on a single payment of a thousand pounds. The Dutch officials in The Hague didn't care what we did, as long as they left Holland. Of course, there were some mayors who were on the wrong side, like the one from Laren who had four illegals brought back across the border. The Gestapo was waiting for them and murdered them. There was a big stir about that in parliament.

It must have been February 1934, because Hitler had just come to power. I was in Groningen, and I called my parents-in-law to tell them I'd be by in half an hour. I get there-it was winter, cold and blustery-and we all go sit around the stove. After a half an hour the doorbell rings and Eduard Gerzon comes in. He also happened to be in Groningen and had had the same idea. So, we're sitting around the stove, and we're talking about Germany of course, and I say, "It's getting dangerous for Jews. They have to leave Holland too. It's all going wrong."

Suddenly Eduard jumps up in a rage and says, "When my niece Mirjam married an engineer, I thought she was marrying a sensible man, but I was wrong!"

I say, "Eduard, I'm not wrong. *You're* the one who's wrong!"

Then her mother says, "Shh, let's not argue. Let's talk about something else."

It wasn't just the Dutch Jews who didn't see the danger, but all of Holland. They said, "We have a declaration from Hitler that he won't invade Holland. And we have the Water Line."[8] Sure, sure, the Water Line! I had lots of colleagues,

---

[8]The Water Line was a line of defense reinforced by inundation of a number of polders in case of an attack by land.

non-Jews, who said, "There won't be any war. We managed to stay neutral from 1914 to 1918, and it'll work out this time too!" That was the kind of mentality there was, and this attitude was even encouraged.

At the beginning of July 1939, we went to Holland again for a vacation. Professor David Cohen, president of the Refugee Committee, called me up. He wanted to talk to me. "We finally agreed to have an illegal ship of *chalutsim* sent to Palestine. We discussed it here with the Dutch government and with the Pilot Service. They thought it was fine, but it had to be hushed up. The ship they bought had space for four hundred people. And what did those guys go and do? From Vlissingen, they first went to Antwerp, took on another hundred people, and then sailed down the Schelde to the sea at night behind the back of the Pilot Service. That was a terrible thing to do![9] I never approved it," Cohen said to me. "What should we do now?"

And I said, "Send another ship after it as quickly as possible!" I looked at it very differently. I thought it was fantastic that they had taken another hundred people, because I knew the situation in Palestine.

In August, I was called in to see David Cohen. He was still with the Refugee Committee. He let me see a drawing. "We're going to make a camp for the German Jews in Westerbork," he said.

I said, "Nice drawing. What a nice camp that's going to be! But it's in the wrong country. You should have it built in Palestine, not in the province of Drente!"

Then he told me about how mad they were and that they didn't want to send a second ship. The Jewish Refugee Committee had given its word to the Dutch government on that. To which the government had said, "If you all want to do something, we won't work against it." But the government couldn't work for or against anything because it wasn't even supposed to know! And then the Dutch Zionists weren't in favor of sending a second ship either. They were afraid and thought it was too risky.

But wasn't it risky to stay? That they didn't understand!

◆ MIRJAM GERZON-DE LEEUW

The war started on September 3, 1939.[10] We left Amsterdam on October 1, 1939, and at about ten in the morning, Abel Herzberg comes to say goodbye to us. He

---

[9]The Pilot Service provided tugboats to tow ocean-going vessels through the treacherous, sandbar-riddled waters of rivers like the Schelde. By taking on too many passengers, this ship ran a greater risk, which the Pilot Service would not have allowed. The decision to illegally navigate the river at night to avoid the Pilot Service further endangered the passengers.

[10]On this date, Britain and France declared war on Germany, which had invaded Poland two days earlier.

was the Jewish Agency representative and had come with a friend of mine, an engineer at Philips.

I said, "Can I give you a word of advice? Get on the train and come with us! Don't you feel it? We've been here for only a few months, and every day is even worse than the one before. Please, why don't you just leave the country? There's going to be war in Holland too!"

Then they laughed and said, "Mirjam, don't you think you're overreacting? There's not going to be any war, certainly not here!"

When we were in Paris, we had to wait because you couldn't get a train to the French-Italian border. You had to wait three or four days, and soldiers went first. So, we went to look for the Jewish Agency office. We met two Zionists there who'd been in the Polish parliament and been smuggled out of Poland by other members of the parliament. The Germans had already invaded Poland. It was now the beginning of October. They told us about unimaginable horrors, whole families, whole villages massacred, just during the first month. So, I said, "They really should hear about this in Holland."

I sent a telegram to Van Blitz in which I asked him to get Sam De Wolff and Kleerekoper and a couple of others together at his place to wait for my telephone call that evening at eight. That evening I told them the whole story, and I said, "I ask that you inform others, because it's important. This is true. The man who told me this is an engineer, his name begins with an R and ends with an S, and Sam De Wolff knows him, he met him lots of times in the socialist party. If that man says it's true, we should believe him."

But they said, "We haven't heard a thing about this here."

After the war, Kleerekoper told me that they hadn't believed a single word of the entire story, even though they knew that Sam De Wolff really was acquainted with those people. But they'd told themselves, "Those folks have really gotten themselves worked up. They're just talking nonsense. It's British horror propaganda!"

1940-1945

◆ Rosa Cohen-De Bruijn

The night before the war broke out there was a performance at the Holland Theater by Sam Englander's Jewish choir. It was a fabulous performance. May 9th it was.

That night I got a call from the Van Amerongen family. They had received a certificate to go to Palestine, and they were so happy and excited. I was also very happy for them.

I knew there were ships going to Palestine illegally and also that Emil Premsela knew about this. When the Netherlands capitulated, I thought, "I have to go. Now!" So, very early the next morning I went to the Premselas' house. I rang the doorbell. The door was opened and I went up the stairs. Somebody appeared and asked me why I had come. I said, "I would like to speak with Mr. Premsela."

To which he said, "Please go. Mr. Premsela isn't here. And don't ever come back."

At that moment, I didn't understand. It only dawned on me minutes later that the entire family had committed suicide. And then I sat for I don't know how long on those stairs.

He had a big family. These are things that can still give me nightmares. The Saturday before the capitulation I had spoken with him, and he had been very optimistic. He couldn't imagine that the Netherlands would capitulate.

I was a member of the *Algemene Socialistische Vereniging van Handels- en Kantoorbedienden* (General Socialist Association of Business and Office Clerks Union). The group I was in was almost all Jewish. But then we had to leave the union. Jews were no longer allowed to be members during the war.

My husband and I went to the union together and asked, "How is it possible that people who are members have to leave, that at the very least they aren't given some kind of compensation? We paid dues for ten years. We helped make this union strong!" Well, it was a German measure they couldn't get around. They didn't want to do it, but they had to.

◆ Liesbeth Van Weezel

I was a member of the *Centrale Nederlandse Ambtenarenbond* (Central Dutch Government Workers Union). I was even on the board of the Municipal Workers

Section. After May 10, 1940, the NSB man Woudenberg came to take over the social democratic Dutch Federation of Trade Unions, the NVV. I resigned from the Federation and was called to task for this by a board member. He started lecturing me, saying, "We never espoused that! We can't go back on our word and become deserters. You must reinstate yourself!"

I said, "You can tell me all you want, but this is the moment desertion is a must. Everyone who stays on the board is doing wrong!"

And he said, "Jews may be persecuted in their livelihood, but certainly not to the degree that it's necessary for you to desert?

There was *such* loyalty to the movement, to possessions, to the buildings, and to money, that those who stood on principle and took a stand were accused of desertion.

Four months later we were not allowed to show up at work anymore, and after another two months I was fired from my job as a government worker. I can still see that man standing in front of me. Later on he was taken hostage, and he came back spiritually broken.

◆ Hartog Goubitz

So many socialists collaborated with the Germans. There's no denying it! I remember that one of my colleagues, who was also on the board of the Cigar Makers Union, worked at a cigar factory with somebody who acted like a really staunch socialist. Then, when the Germans came, he promptly revealed himself to be this terrible anti-Semite. He went to the boss right away and said, "The Jews have to go!"

But then I also discovered in my own neighborhood that people who had always been on a friendly footing with Jews just weren't able to withstand the German anti-Jewish rabble-rousing propaganda.

◆ Aron De Paauw

You can understand what went on in the minds of the old diamond workers when the entire ANDB library was emptied and sold at Waterlooplein a week after May 10, 1940. The NSB man who had taken over the building did that. Verschuren was his name.

One board member, Blesgraeft, stayed. He was a non-Jew. I suspect he made himself serviceable to the new occupier due to a measure of resentment over this.

But all those books were sold at Waterlooplein and at Oudemanhuispoort. Of course they were just library books, not new books, but I thought it was terrible. It was a piece of yourself that they were taking away. And I always told myself that it would all be ten times as good once this was all over, that everything would come back. But, well, what happened, happened.

When I worked at Asscher's, there was a very nice fellow there who worked in maintenance who wasn't Jewish. He was married and had a couple of kids. When Hitler came to power, the truth came out right away. He was a WA man, and he showed up for work in his uniform.[11] That was Willem Koot. He was beaten to death on Waterlooplein. He'd always been a really nice guy.

When the Germans came into the country, Professor Bonger took his own life. Boekman, the Amsterdam commissioner, did the same thing. De Miranda they bludgeoned to death in Holland in the Amersfoort concentration camp. The NSB hated him for everything he'd done for the labor movement. They really did.

◆ WILHELMINA BIET-MEIJER

The Refugee Committee was on Lijnbaansgracht. It was a huge department that had a file on everybody. When the war broke out, my brother-in-law brought me to the Refugee Committee building in the morning. I even heard the eight o'clock news report on his car radio, and when I got there, a lot of people were already busy stoking the furnace with all the refugee files we had. Naturally it was unbelievably hot, the heat was just unbearable. Finally we had to open the windows, and little bits of soot from those files were flying all over Lijnbaansgracht, because we couldn't ever let them fall into the hands of the Germans.

In 1941, when I had to pick up my personal identity card with a J on it from the Apollo Hall, we had to wait in lines, and one line was just for Jews. They called your name when it was your turn. They made a really big demonstration of it. There was applause when I walked by because my name was called: Wilhelmina Beatrix. People were so happy to hear those royal names called out!

◆ ISAAC KISCH

During the latter half of November 1940, all the Jewish government workers, including all the Jewish professors, received a letter that they had been dismissed on the spot. They were already up and dressed to go teach when the mail came with the letter that they weren't allowed to anymore.

I was a lecturer of comparative law and not a professor. They had caught the professors and research fellows, but forgotten about the lecturers because they were strictly instructors, not government workers.

I thought, "Well, they'll probably drop the other shoe. In two or three days they'll notice that they forgot that little group of lecturers, and I'll get a letter too. But as long as I haven't received one, I'm staying on."

I taught one more class in British Law, and at the end of the class I gave the students a little speech about the situation. When I walked out of the classroom,

---

[11]WA = *Weerafdeling* (the Defense Division) was made up of members of the Dutch National Socialist (Nazi) Party, the NSB. It had been outlawed prior to this time, but was able to return when the Nazis came to power in Germany.

Professor Scholten was sitting in the department lounge. He knew me well, and he said, "No doubt you said something."

I said, "Yes."

He said, "You'll get in trouble for that."

I said, "I know, but I wanted to speak my mind."

To which he said, "Write down what you said so that if anybody asks, you can let them see."

So it was typed up and spread around.

I had said that a time of serious reversals for the Jewish population would come. That wasn't such a difficult prognosis to make! I wanted to point out two things. First, for people like myself who had a longstanding familiarity with the urgent situation of the Jewish people, this blow would be less hard. Second, that nobody was going to ask me to support Nazi ideas even though they would start asking non-Jewish students to do so, placing a certain amount of pressure on them. I would have it easier in this respect. I encouraged my students not to give in to the pressure in full awareness of true Dutch tradition.

I really could have gotten into trouble because of it, but evidently there were no snitches among the company, and I never heard anything more about it. After that, exactly what I had expected happened. The next day I also received a letter.

◆ JOËL COSMAN

When the Krauts came here, NSB supporters started popping up out of the woodwork. They harassed Jewish people in the city at various times. Punched them off a cafe terrace or out of a cafe where they were sitting. Then Maurits Dekker, the man who wrote *De laars op de nek* (Boot on the Neck), came to my place one day and asked if it was possible to form a resistance gang to do some bashing in return.

I talked it over with a number of my students, and they unanimously agreed to take part. A few others who weren't students of mine joined us. That's how Jewish boxers formed the first gang in the Netherlands.

We trained three times a week. For those who'd never boxed before, I made it a little easier, and those who by reason of work or being married couldn't come at night, I trained on Saturday afternoons and Sunday mornings.

One of us made a kind of assault car, an old expedition vehicle with a roof and two seats. So, whenever we got a phone call that some Jewish people had been harassed somewhere, we'd go over there to beat up the perpetrators. We got the NSB people at The Crown Cafe on Rembrandt Square. One time we went to Van Woustraat. There was an ice-cream parlor there called Koco. It belonged to a German Jew. The NSB guys were busy beating Jewish people out of there. We went over and really pounded those NSB guys.

One Saturday afternoon, a troop of WA guys came marching into the Jewish Quarter. There was an old woman who sold oranges, Aunt Golly she was called, and they just kicked her cart over. On Sunday morning, the same band came back. They marched across Waterlooplein and then harassed people on Lange Houtstraat. They even forced their way into houses and threw radios and stuff out the windows.

Our gang met Monday, and we were ready. Anybody that we even slightly suspected was NSB was taught a lesson. There was a butcher on Linnaeusstraat, a real NSB fanatic, who ran into the police station, and he was whisked out of the Jewish Quarter in a car. We realized then that the NSB troop would come back. We all met up at the Nikkelsberg Cafe on Waterlooplein.

We stationed ourselves in porticos. It was very misty that night. It was about seven o'clock when we heard the NSB guys approaching over the Blue Bridge, singing *"Juden an der Wand"* (Jews against the wall). There was a playground on Waterlooplein with a fence around it, and when they had gotten close to that fence, all those guys from the gang flew out of the porticos and out of the Nikkelberg, and we really wiped the street with them. They took off left and right, but there were a couple who ran the wrong way in the fog, even deeper into the Jewish Quarter instead of taking Amstelstraat to Rembrandt Square.

The leader of that WA bunch was Koot. He got a surprise welcome from a couple of our boys. They gave it to him so bad that he lay there unconscious. Since he was missing, NSB people went out looking for him the next morning. He was brought in to the Binnengasthuis hospital. He came out again, but he was dead as a doornail.

Then the Jewish Council summoned all the Jews to the Diamond Exchange. They had something to tell us, and we were supposed to turn in our weapons at the same time so the Germans wouldn't retaliate. Baloney, we didn't *have* any weapons! We'd done everything with our hands. Maybe the odd guy had a piece of metal, but for the rest we did everything with our fists.

Because nothing was turned in, all the stores were cleared out the following Saturday afternoon, the Tip Top too. The next Sunday morning there was *another* raid by the Germans, and they dragged all the Jewish vendors in the Jewish Quarter out from behind their stalls. Psychologically that was really stupid of those Krauts of course, because at that moment there were thousands of non-Jewish people there who went to the market in the Jewish Quarter on Sunday mornings. They were caught in the middle, and they started to stand up to the Germans. That became what's known as the February Strike.

In a certain sense, though, that Jewish gang was the first to engage in actual resistance.

◆ BAREND DE HOND

There was an AED soccer club headquarters at the Nikkelsberg. AED stood for *Adorai Een Doelpunt* (Lord, a goal). On Saturday afternoons after playing soccer, all those boys would go there. And then the *Grünen* came.[12] We hadn't expected that. We were expecting the NSB. That was the first raid at Jonas Daniel Meijerplein in 1941. The second one was at Jodenbreestraat. That's when they cleared out the Tip Top too.

The first raid was at the two big squares, Waterlooplein and J. D. Meijerplein. They dragged me out of the Nikkelsberg with forty other guys. We all had to go to the Blue Bridge on the double and then march in lines of four to Meijerplein. There we stood, four hundred of us. I stood out there from three-thirty to six-thirty with my hands up.

I was the only one of that group of four hundred guys who managed to escape. The others were all killed.

◆ BAREND KROONENBERG

The first raid was at our place, the Tip Top Theater, in February 1941. People were dragged out of the theater. My own son-in-law was among them. Not one came back. They were also after me, but our projectionist, Piet Wessendorp, helped me get out over the roof.

I could see the Green Police coming over the Blue Bridge. I was about to go somewhere, but I quickly went into the theater. Then they barged in, and all the Jewish men had to get up and go with them.

They were brought to the prison camp in Schoorl, which I even visited. I got a couple of cases of cigars and cigarettes for the guys who were locked up there. So, I asked the mayor if I could have clearance to go to that camp, but he advised against it because he was afraid that I would be caught, since I was Jewish too.

I ran into a baker who delivered bread to the camp, and I asked him if he wanted to take the cigarettes into the camp. He said, "Mister, for all the gold in the world, I wouldn't dare." So, I went myself. There were two armed guards in front of the door, and I said I wanted to speak with the commandant. Neither of them said anything, just let me keep talking. Then I asked them in German if they were deaf mutes, and one of them said that he would blow me to kingdom come if I didn't go away.

---

[12]The *Grünen* were a branch of the German occupational force, police traditionally dressed in green to distinguish them from other units.

An officer came up, and I tell the same story about wanting to speak with the commandant because I want to give those guys the cigarettes. He says, "Sir, you may go now." But I didn't want to go before I'd given the guys those cigarettes.

Then a higher officer comes over, and he says to me, "Come with me."

We went to his office, and I tell him the whole story again.

Then he says, "The fact that you're doing this is your own business, but you're risking your life." He was extremely polite. "I can easily keep you here in this camp, and you'll join those fellows."

I said, "No, that's not the idea. I only want to drop off these cigarettes."

Then he said, "You have come at the worst possible moment. In a half hour, those men are going to be taken away to Mauthausen."

At that time, I didn't know it was a concentration camp, but I was very upset. While I'm still standing there with that big shot, the transport trucks roll up, and I saw all the guys walking up. I was standing smack dab in front of them, and some of them said to me, "Kroonenberg, say hello to my wife, say hello to my mother." My own son-in-law was among them. Tears were streaming down my cheeks.

Then I got out of that camp with my cigars and cigarettes and went directly to the mayor to try to stop it, but that was impossible. They were all taken away.

◆ ROSINE VAN PRAAG

During the war, I was a teacher at a Jewish school that was a middle school and a high school. That was a very tragic experience. When those kids were taken away, everybody was deeply affected, but you had to go on. There were four hundred kids at our school, and within a year there was nobody left.

I was also caught and brought to the Holland Theater, but because I was a sports teacher, I was able to escape over the roof with the help of one of my Jewish students who was in the underground.

◆ DICK SCHALLIES

In 1940, you noticed how Christian vendors who'd always gotten along so well with the Jewish vendors suddenly changed under the influence of the NSB, like leaves on a tree in the autumn. They bet on the wrong horse, and in 1945, when their cause was lost, they tried to shift gears again.

This was misguided resentment on their part, because Jewish people had skills and experience in business, which a lot of Christian guys didn't have. These guys had no work and thought all they needed to do was unpack their wares and they'd be earning like princes!

In 1940, it slowly became clear that the markets would come under the supervision of the Germans. At one point, I was standing on Dapperstraat when they were getting the market pretty much "swept clean" of Jewish vendors.

A good friend from before the war came over to me and said, "Isn't it time for you to disappear too, you and that Jewish wife of yours?"

And then I thought, "Hey, it's getting a bit dangerous for me too."

The Jewish market slowly shut down because Jews didn't dare go anymore, and there were also regular raids in the Jewish Quarter.

◆ GERRIT BRUGMANS

I stayed in the Jewish Quarter almost the entire time, to the bitter end, I might add. I was in Blok's bakery when I wasn't supposed to be in there because I was not a Jew. I went anyway. They call that chutzpah. I couldn't swallow having those Krauts lay down the rules for me, I was too rebellious. Until the business was closed down, I had the key to the place and went in. They'd already been plundering.

I was in a concentration camp for almost one-and-a-half years. I used to live on that little Marken Square. Everybody came to me to ask me to do all kinds of things, because they knew I had a Jewish wife. I'd come home at night, and my wife would say, "You completely forget that I'm Jewish."

And I'd say, "Well, you know how it goes. They know you. They know me. I can't say no to those people."

At a certain point, they grabbed me anyway. Luckily my wife and kids came out of it pretty well. Those people took everything. There was nothing left. But I returned in pretty good shape.

◆ CAREL REIJNDERS

During the 1930s, we lived above the Vellemans, the family that had a sandwich shop on Rembrandt Square. Every morning the houseboy brought the man's son, who was mentally retarded, to a place where the mentally retarded worked.

When the Germans picked up the Velleman boy one day, that houseboy went with him. His parents waited for the day that they'd be picked up, too, in the hope they would be reunited with their son. They just thought they'd be put to work in Germany and that the circumstances probably wouldn't be great. They didn't expect they would be brought straight to the gas chambers.

When they took a census of Jews in 1941, the information stated that the census was part of an investigation to get people to work in Germany. There was no mention of concentration camps or anything, because people wouldn't have reported in such large numbers otherwise. More Jews were counted at that time than had ever reported to the Official Register.

I couldn't imagine that it would take on such proportions either. I knew the Nazis were anti-Semitic and that they wanted to get the Jews out of their homes and their professions, but not that they were going to murder them wholesale like that. There were rumors in Amsterdam. "The Jews aren't coming back." There were a lot of obituaries during the first months that the Jews were being arrested. A small number committed suicide, but most were killed in the camps. There were stories that made the rounds that Jews were being put to work in zinc oxide plants and other dangerous factories where they were quick to die. But that they were being killed en masse was only gossip and sounded so unlikely to us that it was not to be believed, by the Jews themselves either, I don't think.

◆ HUBERTUS PETRUS HAUSER

I believe the first barbed wire barrier to shut in the *"Judenviertel"* was put up in 1941 or '42 near Muiderstraat.[13] So, every morning when I went to work, I had to go through that barrier-I had gotten a little pass to be allowed to go through-and I saw really miserable things there.

My brother worked at a Jewish company, Trompetter, until the *"Vertreter"* were appointed to run the Jewish businesses.[14] It was a company specializing in leather, rubber, sundries, and such, a wholesaler, on Sarphatistraat. Those people were also taken away and never heard of again.

An awful lot of deplorable things happened, but I was fourteen or fifteen, and I didn't even *know* those people at all, knew them too superficially to say that they were close friends. I was acquainted with them in the day-to-day sense of course, which was very nice. . . .

◆ LIESBETH VAN WEEZEL

There were various people from the Resistance who came from the Transvaal neighborhood, CPN members and Trotskyites as well as an underground press set up by Jaap Nunes Vaz, who was shot by a firing squad. Eli Van Tijn wrote under the pen name of Piet Marsman and, since he was the head of the Kraaipan School, he had a whole Resistance group at work. He took in all kinds of precious books from people for safekeeping, and he also ran a food coupon and ration card clearinghouse.[15] They were denounced—which couldn't be helped of course, it was all too out in the open—and Eli Van Tijn and his whole group were picked up.

The Communists in that neighborhood very consciously took part in the February Strike. My brother trained the Resistance group in East Amsterdam. Now and then he went into hiding at my place. On March 7, he was picked up

---

[13]*Judenviertel* is German for Jewish Quarter.

[14]The German term *Vertreter* refers to the German acting managers.

[15]The occupied population received family ration cards that allowed people to get food coupons to obtain food, which was scarce. A number of individuals, like Van Tijn, illegally produced false cards and coupons for those hiding out.

at home. He was in all kinds of penal institutions and concentration camps, finally in Dachau. He almost made it. He died on April 25, 1945.

The Resistance in East Amsterdam was made up of Jews and non-Jews together, although three-quarters of the CPN were Jews. Gerrit Blom was also a Resistance leader.

◆ MOZES HEIMAN GANS

His Honor Lodewijk Visser, president of the Dutch Supreme Court, was not a typical Jew, although he wasn't at all ashamed of being Jewish. He was clearly a high bourgeois official, a "regent." He acted with extraordinary consistency, and yet the remarkable thing about Visser of course only came out during the war. He was the man who went to the Official Registry with his ID summons, and when they stamped a J on it, he refused to accept it.

The official said to him, "I have to warn you, I received an order. The Germans won't take that."

And he said, "So what if they won't take it. I won't accept it."

The Germans left him alone because they didn't dare get him yet, and he died before they did. He was a figure who was comparable in many respects to Léon Blum of France.[16]

◆ ISAAC KISCH

I was taken away in September 1943 during the last raid on Jews in Amsterdam and brought to Westerbork along with my wife and two children. I was deported as a Jew and not because of my naughty illegalities, since the Germans never found out about them. Until then, I had been protected more or less. However, I belonged to the last group of Jews for whom there was no more mercy. They had to go.

In Westerbork, we were considered slaves. I often had to think of the beginning of *Exodus*, where the Jews also had to lug stones around. We were used for manual work. If some kind of hauling had to be done outside of Amsterdam, we'd be sent out to take care of it. So, I was sent with some twenty others-they had selected married men for this-to Amsterdam. We all had a wife and kids in Westerbork. So, I arrived in Amsterdam with my fellow slaves to load stones from one boat to another. The stones were to be used to build new barracks at Westerbork.

The slaves had accommodations too. There was a little office in Amsterdam that supervised the protective interests of the Jews. You were allowed to stay over

[16]Concerned by the rise of Adolf Hitler, a group of French politicians, including Jewish socialist Léon Blum, formed the Popular Front in 1934. It won in the 1936 elections and Blum became France's prime minister.

at friends' houses, but there wasn't much of a choice. Starting in 1942, there was a regulation that a Jew was allowed to enter a house only if there was another Jew there. After the deportations, though, only those in mixed marriages were left because there were no Jewish families anymore.

◆ ABRAHAM VAN SANTEN

In January 1943, I visited Henri Polak. He was just back from his arrest in the city of Wassenaar and was living at home in Laren again. A request had come from I. G. Keesing, who was also from Laren, whether The Jewish Invalid could take him in. People at that time thought staying there offered a measure of protection against deportation.

I was one of The Jewish Invalid's youngest board members. I asked for the Jewish Council's permission to be able to discuss Keesing's possible admission and to go to Laren, because you needed special permission for that at the time. So, from the Weesperpoort station, I took the steam tram heading for the Gooi area to Laren with a big star on my coat to visit Keesing,[17] but particularly to visit Henri Polak and his wife, who were good friends of mine.

The first person I met when I stepped out in Laren was Willem Vogt whom I'd known for twenty years, and he said to me, "If you want one of your children to go into hiding, I'll take him into my home."[18] That was awfully dangerous back then. So, afterwards I went to see Keesing and finally I went to see Henri Polak and his wife. I had brought a little box of cigars for him, and he was incredibly pleased. During our conversation he told me, "Bram, I may be bent, but I'm not broken." He died shortly after that.

Those words he said to me always stayed in my mind. In May 1943, I went into hiding. For two years, I lived in an attic in an alley near Oudezijds Achterburgwal with my wife, and I never went outside until April 1945. At a certain point, I slipped out anyway because I thought it was already safe. I was wandering down Oudezijds Achterburgwal, in the center of Amsterdam, and I saw a house with large windows, and through the glass I saw drawings and sculptures. I was overcome by such an uncontrollable urge to have something beautiful to look at! I had lived in an attic for two years, with a view of windows painted white. Very imprudently I rang the doorbell and asked if it was a museum.

---

[17]Starting in May 1942, Jews in the Netherlands were required to wear a yellow Star of David with the word "Jude" (Jew).

[18]Willem Vogt was the president of AVRO, one of the main broadcasting companies in the Netherlands.

It turned out Cefas Stouthamer, the sculptor and draftsman, lived there. His wife said that I could look around if I liked. I quenched my thirst on his work. He had a gorgeous bronze sculpture of a woman kneeling over on the ground. He called this piece "Bent but Not Broken."

I told him, "I have to buy that sculpture from you!" Which I did later. One of the kids has it now. It was that sculptor's perception of the Netherlands: a woman who was bent, but not broken.

After 1945

◆ MAURITS ALLEGRO
I think I'm the only one on all of Rapenburgerstraat who originally lived here *and* came back. For the rest, everything's new. All the old residents were taken away and never came back. I'm living here again, in the same apartment. After the war, it did take some effort, a few pennies, and a lawyer.

First, the court ruled against me, even though my lawyer had been sure to ask for a five hundred guilder retainer to start. So, I went to another one. It was my own apartment, wasn't it? This time it was taken care of in two days.

◆ LEEN RIMINI
After the war things were so bad that there were hardly any Portuguese Jews. I'd be behind the counter of the Cooperative grocery store on Jodenbreestraat, and they'd come get me because they didn't have ten men. I'd stand there in the synagogue wearing a raincoat over my white jacket to do those people a favor, so they could say their prayers-although I had no affinity for that religion, I might add!

◆ BAREND DE HOND
After the war, I was sitting out on Rembrandt Square in front of the door to Monico's, and a guy sits down in a chair across from me and says, "I'm sick to death of you."

I say, "Well, I didn't happen to call you over, so take a hike." That was polite of me, wasn't it? I was able to use my hands very well because I'd been a wrestler for twenty years.

That man says, "If you want to know, I'm sick to death of all Jews."

I say, "Stinking NSB filth, you don't belong here, *you* should be in a camp."

Then he says, "You want to try me over here on the sidewalk?"

Well, he didn't know me, or he wouldn't ever in his life have dared to say that. I got up—he was sitting in one of those wicker chairs—I pick up that chair with him in it and throw him off the terrace, over a car, right onto the tram rails at least twenty feet away. Then he came back. I hit him in the jaw, and he lay unconscious for two hours in front of the door to Heck's.

Then some officers, five or six of them, come over from that police post on the corner of Halvemaansteeg, and they ask me, "De Hond, what happened?" So, I tell them what happened, and the police officer says, "Well, let's just leave the bastard lie."

After the war there was anti-Semitism *again*. I'm no tough, but after the war I must have appeared six or seven times in court with Mr. De Blécourt, my attorney, for fighting anti-Semites.

◆ ISAAC LIPSCHITS

During the war, I was in hiding in Friesland. After Liberation in 1945, I went to Rotterdam—I was fifteen then—to the first address where I was in hiding before I went to Friesland. That was Piet Van Maris's place. He was a Communist Party leader who had been very active in the Resistance. I stayed there, went to high school, and under his influence I became a great admirer of communism. So, I left school and started working for the daily paper *De Waarheid* (The Truth).

My parents had also gone into hiding. They were caught. One of my sisters was deported with her husband. One of my brothers and his wife and their baby were deported. Another brother reported to have himself deported. He said, "It's not so bad. We'll only have to do some work in Poland." Another brother who had been in hiding was caught. A brother who was younger than I was in hiding and he made it through the war, like I did.

I don't think I wondered for long after the war whether I still had any family members. I went to all the addresses I got from the Red Cross. When I think back on it now, it's just a nightmare, a building like that with all those lists. You'd be there with a dozen or so other people, and it was all posted alphabetically. Well, under C for Cohen there was a long list, of course, so you'd have to wait for each other a little. To think that you're standing in line, as it were, to see if your parents are on the list of those who are still alive. And to think, I was still a kid!

My communism cooled off pretty quick. I had just started at *De Waarheid* when that fuss broke out between Paul De Groot and the editor in chief, Koejemans.[19] The fog lifted for me at that point. In 1945, though, I was moved by that kind of struggle for one large labor organization with huge First of May gatherings.

So then I came into contact with people from the Jewish guardianship foundation Le Ezrath Ha-Yeled (Assisting the Child). I met a social worker there who impressed me. She would talk about Jews and Judaism, and I started thinking about that. So, I started staying at the Jewish Boys Home on the Amstel, number 21, near the Blue Bridge. That used to be the Dutch Israelite Orphanage. Practically all the residents there were war orphans whose parents had been deported. The director, Van Moppes, was a very exceptional man. I was struck by

---

[19]Paul De Groot, who was Jewish, led the CPN as party secretary.

the atmosphere there. And I became convinced that my solidarity should lie with the Jews.

My parents weren't Orthodox. They were conscious of being Jewish only insofar as they were labeled as Jews by those around them. After staying there, I made the decision to live in a Jewish environment, in Amsterdam in the Jewish Boys Home. That must have been at the beginning of 1947. I also went back to school again.

The Jewish Boys Home—Waterlooplein was just around the corner—stood in the middle of the ruins of the Old Jewish Quarter. It was a very sad neighborhood, not because there were ruins, like in Rotterdam where I'd been born, which had been bombed flat, but because there were spiritual "holes" in the neighborhood.

The Jewish congregation there was in need. It was a regular occurrence that somebody rang the Jewish orphanage bell to ask if a boy could come to make a *minyan*. Just imagine, a person in the middle of the Jewish Quarter having to go to the orphanage to look for a "tenth man." Before the war, you'd be looking for at least the "thousandth man!"

There was also a negative aspect to the attitude at the orphanage. They tended to immediately label remarks as anti-Semitic and to want to fight with non-Jews. You're fifteen, sixteen, seventeen years old, you're in a community of Jewish boys—there were also boys who worked instead of going to school—and now and then one would come home with a black eye. He'd have been taunted for being a "Jew." Considering the environment I was in at that Jewish Boys Home, you didn't take that lying down! No, you grabbed a stick or a stone and went at it full force. Maybe Director Van Moppes was also partially responsible for that. In that environment, you were always being told, "We're Jews and we're proud of it." A number of boys, and I was certainly one of them, had the notion we had stolen part of other peoples' lives. You had survived, and the others hadn't. You felt guilty because you'd made it through.

At a certain point, I noticed that something was going on in the place, but what it was escaped me. There was something secretive, until I was initiated into it as well. The boys' orphanage was one of the centers in Europe that provided illegal support for the still-to-be-founded State of Israel. Palestine was under British mandate at that time, and no weapons—certainly not for the Jews—or money or people were allowed in. It was all regulated. In Europe, however, there was soon an organization that illegally transported Jews from the DP (displaced persons) camps to the Middle East, to Palestine.[20] The Jewish Boys Home was a link in the illegal chain, and that couldn't be kept secret for long from the people

---

[20]Displaced persons were people who had been detained or imprisoned during the war and who did not want to go back to Eastern Europe.

who lived there. I thought that was terrific! For me it meant opposing the government and its regulations, which I didn't trust at all after the war. On top of that, all of us at the Jewish Boys Home already had that negative attitude of wanting to oppose something.

The leadership of that illegal route was in the hands of the Jewish Brigade. That was a division of the British army that consisted of Jews from Palestine. So, they were our big heroes. They'd come in a truck—they could obviously go to a Jewish orphanage for boys without any problem, that was very normal—and they'd bring candy or something. But a few other men would always get out of that truck too (albeit in uniforms, which they had to take off to avoid suspicion), and they would get other clothes from us.

I should also point out that we did receive support from non-Jews. There was somebody in the immigration police force, a highly placed individual, who would warn us. We were also raided by the Dutch police once in a while. They weren't just looking for people though. Those members of the Jewish Brigade were soldiers who lost their weapons now and again.

That orphanage was a center for everything involving Jews and Palestine. That was Director Van Moppes's work. When the *NIW* (New Israelite Weekly) came, Van Moppes would snatch that paper out of the mailbox and go and study it. That's the way the man was. He could create such an atmosphere! At four o'clock, we didn't drink tea. No, Van Moppes thought, "All of you need to drink milk, boys!" and everybody who was going to school would be sitting there. He'd rush in, wildly outraged, shouting, "What's the *Limburgs Dagblad* saying this time?!" There'd be an article with an obvious anti-Semitic slant. This was typical of the fierce revival of anti-Semitism after the war, in the Catholic south of the country as well as elsewhere. The *Leidsche Courant* wrote: "No anti-Semitism and no pogroms, but those dear little Jews shouldn't get nasty!" That text would come to us by way of the *NIW*.

What amazed me was that we'd listen in dead silence to the news reports! It was after all just a boys' orphanage with boys from about twelve to about twenty-two. I can't say that people were incredibly interested in politics, but much of the time back then there was news about the Middle East, and they'd listen to that without saying a word. They'd discuss it. Their attitude was a combination of serious involvement and a yearning for adventure. Back then there were all those tall tales about illegal Dutch Resistance fighters during the war. They were heroes. You felt you were part of that spirit a little bit. Then, all of a sudden, Van Moppes up and clandestinely emigrates to Israel with his wife and kids.

My younger brother had been in hiding in the province of Zeeland. During the war, I went with him to see the man at whose place he would be going into hiding. The man got money under the table. I saw my father give him money, and Uncle Piet Van Maris said to that man, "For that, you have to take the other boy too."

The man said, "I'll take one of them Heebies, not two." So, I went back with them. "One of them Heebies," that's what he said!

When I heard that my little brother Alexander was still alive after the war, I went to Zeeland to visit him. Uncle Piet said to me, "During the war, we had some trouble with that gentleman in Zeeland! He started making too many demands for payment, but we don't think you should talk to him about it. He did save your brother after all." I still went there with a certain prejudice though.

When my little brother arrived there in 1942, he was two and a half, and when I was there after the war, he was about six. Those people thought of him as their own child. He went to the same parochial school as their children did.

But then, when I was back at the Jewish Boys Home, I'd think, "I'm sure my parents would have preferred that Alexander grow up in a Jewish environment rather than in an orthodox Christian family!"

So, I went to the OPK (War Orphans Committee), and they said, "You really shouldn't involve yourself with that family because those people put their lives on the line for that little boy, and that little boy is very happy there!"

One time I went to the OPK social worker, and she said, "Listen, Ies, the next time you go see Alexander, please don't place so much emphasis on the fact that you're his brother, because you're getting the boy very confused!" She didn't forbid me to go, but. . . . I went there a few more times, and I told that man, Haamstede, anyway that I wanted Alexander, my brother, closer to me, that I lived at the Jewish Boys Home, and that he could live there as well. But the man insisted that wasn't going to happen and that it shouldn't happen.

At a certain point, I get a letter from the man in Zeeland in which he wrote that he did see something to my point of view. He wanted to become a truck driver, and there was a truck he could buy, but that he was two thousand guilders short, and if I could have the Jewish organization disburse two thousand guilders to him, he was prepared to give up my little brother.

That was a shock for me, but also a triumph. I went to Le Ezrath Ha-Yeled with that letter, and they immediately made a photocopy of it and stuck it in the safe. Then I went to that OPK social worker, and she had the nerve to tell me, "You're looking at it all wrong, Ies. That letter, his asking for money, is a primitive expression of love for the child!" Then something in me snapped.

I immediately made a decision, "I'm going to Israel, and I'm taking my little brother with me!" Later I went to see Haamstede one more time and said, "I'm taking Alexander to Middelburg for the afternoon," and I never went back. That was in 1948. I kidnapped him. He was nine years old, and I said to him, "I'm going to Israel. All kinds of Jews live there, and I want you to come with me." Highly irresponsible, looking back, because you can't let a boy of nine make a decision like that. He thought it was great, though, and a real adventure.

There was a little place called Putten on the Belgian border. I had some twenty-five thousand guilders I was to transport for the illegal Haganah. The route was perfectly planned. There is a Jewish cemetery in Putten where the Antwerp Jews bury their dead. I was met by a smuggler who had to be paid a certain sum of money. He brought you into a little back yard, and then you walked out the front door of a shop, right? So, you were outside! Then a tram to Antwerp, and on to Brussels. In Brussels, there was a place just like the Boys Home in Amsterdam. We stayed there overnight, and the next day we took a train to Kortrijk, crossed the French border (where the French customs people let you cross without checking your papers, if you gave a particular signal), and went to Paris. The next day we took a train to Marseilles. There was a Haganah military camp there, a so-called sports camp for Jews, but there was already good training there.

Then you went on board the ship with two or three thousand other people. The State of Israel had just been proclaimed, but the United Nations controlled it. We arrived in Haifa. It had just been determined that men of military age were not allowed to set foot on land. So, all the older people, all the women and children disembarked from the front of the boat, and we men disembarked from the back by means of a rope ladder, my little brother and I too.

If you left Europe and were of military age, you immediately became a soldier in the Israeli army. This meant that I had to report to the front immediately, even though I thought I would get three weeks to help my brother-whose name they changed to David-find his way. But I lost him there. I handed him over to a social worker and went to the front. It took five months before I found out where he was. He had ended up in some place where they didn't know what language he spoke. That was very upsetting for him. He turned out well in the end. He is a very nationalistic Israeli now. But a thing like that can just as easily go terribly wrong.

In the Israeli army, I came down with something, so they rejected me. We were surrounded for too long, so I went without water for too long. I had to get medical treatment. I was rejected for all services and had to go back to the Netherlands. So, a year later I was back in the Netherlands, and I went to the Jewish Boys Home and back to school again.

One day the headmistress said, "There are two gentlemen waiting for you." Those two gentlemen, who were from the police, took me with them because after all I was guilty of abducting a minor, and on top of that I had been in a foreign military service.

I was brought to court in Middleburg, charged by the OPK. My lawyer, Mr. Levy from Rotterdam, said, "You'd better plead guilty!" And in front of the court he disclosed the whole business, about the letter, about the two thousand guilders, and OPK's reactions. A huge discussion started up between the defense attorney, the judge, and the prosecuting attorney about how they could give me the lightest possible sentence; because I *had* to be punished! The judge went into such a tirade against the OPK that the woman representing the OPK was shaking with rage! He was a good judge. I received a one-month suspended sentence, with several years' probation.

So, that was my return. Later I went to Israel a few times for my work, and I lived there from 1966 to 1968 as a guest lecturer. I have the same problem that the poet Jacob Israël De Haan describes: being here and longing to be in Israel and being in Israel and longing to be here.

◆ SALKO HERTZBERGER

I would never have put up with fifty-eight years in the Netherlands. In 1967, we crammed our car full of suitcases, and we drove to Marseilles, and from there took the boat to Haifa. When I crossed the border at Zundert, the waterworks really started gushing, I couldn't stop them. I still remember that very well. Emigration in itself is an awful business, but you have to find something you can weigh against it, and we found that here in Israel. Despite all the trouble and the problems, we're fine here. It's something you've turned into a reality, and that gives you a lot of satisfaction. Imagine if I were still in the Netherlands!

One of my patients told me when I was planning to go to Israel, "Doctor, I don't understand you. Why don't you get a nice little house in Nice? I can well understand that you're leaving after everything you've been through here, but why don't you have your children go there instead of going to that dangerous country where all they do is shoot?"

After the catastrophe of Hitler, two large groups went to Israel. One group went because they couldn't stand looking at Weesperstraat anymore, and the other because they wanted to find Weesperstraat again in Tel Aviv.

◆ AARON VAZ DIAS

I always used to like to walk down Weesperstraat and Jodenbreestraat. I knew almost everybody! Yes, I miss that terribly. Just walking down the street you always heard a joke, and you'd laugh if it was a good joke. I liked that a lot!

Now I live in Israel. I live here with all kinds of Jews. I live in a building with four families, two above and two below. I have no contact with them though. Maybe it's me, I often think. But if I look back at how we used to live and work in Holland, and how we get along with the people we see and work with now, then I say, "It's the people!"

◆ BEN SIJES

I was an anti-Zionist for a long time. I used to have discussions with Jopie Melkman who's now in Israel. That was before the war. I was anti-Zionist due to my socialist leanings. We were for internationalism, doing away with borders, the fraternal joining of all people. So then you're not going to set up a separate State based on religion, of all things! Those were very pragmatic, political reasons why I was not a Zionist and why I'm still not a Zionist.

During the war, however, whether you wanted to be one or not, you were hammered into being a Jew if you had four Jewish forebears. Well, I must have had four hundred! In any case, I was forced together with all the other Jews with whom I had fundamental differences, both politically in a narrower sense and regarding worldviews in general. I can't say that I started to "feel" more Jewish because of the war, but I was conscious of belonging to a community of destiny where the hatchet had to be buried.

To put it in Maurits Dekker's terms, *"de wereld heeft geen wachtkamer"* (the world has no waiting room).[21] We can't wait until a whole new "clean" world, where there is no more persecution, has come about. There *is* urgency and we have to help *now*. The world has no waiting room in which you can put people so they can wait until the world is well organized. That's why I stand, as they say nowadays, "behind Israel," although I do maintain my political views.

---

[21]The Jewish writer Maurits Dekker (1896–1962) wrote a play with this title in 1949 to warn against the dangers of a nuclear war.

Illustrations

Nieuwmarkt with Jewish vendors' stalls (Jewish Historical Museum, Van Velzen Collection)

Waterlooplein markt in the Old Jewish Quarter (Jewish Historical Museum)

Pre-Passover rummage sale held on Korte Houtstraat (Jewish Historical Museum)

J. Goudeketting sells herring and pickles on Saint Anthony's Sluice (Jewish Historical Museum)

Sunday market on Oude Schans near Jodenbreestraat (Jewish Historical Museum)

Jewish pushcarts on Jodenbreestraat (Jewish Historical Museum)

Crowd of working-class Jews on Foeliestraat (Jewish Historical Museum, Van Velzen Collection)

Burning leftover bread before Passover (Jewish Historical Museum, Van Velzen Collection)

Batavierdwarsstraat on Uilenburg in the Old Jewish Quarter (Jewish Historical Museum, Van Velzen Collection)

One of the many decrepit alleys on the island of Uilenburg (Jewish Historical Museum, Van Velzen Collection)

Hachnosas Orchim (Jewish Historical Museum, Van Velzen Collection)

De Bijenkorf/The Beehive, founded by Jewish entrepreneurs, on Dam Square, across from the Royal Palace (Waanders Publisher)

The factory of I. J. Asscher, the most prominent diamond merchant of the time (Jewish Historical Museum, Van Velzen Collection)

Jonas Daniel Meijerplein (Jewish Historical Museum, Van Velzen Collection)

Building designed by J.F. Staal for The Jewish Invalid (Jewish Historical Museum)

Crown Princess Juliana receives flowers from a Jewish girl (Jewish Historical Museum)

Funeral procession of Isaac Gans (Jewish Historical Museum)

The Sephardic chazzan and composer David Ricardo (Jewish Historical Museum)

The interior of the Portuguese Synagogue (Jewish Historical Museum)

The choir of the Great Synagogue (Jewish Historical Museum)

Chazzan Abraham Katz (Jewish Historical Museum)

Diamond polishing hall (International Institute of Social History)

Small diamond-working studio (International Institute of Social History)

Henri Polak (International Institute of Social History)

David Wijnkoop (International Institute of Social History)

Owners and personnel of Koco, an ice cream parlor (Museum of Dutch Resistance)

The Young Boxer association (Waanders Publisher)

Anne Frank in 1939 on her tenth birthday in Merwerdeplein in South Amsterdam (Anne Frankhuis)

Three-hundredth-anniversary service of the Amsterdam Ashkenzaic Congregation, drawing by Martin Monnickendam (Jewish Historical Museum)

Sukkoth Service at the Portuguese Synagogue, painting by Martin Monnickendam (Jewish Historical Museum)

Socialist diamond merchant Jacobus Batavier, painting by Jacobus Van Looy (The Hague Municipal Museum)

Max De Vries van Buuren, painting by Thérèse Schwartze (Jewish Historical Museum)

Ad for De Haan ("The Rooster") matzos factory in Amsterdam (Waanders Publisher)

Labels from the fashionable Maison Gerzon clothing store (Waanders Publisher)

Appeal to sign a petition drawn up by Jewish organizations (Waanders Publisher)

Poster by Mommie Schwarz announcing a benefit at the Amsterdam Opera House (Waanders Publisher)

Poster by Jewish painter Meijer Bleekrode for the Independent Socialist Party (OSP) (Waanders Publisher)

Social Democratic Labor Party (SDAP) campaign poster (Waanders Publisher)

Cover to the sheet music for "Izak Meyer's Lullaby" (Waanders Publisher)

Cover to the sheet music for "Amsterdam, You're the City of Cities" (Jewish Historical Museum, Van Velzen Collection)

Upper portion of the stairwell in the Dutch Diamond Workers Union (ANDB) building (Museum of Trade Unions)

Portion of the restored ANDB board of directors' meeting room (Museum of Trade Unions)

Place Names

Amstel. Canalized river for which Amsterdam is named

Amstelveld. Square in the center of the city where a lively outdoor market was held on Mondays

Amsterdamse Stadsschouwburg. Amsterdam Municipal Theater

Blauwbrug. Bridge crossing the Amstel that connected the city center to the Old Jewish Quarter

Burgerziekenhuis. Nondemoninational hospital built by Jewish banker and philanthropist A. C. Wertheim

Centraal Theater. Theater on Amstelstraat, between Rembrandtplein and Blauwburg

Concertgebouw. Concert hall built in 1888, known for its magnificent acoustics. Home to the Concertgebouw Orchestra

Damrak. Important shopping street between Dam Square and Central Station

De Bijenkorf. Bee Hive, longstanding upscale department store

De Bisschop. A popular café and pub

De Joodse Invalide. The Jewish Invalid, home for the elderly and sick on Weesperplein

De Kroon. The Crown, a popular café-restaurant that opened in 1898, the year Queen Wilhelmina was crowned

De Pijp. A working-class neighborhood in South Amsterdam

Diamantbeurs. Diamond Exchange

Diemen. Village, now a suburb of Amsterdam

Gebouw van de Werkende Stand. Building of the Working Class

Hollandsche Schouwburg. Now a Holocaust memorial. From 1942–44 this theater was the collection point for Amsterdam Jews before they were deported to death camps in Eastern Europe.

IJ. Formerly Amsterdam's harbor area

Jacob Obrecht Shul. Ashkenazic synagogue built in the 1920s in the then new residential area of South Amsterdam

Jodenbreestraat. Formerly Breestraat. Main street of the Old Jewish Quarter since the seventeenth century, when Rembrandt lived there

Joden Houttuinen. Narrow street, parallel to Jodenbreestraat, at one time densely populated with poor Jews

Jonas Daniël Meijerplein. This square with its three seventeenth and eighteenth century synagogues was the religious center of the Old Jewish Quarter

Koninklijke Bibliotheek. The Royal Library in The Hague; the largest and most important library in The Netherlands

231

Leesmuseum. This library was once an island of tranquility on the Rokin, a major thoroughfare, with its heavy traffic

Leidseplein. Leiden Square, an area known for entertainment

Manegestraat. Narrow street behind Weesperstraat, where starting in 1900 mainly poor Russian Jewish immigrants settled

Marken. Island in the Old Jewish Quarter. Also called Valkenburg

Muiderberg. Small town near Amsterdam where the Ashkenazic Jews' main cemetery is located

Neye Shul. Nieuwe Sjoel. One of the two major Ashkenazic synagogues in Amsterdam. Located on J. D. Meijerplein and built between 1750 and 1752

Nieuwe Amstelstraat. Street between Amstel and J. D. Meijerplein where many Jewish religious institutions were located

Nieuwmarkt. Important marketplace that specialized in fish and fabrics

Oudemanhuispoort. Covered arcade where mainly Jewish antiquarian booksellers had stands

Paleis voor Volksvlijt. Cultural Palace for Industry Workers. This impressive cultural showcase in the city center was built at the initiative of Samuel Sarphati. It was used as a concert hall, an opera house, an exhibition hall, and for mass meetings of political parties and trade unions. It burned down completely in 1929.

Plantage. Neighborhood near the Old Jewish Quarter where many prosperous Jews settled at the end of the nineteenth century

Plantage Franschelaan. Renamed Henri Polaklaan because at the initiative of ANDB president Henri Polak, the ANDB built its headquarters on this street

Rapenburgerstraat. One of the main streets in the Old Jewish Quarter

Rembrandtplein. Important center of entertainment

Rembrandttheater. Rembrandt Theater, which was burned down in 1943 by the Dutch resistance because of its collaboration with the Nazis

Rijksmuseum. National Museum (Amsterdam)

Rijksmuseum voor Oudheden. National Museum of Antiquities (Leiden)

Rooie Leeuwengang. Red Lion Passageway

Sarphatistraat. Named for Samuel Sarphati, the nineteenth-century Sephardic physician and social reformer. Many well-to-do Jews settled on this street

Schiller's. Fancy café-restaurant on the quiet side of Rembrandtplein

Sint Antoniesbreestraat. One of the main shopping streets in the Old Jewish Quarter

Sint Antoniessluis. Sometimes referred to as De Sluis (the Sluice)

Stadsschouwburg. Municipal Theater

Tuschinski. One of Amsterdam's oldest and most luxurious movie theaters, founded by Abraham Tuschinski, a Polish Jewish immigrant

Uilenburg. Island in the Old Jewish Quarter

Uilenburgerstraat. Before World War II, the slum dwellings on this street and the neighboring Batavierstraat were demolished. The two streets then formed Nieuwe Uilenburgerstraat where the slums were replaced by comfortable modern housing

Valkenburgerstraat. Named for Valkenburg (Marken) in the Old Jewish Quarter

Victorieplein. Formerly Daniel Willinkplein, it was renamed in 1945 to commemorate the end of World War II

Watergraafsmeer. Neighborhood in East Amsterdam bordering on the suburb of Diemen

Waterlooplein. Amsterdam's largest flea market is currently held here. Before World War II, food was also sold and non-Jews enjoyed shopping here, especially on Sundays.

Weesperplein. Important square in the Old Jewish Quarter, where the Jewish Invalid and the Diamond Exchange were located

Weesperstraat. Important Jewish shopping street connecting Weesperplein and J. D. Meijerplein

Wertheimplantsoen. Small public park near the Old Jewish Quarter named for Jewish banker and philanthropist, A. C. Wertheim.

Zaan. Zaan River

Zaandam. Industrial town north of Amsterdam

Zwanenburgerstraat. Some of the oldest diamond factories in Amsterdam were located on this street

Organizations and Publications

AJC. Arbeiders Jeugd Centrale, Workers Youth Federation

AJV. Algemene Juweliers Vereniging, General Jewelers Union

Algemene Nederlandse Diamantbewerkersbond. see ANDB

Algemene Woningbouwvereniging. General Housing Association

Algemene Ziekenfonds van Amsterdam. see AZA

AMVJ. Algemene Maatschappij voor Jongemannen, General Society for Young Men

ANDB. Algemene Nederlandse Diamantbewerkersbond, General Dutch Diamondworkers Union

Antirevolutionaire Partij. see ARP

Arbeiders Jeugd Centrale. see AJC

ARP. Antirevolutionaire Partij, Antirevolutionary Party. Political party of orthodox Protestants

AVRO. Algemene Vereniging Radio Omroep, General Radio Broadcasting Association. Independent radio and television station that still exists

AZA. Algemene Ziekenfonds van Amsterdam, General Health Insurance Fund of Amsterdam

Betsalel. Orthodox Jewish workers' association to which several small trade unions were affiliated. The diamond workers' branch was often called Betsalel

Chevra Menachem Avelim. Religious society for visiting and comforting mourners

Cooperative, The. see De Dageraad

CPH. Communist Party of Holland. Communist party before 1945

CPN. Communist Party of the Netherlands. Communist party after 1945

De Dageraad. A manufacturers' and consumers' cooperative established by Henri Polak, sometimes referred to as 'The Cooperative'.

De Jonge Bokser. The Young Boxer. A predominantly Jewish boxing association

De Waarheid. The Truth. Communist daily newspaper published during and after World War II

De Zaaier. The Sower. A socialist youth alliance in Amsterdam

Dico. Diamantbewerkers-Coöperatie-Drukkerij. Merger of the ANDB and a printers' cooperative.

Gemeentelijke Gezondheidsdienst. see GGD

GGD. Gemeentelijke Gezondheidsdienst, Municipal Health Service.

Hachnosas Orchim. Organization for welcoming immigrants and aiding Jews from Eastern Europe in transit to the United States

Haganah. Clandestine Jewish self-defense group in Palestine which became the official Israeli army after the establishment of the State of Israel

Handwerkers Vriendenkring. see HWV

Helpt Elkander. Help One Another. A charity

Het Jonge Leven. Young Life. ANDB weekly newspaper for young diamond-workers that reported on a wide variety of subjects

Het Volk. The People. Social Democrat daily newspaper

Het Weekblad. The Weekly. ANDB weekly newspaper

HWV. Handwerkers Vriendenkring, Craftsman's Fellowship. A longstanding workers' association that worked to improve the educational level and standard of living of Amsterdam's Jewish workers

Instituut voor Arbeidersontwikkeling. Institute for the Education of Workers

Jeugdbond "De Zaaier." see De Zaaier

Jeugdbond voor Socialistische Studie. see JSS

Joods Armbestuur. Jewish Board for the Poor

JSS. Jeugdbond voor Socialistische Studie, Youth League for Socialist Studies

Keren Hayesod. Central fund-raising organization founded in 1920 to support a Jewish national home in Palestine

Koemi Ori. Rise and Shine. Newspaper published by Poalei Zion in Dutch

Kracht en Vlugheid. Power and Speed. Sports association for men and women

Le Ezrath Ha-Yeled. Jewish organization for aiding Jewish war orphans in Holland after World War II

Leidsche Courant. Daily newspaper published in Leiden

Liberale Unie. Liberal Union. Later called the Vrijheidsbond (Freedom Union). More conservative than the VDB, which was more conservative than the SDAP

Limburgs Dagblad. Daily newspaper from the southern province of Limburg

Maatschappij voor de Werkende Stand. Society for the Working Class. Operated a vocational school

NAS. Nationale Arbeiderssecretariaat, National Workers Secretariat. A federation of Dutch trade unions

Nationaal-Socialistische Beweging. see NSB

Nederlandse Verbond van Vakverenigingen. see NVV

Nederlandse Zionisten Bond. see NZB

Nederlandse Zionistische Studentenorganiatie. see NZSO

Nederlands-Israëlitisch Armenbestuur. Dutch Israelite Board for the Poor

Nederlands-Israëlitisch Instelling voor Sociale Arbeid. see NIISA

Nieuw Israëlitisch Weekblad (*NIW*). New Israelite Weekly. Newspaper

NIISA. Nederlands-Israëlitisch Instelling voor Sociale Arbeid, Dutch Israelite Institute for Social Work

NSB. Nationaal-Socialistische Beweging, National Socialist Movement. Dutch Nazi party

NVV. Nederlands Verbond van Vakverenigingen, Dutch Federation of Trade Unions

NZSO. Nederlandse Zionistische Studentenorganiatie, Dutch Zionist Student Organization

Onafhankelijke Socialistische Partij. see OSP

Oorlogs Pleegkinderen. see OPK

OPK. Oorlogs Pleegkinderen, War Orphans. A government-sponsored organization dealing with the predominantly Jewish war orphans

OSP. Onafhankelijke Socialistische Partij, Independent Socialist Party

Pigol. Portuguese Israelite Home for the elderly members of the Amsterdam Portuguese Jewish community

Poalei Zion. Socialist Zionist organization

SDAP. Sociaal-Democratische Arbeiderspartij, Social Democratic Labor Party (1894–1946). In the prewar period, the majority of Amsterdam Jews voted for this party

SDP. Sociaal-Democratische Partij, Social Democratic Party (1909–1919). Marxist offshoot of the SDAP, which became the Communist Party of Holland in 1919

Sigarenmakersbond. Cigar Makers Union. One of the oldest Dutch labor unions

Sociaal-Democratische Arbeiderspartij. see SDAP

Sociaal-Democratische Partij. see SDP

Telegraaf. Daily newspaper still popular today

Totseos Chayim. Society for religious Judaic studies

Typografenbond. Typographers Union. First union in Amsterdam

VARA. Vereniging van Arbeiders-Radio Amateurs, Association of Working-Class Radio Amateurs. Now a national radio and television station

VDB. Vrijzinnig-Democratische Bond. Liberal Democratic League. Offshoot of the SDAP

Vereniging van Arbeiders-Radio Amateurs. see VARA

Vrijheidsbond. Freedom Union. Formerly the conservative Liberal Unie

Vrijzinnig-Democratische Bond. see VDB

Zichron Jakov. Society for religious Jewish studies

Ziekenzorg. see ZZ

ZZ. Ziekenzorg, Health Care. A democratic insurance fund

Glossary

baal tefillah. one who leads the congregation in prayer; does not have the formal training or professional status of a *chazzan*

bateln. to squander, someone who does not work (Yiddish)

beth midrash. a room, usually in a synagogue, set aside for religious study

bracha. blessing

bris. *Brith Milah.* circumcision

challah. braided egg bread used on shabbes

chaluts(im). pioneer(s), referring to the Zionist pioneers

chametz. *chometz* (Yiddish) or *hametz* (Hebrew) . leavened bread

chasseneh. wedding

chazones. cantor's melodies

chazzan, chazzanim. cantor(s)

chazzanut. cantorial art

chevra. society or organization that collected membership contributions and visited member families at births, deaths, and marriages, as well as performing other social services or setting up schools

chevra kadisha. funeral fund and group which prepares the body for burial

cholilleh. a curse

chuppa. wedding canopy (Yiddish), *huppa* (Hebrew); Amsterdam Yiddish for wedding

daven. to pray

gelul. bullshit (Dutch slang)

golah. exile, diaspora (Hebrew)

goy. a non-Jew (Yiddish)

gracht. canal (Dutch)

habdalah. ceremony at the conclusion of the Sabbath and holidays, separating the holy day from other days, which includes smelling spices in hopes of a fragrant week

hachshara. program for preparation—physical and intellectual—of those intending to be pioneers in Palestine, and later Israel

havdalah. see habdalah

kasher. kosher, sanctioned

kashrut. art of being kosher

kesause mangelen. "Curaçaoan almonds," or peanuts (Amsterdam Dutch)

Kiddush. blessing over wine on Sabbath and festivals

kuf-nun. for nothing (Amsterdam Yiddish)

lernen. learning, to learn (Yiddish)

levaya. funeral (Yiddish)

magen David. star of David

Mashiah. Messiah

matzo. unleavened bread eaten during Passover

mazel (tov). luck (good luck), congratulations

menachem avelim (chevra menachem aveilim). pious society or association whose function was to visit and comfort the bereaved

meshugge. crazy (Yiddish)

minyan. a group of minimally ten men to perform a religious service

mishpocheh. extended family, relatives, ancestors

mitzvah. good deed, or commandment

nebech. alas, unfortunately (Yiddish)

neshama yeterah. extra soul. Refers to the kabbalistic image of the special angel which descends from Heaven to celebrate the Sabbath

oma. grandma (Dutch)

pegime. nick, irregularity (Yiddish)

Pesach. Passover

ponum. face (Amsterdam Yiddish), also *porum*

porschen. to devein meat in kosher processing

porscher. one who deveins meat in kosher processing

Purim. Festival celebrating the triumph of the Jewish people over Haman, who attempted to destroy them

rebbe. rabbi (Yiddish)

rishut. evil, sin

Rosh Hashana. Jewish New Year

Shabbes. Sabbath

shamash. caretaker of a synagogue

Shir Hamaalot. Psalm 126, sung before grace after meals on the Sabbath and festivals

shiva. Seven-day period of mourning

shlemiel. unlucky person or a foolish, awkward or gullible person

shochet(im). *shohet*, ritual slaughterer

shomer. supervises kashrut

shul. synagogue, school (Yiddish)

Simchas Torah. festival celebrating completion of the annual cycle of reading the Torah

Snog(g)e. Dutch Sephardic version of the Portuguese *esnoga* or synagogue

sof. e(i)n sof, without limit (Yiddish); commonly used in Dutch when referring to an unpleasant or awkward situation

steeg. alley (Dutch)

straat. street (Dutch)

tallith. prayer shawl with fringed corners worn by Jewish men during morning prayers

Talmud. encyclopedic collection of legalistic interpretations based on the Mishnah

Talmud Torah. study of the Torah

tefillim. prayers

tefillin. phylacteries; small boxes containing Torah texts that are strapped to forehead and left arm and worn by Jewish men during morning prayers (except for the Sabbath and festivals)

Tenach. Old Testament

Tisha Bov. ninth day of the month of Ab or Av; day of fasting and mourning commemorating both the destruction of the First Temple (by Babylonians) and the destruction of the Second Temple (by Romans)

todiskeh, todisko. a derogatory term for an Ashkenazic Jew in the Dutch Sephardic parlance

Torah. the first five books of the Old Testament, the so-called "Books of Moses,"

treyf. not kosher (Yiddish)

tsholent. *cholent*, a Sabbath dish (a stew often containing potatoes and beans, sometimes meat)

Tu Bishwat or **Tu BiShevat.** the fifteenth day of Shevat; Jewish Arbor Day

vershteren. to destroy, ruin (Yiddish)

Yehudi. a Jew

Yid. (pronounced "Yeed"), a Jew (non-derogatory)

Yiddishkayt. all things Jewish (Yiddish)

Yom Kippur. Day of Atonement

yontif. festival (Yiddish)

zichrono liverachah. bless (his) soul, in blessed memory (Hebrew)

As a rule, the Ashkenazic spelling (s instead of t for th; ch instead of h or kh) has been chosen for both Yiddish and Hebrew as most Jews in Amsterdam were of Ashkenazic background.

Biographical Notes on the Interviewees

Emmanuel Aalsvel (b. Amsterdam 1914)—pickle-maker, 3, 10, 43, 119, 126

Maurits Allegro (b. Amsterdam 1906)—pickle-maker, 9, 74, 220

Jeanette Alvarez Vega-Keizer (b. Amsterdam 1908)—stenographer, later worker at a kosher butcher shop, wife of Eduard Charles Keizer, 129

Lodewijk Asscher (b. Amsterdam 1900)—diamond manufacturer, son of Abraham Asscher, 120

Bertha Barnstein-Koster (b. Amsterdam 1896)—daughter of the manager of the Boas Brothers diamond factory, niece of Handwerkers Vriendenkring president Heiman Barnstein, 92, 113, 116

Wilhelmina Biet-Meijer (b. Amsterdam 1920)—homemaker, 33, 143, 162, 180, 210

Barend Bril (b. Amsterdam 1900)—merchant, 2, 124

Gerrit Brugmans (b. Amsterdam 1884)—kosher baker, 43, 86, 117, 125, 141, 158, 215

Werner Cahn (b. Ohligs-Solingen, Germany 1903)—publisher, 174

Rosa Cohen-De Bruijn (b. Amsterdam 1916)—office worker, later homemaker, 33, 130, 168, 193, 208

Joël Cosman (b. Amsterdam 1903)—sports instructor, 124, 164, 211

Barend De Hond (b. Amsterdam 1907)—market vendor, metalworker, 3, 76, 213, 220

Abraham De Leeuw (b. Hilversum 1898)—professor of engineering, husband of Mirjam Gerzon-De Leeuw, 204

Mozes De Leeuw (b. Amsterdam 1912)—textile wholesaler, 12, 19, 80, 121

Aron De Paauw (b. Amsterdam 1903)—diamond worker, 20, 49, 87, 93, 120, 133, 148, 200, 209

Jan De Ronde (b. Rotterdam 1899)—laborer, former president of the free-thinkers' association, De Dageraad, 89, 192

Salomon Diamant (b. Amsterdam 1891)—diamond worker, office worker, 87, 88, 201

Barend Drukarch (b. Amsterdam 1917)—rabbi, 44, 47, 61, 171

Carel Josef Edersheim (b. The Hague 1893)—lawyer, 131

Joop Emmerik (b. Amsterdam 1909)—dealer in second-hand clothing, 3, 10, 43, 77, 125, 158

Max Emmerik (b. Amsterdam 1894)—diamond worker, 18, 37, 94, 113, 133

Simon Emmering (b. Amsterdam 1914)—antiquarian bookseller, 9, 140

Suze Frank (b. Amsterdam 1907)—diamond worker, 21

Arthur Frankfurther (b. Breslau [Wroclaw], Poland) 1894)—banker, 30, 133, 182

Mozes Heiman Gans (b. Amsterdam 1917)—antique dealer, professor of Dutch Jewish history, 67, 134, 173, 183, 200, 217

Mirjam Gerzon-De Leeuw (b. Groningen 1891)—active in Zionist movement, wife of Abraham De Leeuw, 14, 186, 206

Simon Gosselaar (b. Amsterdam 1908)—teacher, husband of Toos La Grouw-Gosselaar, 36, 54, 103, 111, 125, 145

Hartog Goubitz (b. Amsterdam 1889)—cigar maker, union board member, 17, 74, 85, 94, 105, 115, 124, 152, 209

Alexandre Joseph (Lex) Goudsmit (b. Amsterdam 1913)—diamond worker, actor, singer, 75, 113

Joannes Juda Groen (b. Amsterdam 1903)—professor of internal medicine, 96, 104, 172, 191

Ruben Groen (b. Amsterdam 1912)—diamond worker, musician, husband of Johanna Wilhelmina Louman-Groen, 19, 24, 35, 43, 99, 145, 157

Hubertus Petrus Hauser (b. Venlo 1923)—customs official, 40, 154, 216

Julia Heertjes-Van Saxen (b. Hertogenbosch 1912)—teacher, wife of Max Van Saxen, 59

Hermine Heijermans (b. Katwijk aan Zee 1902)—author, proponent of women's rights, daughter of playwright Herman Heijermans, 151

Salko Hertzberger (b. Amsterdam 1913)—physician, 134, 155, 171, 193, 226

Abel Jacob Herzberg (b. Amsterdam 1893)—lawyer, writer, 32, 46, 131, 170, 189, 201

Henri Isidore Isaac (b. Amsterdam 1903)—director of De Bijenkorf, the department store, 15

Jo Juda (b. Amsterdam 1909)—violinist, writer, 87, 99, 126, 145, 148, 153

Eduard Charles Keizer (b. Amsterdam 1903)—kosher butcher and poulterer, later also kosher bread baker and pastry chef, husband of Jeanette Alvarez Vega-Keizer, 44, 47, 52, 62, 129, 181

Isaac Kisch (b. Amsterdam 1905)—professor of law, 186, 210, 217

Barend Kroonenberg (b. Amsterdam 1901)—manager of the Tip Top Theater, 158, 213

Toos La Grouw-Gosselaar (b. Amsterdam 1912)—saleswoman, later homemaker, wife of Simon Gosselaar, 146

Loe Lap (b. Amsterdam 1914)—merchant, 4, 26, 35, 54, 60, 79, 140, 143, 160

Marius Gustaaf Levenbach (b. Amsterdam 1896)—professor of law, 26, 34, 144, 180, 201

Isaac Lipschits (b. Rotterdam 1930)—professor of contemporary history, 221

Johanna Wilhelmina Louman-Groen (b. Amsterdam 1913)—homemaker, wife of Ruben Groen, 145

Barend Luza (b. Amsterdam 1893)—physician, 55, 105, 132, 194

David Mindlin (b. Amsterdam 1908)—tailor, 7, 168

Meijer Mossel (b. Amsterdam 1909)—cantor, 51, 155, 187

Aron Peereboom (b. Amsterdam 1896)—diamond worker, market vendor, 100

Ben Polak (b. Amsterdam 1913)—professor of medicine, member of parliament, 195, 202

Karel Polak (b. Amsterdam 1906)—salesman, window dresser, diamond worker, 14, 19, 37, 65, 73, 88, 149

Sylvain Albert Poons (b. Amsterdam 1896)—actor, 150, 161

Carel Reijnders (b. Amsterdam 1916)—teacher, 24, 41, 73, 215

Max Reisel (b. Amsterdam 1913)—teacher of Dutch and Hebrew, 49, 172, 187

David Ricardo (b. Amsterdam 1904)—composer, cantor and choir director of the Portuguese congregation, 53, 81, 156, 188

Abraham Salomon Rijxman (b. Amsterdam 1926)— history teacher, biographer of A. C. Wertheim, 27

Leen Rimini (b. Amsterdam 1898)—diamond worker, later a grocer, 2, 40, 78, 88, 95, 101, 112, 200, 220

Ben Sajet (b. Amsterdam 1887)—physician, Amsterdam city councilor, 63, 79, 190

Dick Schallies (b. Amsterdam 1901)—market vendor, 7, 214

Hijman (Bob) Scholte (b. Amsterdam 1902)—singer, 24, 51, 117

Ben Sijes (b. Amsterdam 1908)—professor of contemporary history, 17, 116, 128, 137, 170, 226

Jacob Soetendorp (b. Amsterdam 1914)—author, rabbi of the Amsterdam Liberal Jewish congregation, 42, 56, 63, 66, 109, 142, 190, 203

Nathan Stodel (b. Amsterdam 1911)—office worker, husband of Elisabeth Van de Kar-Stodel, 39, 65, 80, 118, 125, 143, 202

Max Louis Terveen (b. Amsterdam 1927)—textile wholesaler, 11

Eduard (Eddy) Van Amerongen (b. Amsterdam 1912)—journalist, former editor of *Nederlands Israelitisch Weekblad*, 54, 81, 139, 154

Elisabeth Van De Kar-Stodel (b. Amsterdam 1912)—homemaker, wife of Nathan Stodel, 130, 144

Rosine Van Praag (b. Amsterdam 1915)—sports instructor, 138, 166, 214

Abraham Van Santen (b. Amsterdam 1897)—merchant, 218

Max Van Saxen (b. Amsterdam 1914)—teacher, husband of Julia Heertjes-Van Saxen, 55, 60

Bernard Van Tijn (b. Haarlem 1900)—lawyer, scholar of Marxist theory, active in Poalei Zion, 26, 86, 139, 191, 196

Alexander Van Weezel (b. Amsterdam 1886)—office worker, 24, 106, 144

Liesbeth Van Weezel (b. Amsterdam 1908)—journalist, former editor of *Nederlands Israelitisch Weekblad*, 18, 115, 138, 191, 195, 208, 216

Aaron Vaz Dias (b. Amsterdam 1911)—merchant, 10, 54, 135, 149, 226

Joop Voet (b. Amsterdam 1909)—Dutch consul in Israel, 18, 95, 102, 118, 128

Ali Voorzanger-Suurhoff (b. Amsterdam 1907)—widow of Minister of Social Affairs J. Suurhoff, 107, 119

Sal Waas (b. Amsterdam 1899)—active in Jewish funeral organization, 37, 166, 173

Temple Israel
Minneapolis, Minnesota

IN MEMORY OF
DR. LUSIA HORNSTEIN
FROM
MR. & MRS. EDWIN HARRIS